Accidental Missionary

ENDORSEMENTS

Stories tell us many things. For most of us, other people's stories are the easiest way to learn life's lessons. *Accidental Missionary* happens to be a true life walk by Pam and those who chose to walk a road less traveled. It illustrates in living detail a life well-lived, and the impact that faith and action can bring when they collide on earth. It is my honor to call Pam McCormick, not only my friend, but an exceptional human being who has lived bigger than life. This journey, and how it has been written will leave you spell bound.

Jean Kaye Wilson
CEO and Founder of H.E.L.P. International!

Pam is an inspiration and the proof that every normal church attender can make an impact in this world. Pam's heart for God and obedience will be an encouragement for many readers that want to step out from the comfort zone and do more for the Kingdom of God in the community and around the World. Pam's book brought tears to my eyes with so many beautiful stories of how God is revealing himself in places with extreme poverty. I encourage you to read this book with an open heart. It may change your life!

Samuel Brum
Resurrection Fellowship Associate Lead Pastor

One woman's beautiful story of hope, hard work and dedication! My husband and I walked through Masese in 2005 after being asked to scout out the land by Pam and Bruce McCormick. We witnessed a community in overwhelming poverty and hardship. What started with a few committed people willing to sow small seeds of help turned into a dynamic organization with an eternal impact on the Masese community in Uganda. Over the years living in Uganda, we were able to visit Masese and the work of Help International and witness a truly remarkable community transformation! We saw healthy children laughing, playing and attending school and men and women empowered with changed lives!

Katie Bouchard
Friend; Adoptive Parent of Four African Children

Reading *Accidental Missionary* was like participating in a supernatural miracle as it unfolded right before my eyes! As an American, I find it so easy to get caught up with my busy life and take for granted all God has blessed me with: abundant food, shelter, education, medical care, and freedom to believe in and worship my precious Lord. Through this wonderful book, I took time to vicariously walk in Pam's footsteps over many years of ministry. My heart softened and I wept in appreciation for both the ministry team members and the wonderful African adults and children who must work so hard to exist, let alone move forward. Praise God for Pam and her team!

Barbara E. Haley
Author, Editor, Teacher

Pam McCormick's testimony of how God led her to make a difference in the lives of children in Uganda will inspire you and, hopefully, call you to action. This book is a must-read for anyone interested in ministering to the needy in third-world countries!

Marlene Bagnull, Author, Speaker, Editor, and
Director of Write His Answer Ministries

Accidental Missionary

by

Pam McCormick

Accidental Missionary

Copyright© 2019 by Pam McCormick

Published by Boatloads Press

Loveland, Colorado

ISBN 978-1-7343675-0-8

Some of the names, places, and settings have been changed to protect those involved. The author's intent is to be truthful about God and His role in this story of redemption.

DEDICATION

I dedicate this book to Jean Kaye Wilson. Jean Kaye has mentored me, been my good friend, and led the way through this walk of faith called Help Uganda. Without her leadership and faithfulness to follow God's leading, this project would have never made it to this day. I am eternally grateful for the path we have walked together. This village empowerment program, this primary school, this bead business, this entire story would not have happened if she wasn't leading the charge. My life and the

lives of countless others has been enriched by knowing her.

Accidental Missionary is also dedicated to my husband Bruce McCormick. Bruce is my big picture partner. We bring different strengths to this African endeavor both of which are important to the overall good. We have learned, cried, laughed and loved together each step of the way over the years. He protects and supports as we navigate our way walking in God's footsteps both in Uganda and in life at home.

A cord of three strands is not easily broken.
Ecclesiastes 4:12

Praise Report
December 2019

We have achieved a lot of things this year ... the highlight is the New School Building that has taken our profile to a new level. It is the talk of town. We return the glory to God!

We thank all of you who have worked tirelessly to raise the construction funds through your generous contributions, fundraising campaigns, and reaching out to individual donors. God bless you all.

The once despised Masese is on the road to becoming a center of excellence in community empowerment, and lives are changing. Together, we have formed a formidable team both here and on the other side of the ocean, and truly God is using us. The tag "slum" that used to be the main description of Masese is surely becoming obsolete.

Ronny Sitanga
Country Director for H.E.L.P. in Uganda

Religion that God our Father accepts as pure and faultless is this: to look after orphans and widows in their distress and to keep oneself from being polluted by the world.

James 1:27

TABLE OF CONTENTS

Foreword

Accidental Missionary is the extraordinary story of lives being rescued and encouraged, impoverished people given hope and a future, of marriages deepened, cultures shared, and faith built. God shines on every page. His faithfulness is beyond compare.

My daughter Leah and I first visited Masese in 2015. Our lives were forever changed.

The first thing you notice at Masese is, of course, the hundreds of exuberantly happy children clad in their red and yellow uniforms. The second thing you notice is the quiet and humble way that H.E.L.P. International founders slip into this environment as if they've always been there, and more impressively, as if what they've done is nothing special. For a newcomer like me, this was just one more (pleasant) shock of many.

What's happened at this school and community is nothing short of a miracle on earth, playing out in real time, with real people. The poverty and abandonment of the village slum is heartbreaking. If not for the work of a small core group from America, these children would be condemned to a lifetime of squalid conditions with no right to hope for anything better.

Education and a regular meal is likely the most powerful tool in elevating these individuals above the plight they were born into. The Masese School, built over the last decade, may be the only chance to break this cycle. If not for the ongoing focus and devotion by H.E.L.P. International, it would neither have become what it is or continue to thrive. And all this is possible because individuals like Jean Kaye, Pam, Don, and Bruce, in their unassuming way, are quietly going about their business, making a small forgotten part of the world a little better, 500 children at a time.

Dr. Harry Ross—Retired Emergency Medicine Physician
International Medical Relief Volunteer

Acknowledgements

A myriad of people has helped both now and through the years as God brought this labor of love about. To each of them I am eternally grateful. This is a team effort spanning two continents.

The Uganda team on the ground in Masese made our work doable. Ronny Sitanga, Richard Mugeni, Ritah Kisakye, Pastor Frederick Ojiambo, and Arthur Nsubuga guided us every step of the way. Their patience and wisdom paired with their knowledge of their people were invaluable to the success of this program. Our headteachers and teachers are the true heros. Each one brings education to the children vital to the furtherance of those children's lives and the future of their community and beyond. Support staff for the school; Robert, Bonny, Edmund, Paul, Patricia, our cooks, and office staff, Loyce, take on the day-to-day challenges. Without them there would not be a HELP Primary School. What a difference you all are making in your community and in Uganda as the future leaders of your country may be going through your doors.

The H.E.L.P. Uganda Board has been the center foundation. Jean Kaye and Don Wilson, Bob, Diana and Corryn Silon, Delia, Peter and Patricia Garrity, Renee and Jon Jelinek and Kate Ditchik have all contributed more than I could ever relay. Their time, money, expertise and love are truly the reason this project is what it is today. Many times we have fumbled our way, not knowing just how we were going to manage. Reliving the story as I wrote this book brought fond memories of each of you I have traveled with over the years and a great appreciation of the work all of you contributed to the village of Masese and particularly the HELP Primary School. Thank you from the depths of my being.

I owe an enormous amount of gratitude to all those who helped me write *Accidental Missionary* and get it published. First of all, my dear husband Bruce encouraged me to get the story recorded, helped write parts of the book that he was more involved with, edited, and provided all my computer support. Barb Haley and Marlene Bagnull encouraged me to write my story and introduced me to the Colorado Christian Writers Conference where I learned an incredible amount about writing, publishing and marketing. The Tuesday morning's Writer's Group at the Senior Center in Ft. Collins, CO listened to me and guided me for two years. Dave Arns' critique group encouraged and brought me extremely helpful and constructive criticism. Renae Burt did a wonderful job finalizing my cover. Luann Benefiel and Sandy Andrews read through the manuscript with fresh eyes for a final edit. Their contribution made for a better presentation for the readers.

I want to thank everyone who sponsors children anywhere in the world or otherwise supports the efforts of those in the field. There are many good organizations fighting the good fight to make the world a better place. God made this world to be a Paradise but for so many it is anything but.

Most of all I want to thank my God for His blessings and favor on both this work and my life. He does truly bring "boatloads of provision" and for that I am forever grateful. It is an honor to serve such a loving Father.

~Pam McCormick

AFRICA

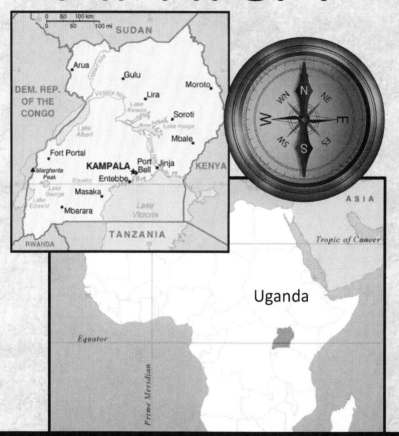

Uganda

Father God, we pray Your Word will go forth with favor from the North, South, East, and West.

Prologue

As we sit in our event tent, surrounded by Ugandan jewelry and crafts, I am telling stories. The weather is in the low 90s. A slight breeze carries enticing street-vendor food aromas through the air. The pavement where we are standing is hot and tiring to our bodies, but the streets are teeming with people. Our particular avenue is lined with tents. Most patrons with something to sell hope potential customers will wander in. Those passing by are on their way to an outdoor concert, or the children's play area where there are carnival rides, or looking for something fun to eat. Summer outdoor festivals are a popular way to spend an afternoon in Colorado. My stories are an unexpected bonus for those who stop and listen.

The banner across the front of our tent reads "Bigger Than Beads," with a subtitle of "Bringing Hope from Paper." There are large photos of Ugandan children from our Help Uganda Primary School, and of proud Ugandan jewelry artisans showing their creations, further identifying our mission as you scan the tent.

Dozens of necklaces, bracelets and earrings for young and old fill the table tops or hang from grid walls. People are amazed when I describe the time and expertise it takes the village women in our project to hand roll every bead from recycled paper and craft into jewelry, especially when I explain the circumstances in which these women live. Often our poverty-stricken artisans are sitting on hand-woven grass mats outside their mud and wattle huts.

Handcrafted baskets, made from natural grasses and banana leaves woven into appealing, colorful designs, add to the display.

The biggest draw to the tent is the collection of handbags, also crafted with the beads. These bags are truly amazing. If you purchase one someone will stop you on the street to exclaim over it. We hang these right out in front to get the attention they deserve.

There are smaller beaded wristlets and colorful cloth ones adorned with bigger paper beads. Small stuffed animals, in bright African fabrics, and ornaments, made from the beads, sell quickly.

Our tent is pretty well attended by the festival public. With our five-hundred and fifty student Ugandan primary school and the village empowerment program growing by leaps and bounds, profit from our sales is critical to our ministry.

The Bigger Than Beads name gives us a chance to tell our stories. This endeavor is much more than just about the beads. It is about saving lives, educating the impoverished, feeding the hungry, empowering villagers, bringing hope and opportunity to a people group living in the Pearl of Africa, otherwise known as Uganda.

My favorite activity during these events is answering the question, "How did you ever get started in this?" My biggest problem is curtailing my answer. I could talk all day about this project I love.

The cacophony of the festival fades into the background. I find a chair and begin to spin my tales.

As I talk, I am aware of my passion. My storytelling is full of exuberance and pathos, humor and challenge. I am animated and fully alive. My audience listens, spellbound, as I transport them across the ocean. I have to make sure I have helpers in the tent so someone is attending to the business of selling our wares. While I talk! Their faces reflect their enchantment as they begin to experience a bit of what I get to live as I labor for the betterment of the village of Masese, Uganda. I always invite my listeners to come to Uganda with us. Most have wistful expressions as if they would love to come, but may not be able. That is when they say, "You should write a book!"

* * *

I was in my senior years. God woke me up one morning with the beginning of the story: the tapestry of God's faithfulness. Since this is really His story, I looked at other writers and saw they all wrote through their own personalities and history. While I wouldn't ever compare myself to the writers of the Bible, I looked at my own life to see how God has woven together my being so He could use me.

Me, a woman leading an ordinary life.

I wasn't a prostitute like Rahab, a judge like Deborah, or a priest's wife like Elizabeth. I was just living an ordinary life, more like Ruth. Once God's plan for her life (and mine) was in motion big results happened. In the midst of ordinary lives, God is extraordinary!

I am in awe of what God can do with an everyday person like me.

A finished tapestry is incredibly beautiful. However, in the beginning, there is just a jumble of thread and the weaver. The weaver may have a pattern in mind, or the weaver may design as he goes along. Maybe both approaches are engaged as the weaver uses his creative license. Each thread a weaver uses is important to the design. Intricate patterns develop as the tapestry design evolves. While some threads are included throughout the design, others are inserted for a short portion of the whole. Interestingly, no thread is ever wrong in the hands of the weaver.

My life seemed "wrong" at times. It didn't always seem coherent, or on the right track. I, as the tapestry, couldn't comprehend what the overall design would be. I only saw a jumble of thread. The unraveling was not up to me.

Since I've acknowledged that God is the weaver, my life has been incredible, even when I couldn't fathom the reasons and seasons of it.

A village called Masese, in the country of Uganda, in East Africa, became a focal pattern in my Weaver's design. Suddenly, my life made sense and I began to see (at least a thread or two) what God had been working in me all along.

Joseph had a coat of many colors, provoking envy in his brothers. The coat showed that Joseph was his father's favorite son. I delight in thinking of my Father's love for me as He weaves my multi-colored garment.

Maybe, this is what I will be given to wear throughout eternity.

So, I spin my tale.

"Well, this is really a story of God's faithfulness," I begin.

The Story Begins . . .

A Bit of My History

I grew up in a small town in Missouri, the heartland of America, in the fifties. Our country was struggling to accept black people as equals. As a three-year-old, I saw my first black person on a train in Kansas City. The conductor was African American. My parents taught me the polite term for them was "Negroes." Some people had different names like "colored" or "darkies" or worse names I don't even want to repeat. I thought "colored" was an inaccurate name because they weren't blue or green or red.

When I saw this train conductor, I was openly curious. I asked why he looked different, loudly enough to embarrass my mother. She gave me some explanation that must have satisfied me as later she said I sat and played with his little son as though he was one of my white playmates from home.

I don't remember seeing another Negro until I started junior high school. My mom once said if Negroes were given the chance to clean up and get good jobs, they would do just fine. In my junior high school, there was a Negro sewing teacher. Mom was right. Mrs. Brown was, in my mind, just like all my other teachers. I loved her and she taught me well.

I grew up watching stories on TV about struggles with desegregation in the South and was appalled at the meanness and injustice I witnessed. There were a few Negroes in my high school. I wasn't aware of them being mistreated, though they may have been. They seemed like they would be fun people to know, but they kept to themselves most of the time.

There was a separate swimming pool and park for the Negroes. When I asked why this was so, I was told some people thought it would be bad to be in the same water with "those people" since there was oil on their skin that would be in the pool water. It was also implied that they were dirtier than we were.

When I was in seventh grade, I met my first African. His name was Titus Solomon. I don't know if his first name was Titus or Solomon because I learned later that Africans say their last name first. I thought his name was cool since it was from the Bible. He was a student at Ozark Bible College, and my parents invited him to our house for dinner. We made sure he felt welcome in our home.

As I look back, though, I realize my dad was uncomfortable with Negroes, whether they were from Africa or the South. My father hadn't been around them when he was growing up, so I think his discomfort was a fear of the unknown. However, as the years went by, I saw more prejudice from him than I liked.

My dad was a huge influence in my life. I will love him forever. I often disagreed with him, but his love for me was the overriding factor in my life. He thought I was special and treated me as an important and valuable person. I get a lot of my relationship with my heavenly Father from this very human man. I don't doubt God loves me because I never doubted that my dad loved me. He had an unconditional love that I never wanted to disappoint. Admittedly, he was flawed, but that didn't matter. He loved me and believed in me.

One of his flaws was this prejudice I mentioned. I didn't see it when I was young. I think he kept it quiet as he knew my mom would disapprove. In later years, he would let slip some of his intolerance. Mom saw all people as good. Daddy had a mistrust of most people. Only his immediate family passed the test. We could do no wrong. We should avoid others. Even our spouses were outsiders. He wanted nothing to do with anyone who wasn't white. Having fought against the Japanese in World War II, he developed the view that all people who looked like "Japs" were enemies. He saw Orientals and Negroes as less than whites. My mother didn't think God meant for the races to mix in marriage, but Daddy didn't think we were to mix in any fashion.

Because my dad pastored small churches through my teen years, I considered attending Ozark Bible College. But I had no desire to be a missionary. I wanted to become a teacher.

In 1965, a year after my high school graduation and a year into my elementary education undergraduate degree, I married my high school sweetheart. I finished my degree in three and a half years, received my Bachelor's degree in Education at Southwest Missouri State Teachers' College, and then set about raising my own kids.

By my twenty-first birthday, I was out of school, started my first teaching job and was pregnant with our first baby. In 1970, I birthed our second son, nineteen months after my first son was born. Our last baby came several years later in 1976. I was lucky because I could stay home and care for my three boys. I set a career aside and focused on my family.

While my boys were small, my church hosted a Women's Bible Conference with a conference speaker named Dorothy Keister. I thought she was phenomenal. Very few women were in leadership positions in the church at that time. My mother was a respected career woman. I didn't realize just how special this woman (and my mother) were at this time in history. Dorothy Keister's teaching captivated me. I was part of the team hosting her so I followed her around and learned even more from her than she taught during her teaching sessions. I heard that on Friday night we would hear an invitation to dedicate our whole lives to the Lord.

Well, I had been a Christian as long as I could remember. I was baptized after church camp when I was eleven. I always believed in and loved God, but the idea of turning my whole life over to Him scared me. I envisioned He might send me to Africa to be a missionary. Unwelcomed visions of uprooting my family to go back to the Bible college I had already rejected plagued my thoughts.

Becoming a missionary to Africa did not appeal to me in the slightest. I almost couldn't make such a dedication that Friday night. I didn't trust God enough. I still needed to be in control of my life.

After wrestling all week (seven days that seemed like an eternity!) I finally said, "Okay, God! Whatever you want me to do I will do. But I don't want to go to Africa!"

I am sure God must have laughed, knowing my future as He did. He graciously told me my mission field was my neighborhood and set about defining that for me.

I was ecstatic. My fears were put to rest. I served Him with all of my being until I started having trouble in my marriage.

A Rocky Beginning

My husband and I met at church camp when I was fifteen. We had been leaders in our church after marrying and starting our family. Those were happy years for me. My whole world centered around Jesus. All my friends, all my music, all our activities revolved around our faith. Then marriage troubles distracted me from my mission, and I began to focus more on my marriage than on Jesus.

During those years I wasn't a very good Christian. I still had a humanitarian nature. God had instilled this in me from early on. My dad used complain that my mother would "give the shirt off her back" to a bum begging at the door. I, on the other hand, thought that was pretty great of my mom. Every year she would make sure my cousins, who all had less than we did, had special things to eat at Christmas and nice presents. I loved helping her take care of others as I got older.

As an adult, I continued to follow her lead. I took on short-term fostering of teens in crisis and became a foster mother for a sixteen-year-old girl for a couple of years. I was a friend to young moms pregnant with unplanned babies through a program at the hospital.

I was a chaplain at a home for emotionally-disturbed girls. I loved delivering Christmas baskets from our church to needy families. I mentored friends of my boys and sometimes helped negotiate peace between their parents and them.

Through this time God was preparing me, even when I was pretty far from Him.

His faithfulness from the very beginnings of my life amazes me. That is why I consider this to be our story and not just mine. When I finally surrendered to His will in my life, He used every thread of the life I had lived, weaving His good plan for me and for the world in which I live.

My Second Marriage

Fast forward, a lot of years, to my second marriage. I asked God to bring me a Christian man to be my husband. I met Bruce when I was forty-two and married him a year later in 1990. He wasn't actually a Christian when we met, but I felt very clear Bruce was the man I was to marry. I could sense a desire for God in him, but for a while, he resisted.

As a child, Bruce's family's religion was the Navy. Neither parent attended an organized church. His mother was bitter against the Catholic religion in which she had been raised. She had her babies baptized, but that was the extent of her religious connection. Bruce had looked for God in Eastern religions when he was in college. Most of his late teens and twenties were filled with partying and trying to find his way through the sixties. His only attempted connections to spirituality came through drugs. After he was married to his first wife, he attended her church. Feeling like everyone was trying to "save" him, he was put off. He would accompany me to church but stay aloof, often belittling and judging what he was experiencing.

When we were first married, we joined a "Kinship" connected to our church. This was a small group focused on sharing our lives while studying the Bible. Bruce worked on Sundays, but attended the group meetings held during the week. He would argue and challenge, but he kept coming. Then one day he decided to be baptized. We met at the Poudre River. Bruce's parents attended but were confused. In their minds, he had already been baptized. My dad did the immersing, with Buck, our Kinship leader, assisting. Our Kinship and family members had a celebration party afterward on the banks of the river. I think the Heavens were partying too! Now Bruce and I could really become one in our spirits. That was a glorious day for me!

Compassion International

I asked God for a ministry but was told to wait. Wow, waiting was hard! I had read that Joseph waited thirteen years, Abraham twenty-five years, Moses forty years, and Jesus thirty years. If God was making me wait, I was in good company. Even so, I was not at all patient. God even wove that personality trait into my tapestry.

Knowing waiting would be difficult for me, God said He would bring my ministry to my door for that period of time. My years of humanitarian activities had helped to prepare me. All through my life I had been helping people in difficult circumstances. Now I was waiting for God to show me when and for whom to do His work. I began to see everyday episodes of Jesus ministering through me, from my home. This was different than what I perceived ministry to be, but it was all I had. I embraced these opportunities!

During this time, I sponsored a child through Compassion International. I attended a Christian concert where the performer talked about sponsoring and the organizers had child packets available. I had seen ads in magazines showing kids that needed sponsoring in third world countries. My heart was touched. However, I was leery of my money being used for administration purposes instead of ever getting to the child. I didn't trust these organizations until I heard that singer tell of his experiences with Compassion International. This was something I could do from home, while waiting for whatever else God meant for me to do. This was the beginning of God moving me from home to the world. I wrote letters. I reached out across the miles to bring God's love and provision to children through those letters.

My first Compassion child was a little girl from Haiti. Elmithe was nine when we first started sponsoring her in 1992. We wrote letters and sent money for several years until her family moved out of the Compassion region. She was a teen at the time they moved. Elmithe was taking a tailoring class to learn to sew before they left. Remembering the skills my sewing teacher, Mrs. Brown, taught me (at about the same age as this young girl), I hoped she would be able to make a good life for herself. I often wonder about her.

Since I couldn't sponsor every child from Compassion that touched my heart, I also became an Advocate for Compassion in 1992. I spoke to churches and youth classes, hosted tables at Christian concerts, and encouraged whoever would listen to sponsor children Compassion had identified as ones they could help in their program. Over the years I was blessed to assist in sponsoring of 447 children with Compassion International. I was passionate about helping as many children as I possibly could to have a better life. These children melted my heart.

Samson Kaboko ...

Having sponsored a young girl for my first Compassion child, I asked for an older boy for my second child. In 1997 Compassion assigned me a fourteen-year-old boy from Uganda, whose big smile won my heart before I ever received a letter from him. His name was Kaboko Samson. I still didn't know yet that Africans put their last name first so I called him Kaboko, thinking that was his first name. He didn't seem to care which name I used. He had lost his sponsor and told me he was really thankful I had agreed to sponsor him. Compassion had given him a chance to go to school and taught him about Jesus. Unlike most sponsored kids who wrote short, almost form letters, he wrote me long letters, sharing his heart with me. I didn't know it at the time, but he had to hand copy every one of his letters. The Compassion project needed a copy for his file, and they didn't have access to copying machines. I expect Kaboko's hand got tired since his letters were long.

Kaboko's correspondence helped me see his struggles and his dreams. I sent letters back sharing what light I could shed on his journey. I also shared details of my life. I grew to love this young man. At one point he asked if he could call me "Mom," but I thought that would be disrespectful to his own mother. We decided I would become "Auntie Pam."

At that time, he was angry with his own mom. Kaboko's father died when he was very young, and his mother had left him to be married to a second husband. Kaboko was being raised by his grandmother. He has since forgiven his mom and they have become close. Kaboko told me that he took some of my letters to his village chiefs to share my wisdom with them. That always made me wonder what I had written that he thought was so wise. I knew God must have been in the translation!

Once I got a collection of Sunday School materials together, along with some snacks and small Christmas presents, and mailed them to his church. I think I mailed them in October, but they didn't arrive until Easter! After the box arrived, the attendance of the children in that little village church increased greatly. Sweets were hard to come by, and I had loaded them up! That was fun for me and made me wish I could do more. However, now that I knew I couldn't trust the package to arrive, I didn't mail anymore.

Compassion has a policy that a sponsored child is not allowed to contact the sponsor except through monitored letters. Our return addresses were blotted out and any requests for money from the child were not allowed to be sent. This policy was meant to protect the sponsor from having a child, or one of his or her relatives, one day show up on the sponsor's doorstep begging for money. This was a good policy, but I was unaware of it until much later. Somehow Kaboko got the phone number I sent him. It slipped through the Compassion watchdogs. Probably another of God's little interventions. When we connected by phone, I could hardly conceive of the fact that I was speaking with this young man who lived what seemed like a whole world away. He spoke English, but I had a hard time understanding him because of his very strong accent and the poor phone connections. Nevertheless, connecting with Kaboko from across the ocean, was a profound experience.

I wanted to visit him!

Once Kaboko finished his secondary schooling, his sponsorship with Compassion was over. However, he qualified to receive additional sponsorship help while he was at the university. He had also been awarded a full scholarship from the Ugandan government because he was such a bright student, but he had to choose between the two offers. The government offer was more than the Compassion program could offer so he reluctantly withdrew the scholarship.

Even though a direct sponsorship through Compassion was no longer possible, I was able to continue to help because we had our own connection via the telephone. He needed help with living expenses which were not covered by his scholarship. I wired money through MoneyGram. He couldn't take a check, and sending cash through the mail is never a good idea. I no longer had the intermediary of Compassion International. I kept sending about the same amount of money I had been giving through Compassion, but this reached him directly now. The little money I sent was all he had for living expenses. For a while, he lived in a slum area. But after he was attacked and beaten up, he moved to a better place. I couldn't understand at the time why he couldn't get a part-time job to help himself. Now I know there was eighty percent unemployment in Uganda. There were simply no jobs to be had.

Kaboko invited me to come to his university graduation. I had never traveled internationally and regretfully declined. Traveling by myself seemed daunting and my husband would never be okay with me traveling to a foreign country alone. In the video he sent me of the graduation ceremonies, I was able to see Kaboko credit me for being able to accomplish this amazing milestone. He sold himself short. I provided a little bit of money, but he did all the rest. I was truly happy to help so this young man could make his mark in the world.

A year of struggle ensued after graduation. Jobs were hard to come by in Uganda, even for bright college graduates. Kaboko tried

several avenues to find a sustainable income, but none really supported him. Then, miraculously, he got a job with Compassion in the Kampala office. Being chosen by Compassion made a big statement as to his potential and determination. Now he helped children get the same assistance he had received as a child. My heart burst with pride! I could envision him as the President of Compassion for his country!

In one of his letters, he confessed that he had met his rib. His rib? Oh, of course, Eve was formed from Adam's rib to be his helpmate and keep him from being lonely. He had found a girlfriend! I never thought of myself as someone's rib, but I remember reading something about not wanting to walk ahead of or behind the husband but right beside him. There was a reason the woman was formed from the side of a man. I was happy for Kaboko and his new special friend. Next, I got a wedding invitation. Oh my. I really wanted to go to this wedding!

2005—2006

Meeting Jean Kaye

In Colorado, the summer of 2005, shortly after I heard of Kaboko's upcoming wedding, I was invited to a performance by a Ugandan singing group called "Afritendo." I attended and was delighted to hear them. I could almost see my Ugandan young man in their faces. The performers seemed happy and full of God. I loved their music; their bright colorful costumes, and their upbeat dancing. Keeping the beat with drums and singing with all their hearts was like nothing I had seen or heard before.

After the performance, I looked around at the Ugandan crafts for sale, thinking I would like to support these performers in some way. My heart was also full of images of Kaboko and how I would love to be able to see his smiling face in person. I ran into Mike Wangolo, the leader of the singing group, and asked him if he knew Kaboko. Since Uganda is a pretty big country, of course, he hadn't met him.

As I laughed at myself and milled around, a woman came up to me.

"I think I am supposed to meet you," she said directly.

Well, this was strange. "Do you know why you are supposed to meet me?"

"No. Do you do anything internationally?"

Her questions surprised me. "No, except I am an Advocate for Compassion International. I don't do anything international myself, but I wish I could go to a wedding in Uganda."

Her eyes lit up, and then she said something that changed my life forever. "I know a lot of people in Uganda. Maybe I can help you."

What? A shock went through my body of surprise and hope. Well, now I was very interested! "Can we meet for lunch next week?"

"Yes, come to my warehouse, whichever day you choose," she responded.

I fumbled with my words as I struggled with a sense of disbelief. "You have a warehouse? Where? Why?"

She seemed not to notice my bewilderment. "I have a non-profit called H.E.L.P. International. H.E.L.P. stands for His Everlasting Love Prevails. I collect medical supplies, equipment, and humanitarian aid and ship them to clinics or missionaries all around the world."

A ministry? Sounded fascinating. We exchanged contact information and chose a day to meet the following week. Could she possibly help me get to Uganda to meet Kaboko?

When I got to her warehouse I was surprised at how big and messy it was. An older man was sweeping and an older woman sorting. Later, a team from the Larimer County Detention Center came in to work, leaving Jean very little time to visit, let alone get away for lunch. There were no shelves, so the donations were on the floor. Everything from walkers, exam tables, medicines, clothing, and much more was in an orderly space but with no appropriate place for storage. It was an organized mess. The clothing was in piles waiting to be sorted into boxes ready to ship. More help was clearly needed.

I told Jean Kaye, my new friend, I would like to help. I thought I might help sort clothes. She suggested I pray about what I could do. I didn't know it at the time, but God told her I would be a significant person in her life.

She had been praying for a friend. She saw me as much more than a sorter. I went home and prayed. She prayed as well. When we met the following week, we still didn't have any answers. She suggested I shadow her to prompt me where I might want to get involved. Though I didn't even know what a pallet jack was or how to use a tape gun, this was becoming my mission! I followed her around. I became almost obsessed with her. If I saw her lifting something, I wanted to help her lift it. If she needed paper, I found someone to donate paper. If she was talking to someone, I wanted to hear what she said. A friend said there was a word for what I felt, "armor-bearer."

The term is found in the Bible, as well as from history. Jean Kaye further explained that an armor-bearer fights beside a warrior in battle as if they are one and the same. If the warrior is killed or wounded, the armor-bearer picks up the armor and continues fighting.

That sounded like a pretty heavy mantle but the idea had already captured my heart. We became a team. God began to weave us together. In Scripture, an armor-bearer carried additional weapons for commanders. Abimelek (Judges 9:54), Saul (1 Samuel 16:21), Jonathan (1 Samuel 14:6-7), and Joab (2 Samuel 18:15) had armor-bearers.

One day, Stephan, a Ugandan, came to visit Jean. He met her when she was on a trip to Uganda in 2004. She and her team were on their way to a village to hold a medical clinic. After some persuasion, he convinced her to stop by his village of Masese, to introduce her to the extreme poverty there. Now, Stephen was in the United States helping load a container of supplies for a group of youth Jean had met in his village. As Jean had visited with them, they requested vocational training to enable them to support their families. Many of their parents made and consumed the local alcohol. These young men wanted to do better, but they needed help. Jean was glad to send supplies to help them break out of this destructive lifestyle.

I helped fill boxes for the container and added things for Kaboko. It felt good to send him gifts I couldn't send through the mail: a small refrigerator, cooking supplies, a warm jacket, shoes, and other staples. I might not be able to go to the wedding but I could show my love to him and his bride by sending these gifts. I really didn't think I would ever get to travel across the ocean to this small country in east Africa. Still, I was sad I couldn't attend the wedding. Kaboko graciously sent me a lengthy video of the ceremony. I adored watching every minute. I almost felt like I had been there. He even spoke to me, in English, as if I was there.

One day, Jean came to me. "If you would consider going on a medical mission trip with me to Kenya, I will take you on to Uganda to meet Kaboko." Jean frequently led medical mission teams to Africa through an organization called International Medical Relief (IMR). She is a nurse herself and loves Africa. I didn't know what I would do on a medical trip since I wasn't trained or even medically inclined. She said my role would be to play with children while their

parents were visiting the clinic. I could do that. Wow!

I was actually going to Africa!

With Jean leading the trip, I felt safe to travel to this foreign, yet compelling, land to meet my Ugandan son and to help Kenyans with a medical team.

2007

First Kenya Trip—August

Meeting Jean changed my life, but going to Africa set my purpose.

Traveling to Kenya was surreal. I realized, as I was preparing to leave, how such an adventure was inconceivable. Misconceptions about Africa abounded and cultural differences seemed daunting. But my excitement was unparalleled! This was never on my bucket list but was undoubtedly a dramatic opportunity in my life.

In Kenya, I saw poverty all around me I never knew existed. Poverty permeated my being in indescribable ways.

Being able to help in any way possible, large or small, felt so right! Once, when we were on our way to our safari, the bus hit and dropped into a mud hole. Curious Kenyans came by, often trying to help.

A young family passed by and heard we had medical people on board. They held a precious baby girl in their arms. These parents had recently discovered their daughter had a serious problem with her eyes. Without the help she needed, this little girl would go blind. The parents' pleading eyes told us they were frantic to get help for their child. Jean didn't have the supplies she needed, but we scrambled through our medical supplies trying to find some drops to relieve some of the child's discomfort. We found nothing to help.

Caught up in sympathy for the baby and her parents I helped Jean as best I could. I wept uncontrollably after they went on their way because I hadn't thought to pray. I felt like I kept that child from ever being able to see because I didn't pray over her. I know God is bigger than that, but this illustrates how strong my desire was to make a difference in the lives of these people. I felt my own inadequacy but knew God was never inadequate. I needed to rely more on God than on any of my own efforts. I didn't want to miss another opportunity to help. Please God, I pray even today, heal that child's eyes.

During medical clinics, I held classes teaching exercises to strengthen and stretch backs. I was not an expert, but I had learned more than these dear Kenyans. I demonstrated what I knew. We did some stretches and practiced lifting techniques. It was fun to see my onlookers try the stretches, laughing at themselves as they learned this new concept of moving for a reason other than basic living and survival. Some of them came back and told me how much better their backs felt. Even so, one thing I could never change was their practice of sweeping with a short-handled broom. Those sweeping have to bend over to reach the ground, thus straining their backs. I tried to show how using a long-handled broom like we use in the States would help their backs. Unfortunately, I have never seen anyone take my advice.

My original intention was to entertain the children waiting to be seen by a doctor or nurse. I didn't know their language, but I was eager to please the children. I brought stickers and fingernail polish because they fit well in my suitcase. The stickers were for the boys and the nail polish for the girls. Those items were a hit! Everyone wanted both. Giggles sprang forth in that universal language I so appreciate. We played "Follow the Leader" and the adults smiled as we cavorted in a line around the area doing silly things. We sang and danced the "Hokey Pokey" and anything else that came to my mind as I searched my memory for fun things to do.

Such simple pleasures made for a chance to show these impoverished children that someone from America cared, even a little bit. I would have liked to have told them I was doing this because I wanted them to know that Jesus loves them, but I couldn't speak their language. Nevertheless, I believe they received His love from my actions.

Actions are more powerful than words. I felt I was living out the saying attributed to Saint Francis of Assisi: "Preach the gospel at all times, and if necessary, use words."

I touched and laughed with both young and old. Sometimes, the mothers would shyly offer me their hands to hold while I painted their nails too. Those hands were weathered and worn, yet lovely to me. What pleasure I received from providing joy in this seemingly insignificant way.

Love is God's language.

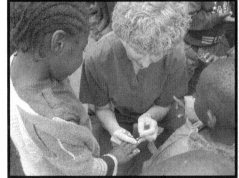

Now, years later, I travel to a place where I bring the children something more lasting. I am helping turn their illiteracy into knowledge. It isn't in pink, red, green, or blue nail-polish colors, and it transcends language barriers. Now I give more than a few minutes of attention. Now I help provide a better life for them. However, I am getting ahead of myself!

I was in love with Kenya. All its slums and poverty, amazing church worship, powerful prayers, orphans, and beautiful resilient people worked its magic on me. I was captivated in ways I couldn't fully explain. It sounds strange to say I loved it all with the poverty and harsh conditions, but God put a love in my heart for this new continent and enabled me to look beyond the poverty and see beautiful people. Each face told amazing stories of resilience. Despite their poverty, the people exude energy and resourcefulness. My heart burst with passion and compassion, curiosity and awe, happiness and sorrow, a sense of purpose and a lack of direction.

I was not the only one. Other people on this trip were impacted as well. One couple decided to look into foreign adoption. One young woman fell in love and cried, brokenhearted, as we drove away. She later married that Kenyan man and lives not far from me with their adorable children.

Meeting Kaboko

Reluctant to leave after a week in Kenya, Jean and I flew to Uganda. Anticipation heightened my senses. Kaboko's heart and my heart had reached across the ocean through the years by way of letters. I had wanted to meet this young man since 1997, with little hope of actually accomplishing that desire. Then, after ten years, there I was in Uganda where I finally got to meet Kaboko and his lovely young wife, Hellen, in person. I first laid eyes on Kaboko at his place of work, the Compassion International office for the country of Uganda.

He came outside to greet us, and we both cried tears of joy. It seemed unreal and incomprehensible that I was actually there holding his hand in this parking lot in Kampala, the capital of Uganda, in east Africa. After all those years of wanting to meet him in person, here he was in front of me. I hardly knew what to say to him.

Dressed in a suit and tie, he looked very distinguished, although shorter than I had imagined. Even though Kaboko was full of emotion, I could see he was confident and self-assured. His smile lit up his face, endearing me to him even more and reminding me of the smile in the photo of him as a young boy. I liked him even better in person.

Kaboko took us inside and introduced Jean and me to the Compassion team. He showed us his desk and the work he was doing with letters written from sponsors to their sponsored children. He seemed well liked and respected by his team. I was proud of him all over again. A little boy from a rural village, with little chance for success, had become a responsible man working for a well-respected international company. Miraculous! Now he was focused on helping others like himself, which seemed right in so many ways.

When Jean asked Kaboko how it was that he had done so well in his life, he told a little story that amazed me. He said when I wrote letters to him I always ended with "Take care." He didn't know exactly what I meant but since I always ended his letters with that phrase he determined to "take care" in all things. I never expected such a little exhortation would affect this young man so profoundly!

I enjoyed seeing his home. It was not a mud and wattle hut like where he grew up but a rented house with a living room, kitchen, and bedroom. Hellen cooked a delicious Ugandan meal and shyly told me she was expecting her first baby. I felt like a mother-in-law, wanting to help her navigate through her first pregnancy and birth.

I kept asking myself, "How is it I feel so connected with these people living a world away?" The answer was clearly that God had knit our hearts together, thus beginning my destiny. This destiny in Africa started with a small monthly commitment to help the life of one child. I'm so thankful for the opportunity to make a difference in this young boy's life. Ironically, the experience made an even greater difference in my own life.

Introduction to Jinja

Frank, our Ugandan driver, drove us from Kaboko's home, situated in the large, busy, smog-infused city of Kampala, to the charming town of Jinja. Jean had business to attend to there. Frank kept us entertained with stories of his life and life in general in Uganda. He was a delight. I learned a lot from him.

After a few hours, we entered the town I would come to think of as a second home. Away from the big city, we saw very few white faces. Some of the littlest children were afraid of us. We must have looked like ghosts to them. Others were just curious. Some were excited, as if we were some kind of celebrity.

Women walked about with baskets balanced on their heads filled with items they hoped to sell. We bought delicious, tiny, sweet bananas. As in many countries in Africa, the women dressed beautifully, even though they were very poor. The vivid colors in the fabric of their dresses were bright and lovely against their dark skin. Reds, oranges, and yellows were especially beautiful. The blues and greens reflected the lushness of the Ugandan countryside. The women also wore jewelry in bold, happy colors. We must have looked pretty dull compared to these women.

Ugandan food was still unfamiliar to us, and we missed our own cuisine. Frank took us to "The Source Café." They served the closest to American food we had seen. This cafe was named after the source of the Nile, which the town is famous for. As I sat and watched Ugandan life pass by, I imagined living in this town.

We visited the source of the Nile where the fresh water from an underwater spring comes up out of Lake Victoria and flows north, becoming what is traditionally known as the longest river in the world. It travels through eleven countries, including Kenya, Congo, Sudan, Uganda, and Egypt, before it eventually drains into the Mediterranean Sea—a total of 4132 miles.

Kaboko attended a secondary boarding school here and had once sent me a picture captioned: Someday we might visit it together. How I wished he could have accompanied us to this site.

First visit to the village of Masese

From Jinja town, we drove to a nearby village called Masese. Masese was a desolate place. Buildings were falling down and everything was in major disrepair. Dust and dirt filled the air. The landscape was scattered with trash and large piles of refuse, frequented by the local goats. Pits filled with water, urine and muck were a breeding ground for mosquitoes. We had to watch where we stepped, as local long-horned cows and scraggly goats often left smelly packages to be avoided.

The villagers looked at us with distrust as we walked about the village, viewing their poverty.

We found the still where they were making the liquor we had heard about. The stench surrounding the still was appalling. There were babies sitting in the mud and filth. Occasional raucous laughter of the people working to make the liquor reached us before they saw us coming and were hushed. I heard that there were drug deals and witchcraft going on in this area we would later call "home."

Smoke from the cooking fires also filled the air. Our eyes stung, and I coughed. There were multitudes of children—dirty and scantily clothed. They fought with each other to touch us, hold our hands, and touch my elbows. I felt honored and, at the same time, grimy since they lived and played in the dirt. When I sat, they reached for my hair, curious about the color and texture. Often a child would rub the skin on my arm or pinch my skin, fascinated with the whiteness. Later we taught them to be more respectful of a person's space.

In this village, and just about everywhere we traveled in Uganda, we were celebrities called "Mzungus" (white people). We heard the name Mzungu being called out wherever we went. I felt what Jesus must have felt as He lived in a village in a not-too-distant part of this world and the crowds thronged about Him. At the same time, I saw His face in the faces of the children. Walking through the village, our eyes were opened to their living conditions. Their circumstances were more difficult than I imagined.

Roads were just dirt, not much more than paths. Some houses were made from bricks, but many more villagers lived in mud and wattle huts. Some lived in a one or two-room dwelling attached in a strip of three or four abodes we might call apartments. When not working, the women sat on woven mats on the ground rather than inside their dark homes. Most homes had no door. There might be a strip of cloth covering the door opening.

There were a few latrines for individual houses, but most of the villagers had to share a common latrine. I was again convicted. I live in a beautiful house in a clean neighborhood with running water, toilets, a bathtub with a shower, a washer and dryer for my laundry, and food to cook in my nice, well equipped kitchen.

The villagers cooked over fires outside their one-room huts with no electricity or water, except what they carried. Their bathing area, commonly used by all, was a small tent-like structure made from scrap material and barely large enough to fit one person. The bather took a pan of water and some soap into this space so they could have some semblance of privacy to clean themselves. Babies were bathed in round washtubs and laundry hung from lines strung between huts. I could see the bloated starvation bellies on many of the children. I saw boredom and lack of hope on most of the adult faces.

We gave away donated shirts and delivered some supplies to the local clinic. Jean had shipped an exam table, baby scales, and bedding for their clinic beds, along with a few other supplies. In that clinic, there were very few supplies, no electricity, or running water, and a nurse with limited knowledge. Her main purpose seemed to be to treat malaria and to help women birth their babies. Jean purposed in her heart to help this clinic that was, at least, trying to help the people of this village.

We were considered heroes. But I felt like an imposter since I had so much compared to what we gave. One teen boy came to tell me he didn't get a shirt. I was devastated to tell him we had run out. The need was so great.

In later years, we took birthing kits to help make childbirth safer. We included a hospital waterproof pad to help keep the women and newborns out of the dirt or otherwise unsanitary situation, some scissors to cut the cord with instead of a dirty knife, a clamp for the umbilical cord, an infant blanket, newborn clothes and some pads for the mother. We also continued to bring supplies for the clinic.

Prayer Walking

We knew God was with us in a miraculous way, but there was also a darkness present when we arrived at Masese. Jean decided we needed to walk around one of the pole barn buildings. It stood vacant and lonely, weeds all around it. I followed and prayed with her. As Jean waded through the weeds, her skirt filled up with burs. I've learned they are often called Devil's Beggarticks. We wore skirts with flowing material that gathered these burs by the hundreds.

Multiplication Miracle

Jean asked Frank to buy papayas and some sweets to give to the children in Masese. Word spread we were in the village and came with treats. A huge group of excited children gathered, many more than we expected. Anguish built in me as I realized there was no way we had bought enough for each child.

"Can you cut each papaya into fourths so everyone would at least get a taste?"

They told me, "No, the fruit is too sticky."

Jean and I sat on the porch watching and praying for a miracle. Jesus multiplied the loaves and fishes so maybe He would help with the fruits and sweets. I was distraught that some children who were desperately hungry and had their hopes up for a treat would be disappointed. I could hardly watch.

The African team helping us set up an orderly system where the children would come in a line, get their fruit, and then move over to Frank, who held their sweets. Then they were to go on home.

Instead, they sat on the ground in front of Jean and me. We must have been a fun diversion from their usual lives. As the crowd at our feet grew, I saw that the line of kids being served was almost finished. There was still fruit being given out. I couldn't believe it! I watched as the last child got his papaya and saw the helpers getting papayas from the bag for themselves. They even offered us one!

This was the first miracle I had ever seen. God actually multiplied the amount we had purchased. He had compassion on those kids and on me. I still get goosebumps when I remember this story. God was setting up His work for this area, promising to be there, as we needed, in ways more abundant than we could imagine. There were even sweets to give out for the remainder of our trip!

That evening, as we picked the burs from our clothing, Jean reflected that they were meant to show us that this project would have some difficult times. We had an enemy that didn't want us there and would make trouble for us.

Helping a Wounded Muslim Man

As Frank drove us from one location to another, Jean noticed a young man limping on the opposite side of the road, his foot dripping with blood. She told Frank, "Turn around! I can help that boy!" Jean carried a medical bag with her everywhere she went. Frank slammed on the brakes and turned the car around. Unfortunately, the wounded man got scared and ran. Frank yelled out to him in Lugandan, the common language of the Ugandans, "This is a nurse from America! She  wants to help your bleeding foot." Reluctantly the young man let us come to him. He sat on our car hood, frightened, while Jean cared for his foot.

The boy's name was Mohammed as so many Muslim boys are named. He had just injured his foot and was walking home. Jean whispered, "If I let him leave his foot will get infected. He might lose his life or at the very least his leg." She cleaned it, put antiseptic on it and bandaged it to keep it clean. Without shoes, he could never keep the dirt out to prevent infections so she admonished him to get to a doctor for antibiotics immediately. Sending him on his way,

Jean turned to the Ugandan audience who had gathered to see how she could help them.

I often think about that young man. Frank told us, "Someday that boy will tell his kids and grandkids about the day an American woman stopped him on the side of the road and saved his life."

Another day the car tire went flat. Pulling off the side of the road, Frank set about changing the flat. For safety's sake, he had pulled to the side keeping the flat tire away from the traffic. This meant he was standing out in the brush. Suddenly he came running to the road stomping his feet and frantically slapping at his legs. Hundreds of small red ants crawled on his lower legs. We joined him slapping and brushing them off. Once he got his ant problem under control, he pulled his socks up over the bottom of his trouser legs and went back to his task. He had no more problems but Jean and I stayed on the road just in case! I suspect Jean left him a bigger tip than usual.

Working Things Out with Bruce

My first trip to Africa ended. As far as my husband was concerned, it was my last trip. But I couldn't get my head or heart out of Africa. Bruce quickly grew tired of hearing about my experiences. I couldn't wait to get back, yet he never wanted me to go again. I not only wanted to go back myself, but I knew he must go too.

He was hostile to the idea of either of us going. He said, "This was your trip of a lifetime, but now it is over!"

I have never known him to forbid me to do anything, but this came pretty darned close. It was apparent that if I went, it would be a problem in our marriage. As we talked, he shook his head and said, "I never signed up to be married to an African missionary!"

"I am not a missionary," I honestly replied. I had never thought of myself as a missionary.

"You sure sound like one!" And he didn't like it!

2008

Jean had another trip planned to Zambia in 2008, and this time several of my friends were going. Not only were they going to Africa, but they were going to Victoria Falls. I wanted to go so badly I could taste it! I knew my husband wouldn't stop me, but I also knew that it would damage our relationship. He didn't think I could stay home without resenting him. Some heavy praying needed to be done. Thinking a wife should honor her husband, but also thinking a husband should love his wife made this an important issue. I could always say I would honor him if he would love me enough, but what about in this instance? I couldn't put this on him even though I would have liked to. It seemed unfair for me to have to stay home when I wanted to go so badly.

Jean counseled me to put this trip on the altar like Abraham who was willing to sacrifice Isaac because he had faith that God would supply the sacrificial lamb (Genesis 22). So, if God wanted me to go to Zambia, He would intervene somehow. Trusting that God held the big picture, I gave up my trip with no (or at least only a little) resentment. I didn't go on that trip, but as I expected, God had different and better plans.

That year Bruce and I struggled. We processed some of our problems in our Kinship group from church. I felt strongly that we should be on the same page in our walk with God, but did that mean I needed to give up my desire to work in Africa? Or did it mean Bruce's heart had to change? When a couple is married and they have the Holy Spirit living in them, they can't be divided and be effective. The same Spirit lives in both. The Spirit isn't divided.

How can we know when is it our own spirit making the calls? Our Kinship friends prayed and stood with us through our struggles. That is what good friends do. They suggested to Bruce that he go with me so he could understand my passion. He really had no interest in going to deep dark Africa.

Changing my focus

My relationship with Jean changed. Instead of idolizing her and seeing her as a mentor, we became partners in the Uganda effort. Before Africa, I spent almost every day by her side working for H.E.L.P. International. I even stopped substitute teaching so I could follow my heart. I enjoyed teaching, but my impact seemed minimal as a sub. My efforts at the warehouse touched people all over the world as well as at home.

Once I was on fire for Uganda, I needed to shift my energy again. Since my heart was full of Africa, I focused my attention on that project. How could I help that village? How could I raise money, enlist supporters, find donations, attract others to become team members, set up trips, research ways to help improve the villagers' lives, and set up social media? Whereas Jean geared her energies toward Uganda, she still had a broader focus. My focus became much narrower. We also redirected our financial support to Uganda. This left a lack in the budget of H.E.L.P. After some discussion, Bruce agreed that we probably needed to shift the emphasis in our funding.

Just after Jean Kaye got back from Zambia, she fell from the top of a ladder and was bedridden for some time. She severely damaged her heel and walks with a small limp to this day. By this time Bruce admired and loved Jean too. We stepped in to care for her with everything we knew to do. Remarkably, in typical Jean fashion, she had already begun planning another trip to Kenya and Uganda for the spring of 2009.

My discussions with Bruce about going back to Africa had softened. He had said if Jean went back to Zambia again, he would be okay with me going. I wanted to go to Zambia, but when Jean told me about *this* trip to Kenya and Uganda, I didn't want to miss it.

Approximately a week before leaving, Jean asked me if it might be possible for me to go with her again. I would have to decide that night. My husband seldom makes quick decisions, especially one this big. I had hope since he had already agreed on the Zambia trip.

"Jean asked me if I could go with her next week to Kenya and Uganda. It is so near the time to leave we need to decide tonight. I would really like to go. I know I was planning on going to Zambia in August, but this trip feels important. What do you think?"

After I presented this option and the need for an immediate answer, I was surprised and pleased at his response: "I think Jean needs you to help her. She hasn't traveled since her fall. You need to go to be there for her if she needs you." His growing admiration for Jean won the day. I doubted she would need me, but I didn't want to argue!

Returning to Kenya and Uganda—April

A week or so later as I was on the plane to Uganda. Bruce heard "I Hope You Dance" by Lee Ann Womack on the radio as he was driving home from the airport.

Through her lyrics, Womack encourages others to consider faith when faced with adversity. To choose to keep going rather than settling for a safer or easier path. To take a chance—to dance in the face of obstacles.

Bruce told me later that at that moment he knew I was dancing!

My heart leapt. He got it! Little did he know this dance was meant for both of us. He didn't need to sit it out either.

That trip was the beginning of more than any of us could ever have imagined!

I enjoyed reconnecting in Kenya. I spent time with a couple on the International Medical Relief (IMR) team during the clinics. Bob was a dentist and Diana a strong Catholic. Serving in the midst of a group of doctors and nurses on a medical mission, she and I spoke the same language. We loved talking about God. I thought if we had lived in the same area we would be best friends. In fact, after I got home, I told Bruce we had to go to Long Island so he could meet them. Little did I know the path we would walk together.

Kaboko's Son and Mother

After the medical team left for home, Jean and I went on to Uganda. We met up with Kaboko for a brief visit. He took us to visit my current Compassion child, Praise Akatukunda, in Western Uganda. I wasn't expecting such a long trip. Nonetheless, it was good to see her. I think she was about seven or eight years old and was shy. I love her name; it's what drew me to choose her when she was five.

We met Kaboko's young son Prince Angelo Kaboko. I felt like I met another grandchild. His smile was even cuter than his dad's had been. In Uganda grandparents are called Jajas. So I became Jaja Pam! We also found out Hellen was pregnant again. What fun!

We went to see Kaboko's childhood home where his grandmother had raised him and the Compassion Project he had been a part of growing up. I met his mother and grandmother and many more relatives and friends.

A few years before this trip Bruce and I bought a new home. I only agreed to move if we could help Kaboko's mother finish the house she had been trying to complete for some years. Over the years Kaboko would mention how upset she was in the rainy season since the house she was staying in had a very leaky roof. I couldn't bear getting such a nice new home when this woman was struggling so. We inquired and found that $400 would finish her house. A small sum to us meant the world to her. We were happy to send enough money to facilitate finishing her house and doing a few "extras."

Upon completion of the house, we learned his mother could sew. She could make a living with that skill but needed a sewing machine.

A treadle machine was only about $100, so we bought one along with a cabinet. This started her tailoring business in her village. We were able to visit this house and see the sewing machine. She made clothes for all the children living nearby.

Her home was no palace, but it was nice compared to the homes around her. She was truly grateful. There were only three rooms, but they were sound and provided enough space for a bedroom, living room and a small kitchen. Her sewing could be done in a small area just between the living room and her bedroom where there was a window to help with the light.

A traditional Ugandan celebration meal had been prepared for Jean and me. Chicken was the main dish. Posho and beans were always on the menu as well as sweet potatoes, peanut paste, kava and Irish potatoes. I felt awful eating such a feast when I knew there was very little food to go around.

Compounding my guilt, there was a crowd outside this home that was not being served at all. I could hardly eat, and even refused some food hoping they would distribute it to others. Even though they were gracious, I found out it was disrespectful to turn away their offering. They were eager to please us and celebrate our visit. I turned down their hospitality and thus was inconsiderate. Jean and I were the guests of honor. Honoring is an important part of the Ugandan culture. This was also their way of thanking me for the help we had been to their family over the years.

To make me feel a little better Frank told me a story about a time he was in another African country that brought him a head of a chicken with the beak open and the tongue sticking out as if it were screaming. It was so grotesque he made up some excuse and didn't eat it either.

As soon as I could after our meal, I sat on the ground with the women gathered outside. I sat with Kaboko's grandmother to honor her for all her efforts in raising him when his mother was married to another man. I wondered why she was outside instead of enjoying the meal inside the house with us.

While I was outside with the friends and grandmother, I saw all the children run to a small mound. They jumped and laughed and grabbed at something in the air. At dusk, flying ants come up out of a hole in the mound. The kids grabbed them and popped them into their mouths, raw and whole! I surely wasn't in Kansas anymore!

When we were leaving, Kaboko's mother brought a live chicken for him to take home in the car. She held it upside down, and for some reason it didn't move or make a peep in the car. Kaboko had it under his feet on the floorboard where I couldn't see it. I was glad I didn't know what was happening. Those from farms probably wouldn't be as shocked as I was. It reminded me of all the times I sent home food with my grown children. Mothers are alike all over the world.

Starting the School in Masese

The night before we were to visit Masese again Jean had a dream in which the Ugandan children were excitedly calling our names, "Miss Jean! Miss Pam!" like they knew us well. I hid that away in my heart, wondering.

When we arrived in Masese, Jean called a meeting with the original "youth" who had asked for her help. She was frustrated because nothing she had done to help had been effective. She asked the group, "What skills do you need? What opportunities are there for you? What skills do you already have? What can we do to do to help you get jobs?"

One man, Ben, said softly, "I am a teacher."

I about fell out of my chair. He didn't need training; he needed a job.

Jean looked at all the children running around outside. These kids were obviously not going to school anywhere. They lacked money for school fees. School in Uganda is free but there are uniforms and multiple fees required that make it difficult for many kids to attend school. If you factor in that the average daily salary is around $1 or $1.50 a day and eighty percent unemployment in Uganda, you can see how a uniform costing around $8 and school shoes costing around $15 are a true hardship.

Jean waved her arm toward the children and asked, "Ben, can you teach those kids?"

He replied confidently, "I can."

I had been looking to sponsor another Compassion child in this area since I could see him or her if we came again. Sponsoring a child was $38 a month at this time. So I asked Ben, "What does a teacher earn per month?"

He replied, "$40 to$100."

I clarified, "You mean $40 to $100 a month?"

He nodded his head. "Yes."

I quickly calculated that I could support a man taking care of his family and educate a classroom of children for not much more than the cost of sponsoring one child. When he said he could teach those children who were unable to attend a regular school, I told Jean I wanted to pay his salary instead of sponsoring with Compassion. I would pay $60 a month.

She offered him the challenge. "Put together a roster of students that would have no opportunity to go to a regular school, get permission from the government to teach, and get the curriculum/syllabus the government schools use. Once that is accomplished we will start paying you to teach."

As we walked out, Jean looked at me and said, "Do you have any idea what we just did?" Neither of us had any expectation of starting a school. I couldn't figure out how Ben would do this. Would he hold class under a tree? With no supplies?

Within two days Ben had a roster of forty-five children and the government syllabus. He was ready to go!

I asked him to keep in contact with me through an internet cafe. He found a few chairs and a box of printer paper from the container we had sent a few years before. He drew pictures and wrote the word under the picture in English. With these crude supplies Ben began teaching first under a tree, then in the corner of one of the dilapidated pole barn structures. At least he had a roof. No walls, floor, pencils, paper, books, or anything else. He borrowed a blackboard from a close-by business since they only needed it for their business during the evenings. Six weeks later he emailed that he now had ninety students.

"Ben," I asked, "why would you let so many kids into your class?"

He explained, "Madam, they come and sit around the perimeter of the building where I am holding class, so I just invite them to come on in. They are eager to learn."

"Ben," I said in astonishment, "I love your heart! But that is too many students for one teacher. Can you find another teacher to help you?"

I tried to envision the little ones sitting around the edge of his wall-less classroom listening so they could learn too. They had been left out and left behind. Ben knew quite well what his class meant for them. He didn't want to leave them behind, so he didn't.

As he looked for someone to be a second teacher, I told this story to a group at Jean's warehouse. Susan Bruns was there sorting clothing to be boxed and shipped in a container. She said she would sponsor this new teacher.

Susan has stood with us in this unplanned, unimagined endeavor for all these years and still sponsors Lydia, the second teacher. This faithful woman's strand of thread in the Weaver's hand must be extra beautiful.

We now had a project in Uganda. Not a planned one, but it felt like God had plans that we hadn't even imagined. "Now to Him who is able to do exceedingly abundantly above all that we ask or think, according to the power that works in us, to Him be glory in the church by Christ Jesus to all generations, forever and ever. Amen" (Ephesians 3:20-21 NKJV).

To this day I marvel that God chose me to be involved in His plans for this village. I laugh when I think of the time I begged God, "Please don't send me to Africa!" Here I was begging to get to go. It all made sense. I knew why I had trained to be a teacher, why I needed to learn to be a salesperson, why I have been an advocate for Compassion, why I had been a sponsor, why I had met Jean, and why so many things in my life had led up to this opportunity. I feel incredibly privileged to be even a small part of this God-breathed village empowerment project! But I am getting a bit ahead of myself again.

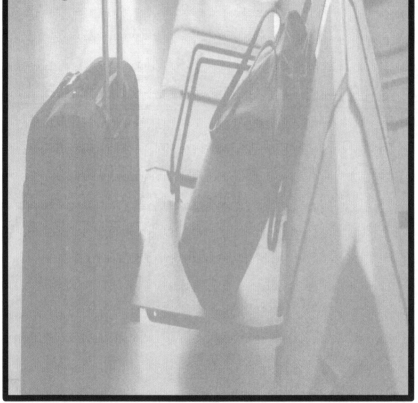

We were in Africa!

It's interesting to see who comes into the country. Early on there weren't many Westerners. Over the years more and more young adults are traveling to Uganda on short term mission trip, coming on their own for adventure, or working with the Peace Corp. They are excited and full of energy. There are Ugandan families entering their homeland. There are more seasoned Westerners just walking through the process once again, and businessmen coming to do their business.

2009

Bruce's First Trip to Africa

I returned from my trip to Kenya and Uganda with a fire in me. Not a little flame, but a full-blown fire, more directed this time. I had been in on the beginning of a new primary school. I could hardly talk about anything else. The village of Masese in Uganda had captured my heart. My teacher's heart was enthralled at the realization we had made a way for unschooled children to be educated. We were having a part in turning illiteracy into knowledge.

These children now had hope they didn't have before. I felt like I was truly making a difference in many lives. Everything in me was consumed with this endeavor.

I had a hard time being at home in the U.S. People avoided talking with me. My brother wouldn't even view my pictures. He said it was like looking at someone else's boring vacation photos. My mother and father worried when I went so far away so they didn't really want to hear about everything. Bruce grew impatient and said I had become a "one-trick pony."

I tried to be sensitive to their feelings, but I simply had no choice. I had to share. I was consumed. God had shown me what I was all about. Once again, this seriously strained my marriage. Bruce couldn't understand because he hadn't been there. He hadn't walked where I walked and seen what I saw. He couldn't possibly feel what I was feeling.

Bruce thought it was a "no-brainer" to pay Ben's salary—to help a man support his family and teach children all in one payment. He still didn't like the idea of me going to Africa, but he saw I was doing what I loved and didn't want to stand in my way. Finally, with so many friends encouraging him to take a trip to Uganda, Bruce joined us on next trip in September. He wasn't very happy about it. He was pretty sure he would die over there. Later, he admitted that he was only going to see if he could stay married to me. He didn't feel like our marriage could work with me being so involved in a mission in Africa. God protected me from that realization until much later. All I saw was my husband finally giving Uganda a chance. As I look back, I see what a love he had for me to be willing to overcome the fear of death to see if he could salvage our marriage.

First Team and Friends

On the 29th of October 2009, our small team left for Uganda. There were five women and my husband. We found wonderful Humanitarian Aid tickets. Each of us could take three fifty-pound bags, along with carry-ons. We packed personal clothes and incidentals in our carry-ons and saved the larger bags for school supplies, clothes, first aid, meds, toothpaste and toothbrushes, books, VBS materials, and Bibles. I was challenged to pack carefully so I wouldn't take any room away from those who needed what we were bringing more than I needed to have a nice wardrobe.

Long Flight

Right out of the chute we had to repack our luggage at the airport. Our scales were inaccurate so there was too much weight in every suitcase. On top of that, the tools the men had received as gifts at the last minute had been added to most of the bags. All of our bags needed to be lightened. If you can imagine, we had to open all eighteen pieces of luggage right there on the airport floor and reposition or offload. It was a mess! The allowance is fifty pounds and overage is expensive. Thinking we wouldn't have to deal with these bags again until we arrived in Uganda once they were the correct weight and all checked in, we breathed a collective sigh of relief.

Unfortunately, we missed our flight in London and had to spend the night before reboarding twenty-four hours later. We had to collect our luggage and recheck them the next day. What do a group of women do when "stuck" in London? We decided it would be fun to do sightseeing!

Not thinking much about all the luggage, we hopped on a train and spent the afternoon running around London. Bruce got stuck with all eighteen pieces of fifty-pound bags and our carry-ons. We helped him onto the shuttle to the hotel, but once at the hotel, he had a huge challenge taking care of all this luggage. He was not a very happy camper. Here he was, alone, on a trip he didn't want to go on in the first place while all five seemingly clueless women went off on a lark in jolly old London! When he finally got all the luggage safely stowed in a room, he went to the bar and had a drink! Probably two!

The flight is really long, even without a twenty-four-hour delay, and crossing time zones compounds the tiredness. We have a nine-hour time zone difference from Colorado to Uganda. Overseas flights do what they can to make your flight endurable. On British Air we received eye masks, socks, a little toothbrush with paste, and a blanket and pillow. The food is tolerable and appreciated. The blankets are thin and not usually warm enough so I bring a little something for warmth to supplement. On top of that, I bring lotion, eye drops, and a moisturizer for my nose. The dry air on planes can be brutal on such long flights. I also take extra vitamins and a jet lag chewable I found at the health food store to minimize jet lag. Thank goodness for the inflight movies. They help pass much of the time.

In keeping with time zones, we might have breakfast at 9:30 at night to coordinate with in the time zone we were heading to. It helps us acclimate to the time zone of our destination.

Bruce fell asleep as the plane was taking off. I think that was remarkable as I can hardly sleep at all on a plane. I often wish God had pricked my heart for a ministry closer to home. We were in the air around twenty hours, not including time spent on layovers, traveling to the airport, arriving three hours early for the international flight, and finally, time driving from the airport to our village Ugh!

On my first trip to Uganda I looked out the plane's window as we arrived. I turned to Jean Kaye and said, "What are we doing over the ocean?" It wasn't the ocean at all but Lake Victoria. I had no idea it was so huge! There was water for as far as I could see. Lake Victoria is the second largest freshwater lake and the largest tropical lake in the world, with a surface area of 26,600 square miles. The single outlet for this lake is in Jinja, which is the northern part of the shore where the Nile river sources.

Arriving

Once the plane stopped, we were ushered off the plane onto stairs descending to the tarmac. The air felt different. A big grin spread across my face.

We get our Visas right there and the luggage usually arrives intact. We unload our luggage from the conveyor belt and get it to a car. There are always plenty of Ugandans who want to help us. We don't have schillings yet to tip them and the exchange rate is not the best at the airport. So we pile our bags on carts and roll them out the door where we find a multitude of Africans waiting to pick up their travelers. They hold up signs with names on them.

Relying on someone to get you from here to there in an unknown locale can be tricky. I've had extremely good experiences in my journeys and believe it's because my heavenly Father takes good care of me as all good fathers would do for their daughters.

We were met by our Ugandan driver and friend, Frank, who had arranged for us to go in one van and our luggage in another to a hotel for Westerners in Kampala. Can you imagine all that luggage? Logistics can be complicated on these team trips. We were bursting at the seams, even in two large vans.

We arrived late at night so traffic was less than we now know it can be, but at the time Bruce's fear that he would die in Africa seemed way too real. Riding in the front seat, Bruce had a clear view of car headlights coming straight for us. At the last minute, each car would swerve to their respective sides (the opposite side of what we are used to) and then take their place back in the middle of the road.

On top of this confusion, there were the bodas everywhere. A boda is a motor bike that carries passengers. These inexpensive "taxis" zipped in and out of traffic. They are called bodas because originally the motorcycles transported goods from one border to the other, thus "boda-to-boda". Men might pack four or more onto one boda. Women sit sideways with nothing to hold onto. Often multiple children hang onto their mamas. Bodas also carry goods—anything from whole beds, huge bunches of bananas, chairs piled to the sky, or even a live cow or pig for the market. It always amazes me the balance these drivers have.

First Morning

The hotel where we stayed that night sat high on a hill overlooking Kampala. Kampala is known as the City of Seven Hills, but it covers over twenty-one hills. It has a transient population of 2.3 million people. I awoke early the next morning all excited to be back in Uganda. Bruce was sleeping. Since the trip had been a long one, I let him sleep while I went outside. Greenery grew everywhere. I soaked in the morning sun and the amazing view of the sprawling city until I couldn't stand it any longer. I woke Bruce. "Get up! We are in AFRICA! How can you sleep?"

"Okay, okay! I'm up!" he responded to my enthusiasm. We had a perfectly lovely breakfast out on the porch with our small team where we could take in the vista overlooking the city and the lush surroundings of the hotel grounds. The melodious songs of the birds and the vibrancy of the tropical flowers teamed with the feel of humid temperate air welcomed us as only Africa can. Uganda is just off Lake Victoria, and with the altitude at nearly 4000 feet above sea level, the temperature is usually in the 80s. If it gets into the lower 70s, the Africans feel cold.

Breakfasts aren't that dissimilar to what we have at home. Eggs cooked how we order, toast, delicious fruit (usually pineapple, watermelon or papayas, sweet bananas) and tea. African tea contains milk, sugar, and tea masala (cardamom and ginger) and is delicious. Coffee is often not as good as Americans are used to. Bruce has learned to bring small packets of his own. Even Bruce relaxed and enjoyed the exoticness of our morning.

Drive from Kampala to Jinja

After breakfast, we set out for Jinja, traveling through a portion of the bustling capital city. Smoke and the thick brown pollution haze that covers the city filled my asthmatic lungs. I had not yet learned to wear a mask. The heavy traffic jams slowed us down considerably.

We traveled through smaller towns beside bicycles carrying unbelievably large loads. Bikes were used for their wheels. The drivers walked alongside and pushed their load via the handlebars. Once in a while we saw a cart being pulled by an industrious man.

It was interesting to see the variety of small businesses alongside the road as we drove. All the billboards have African people on them. I know that sounds obvious, but it surprised me. The small businesses would have hand-painted signs portraying a picture of what they were selling or the name of their businesses. Often those business names are religious in nature, like "God Loves You Hairdressers" or "Jesus Loves the Little Children Nursery School."

Furniture-makers displayed their wares by the side of the road—bed frames, bunk beds up to three levels high, and big overstuffed sofas. Butchers hung their meat among various fruit and vegetable stands, artistically and colorfully arranged. There were crafts like three-legged stools to sit on, splendidly colored fabrics, dresses hung on wire female forms with big wide hips, cell phone charging stations, and many places to buy airtime.

Unlike America, where people stay in their houses or in their cars, Ugandan people walked everywhere, visited with acquaintances on the road, sat outside their houses, purchased their daily needs, and listened to loud music, all adding color to their dusty surroundings with their brightly colored clothes, or as Ugandans say in their proper British accents, "clotheses."

As we got closer to Jinja, we traveled through a forest. During the day it is scenic, but we found out later it is foreboding at night. It was the closest to my Tarzan idea of Africa; jungle, vines for swinging through the trees, snakes and all that—except there is a road through it.

I didn't actually see all of that but where the forest was dense and green with an air of mystery to it, my imagination ran that direction. In contrast to the city and town clamor, this was a quiet stretch except for the sound of birds. No one was walking. People tell stories of finding corpses alongside the road from time to time.

This particular morning a semi had turned over, stopping traffic from both directions. It is hard to explain Ugandan traffic. There is little regard for lanes. Even though it is illegal, many drivers go around on the sides. What should be two lanes often become four, with cars driving in the middle toward each other until they have to move. Where this semi had turned over there were cars sitting nose-to-nose with no possibility of advancing. We were exhausted, and Bruce was certain he was not supposed to be in this foreign country. I can't remember how we ever got unstuck, but Bruce says it took hours of inching and weaving our way through.

Once past the forest, we came upon verdant fields of sugarcane and tea. The favorable climate and richness of the soil enable Uganda to develop some of the world's best-quality tea. I love the carpeted look of tea fields. Their beauty is hard to surpass. We passed a large sugar mill named Kakira Sugar Works. This is one of three sugar mills producing, between them, over 200,000 tons of sugar per year.

History of Jinja

Before 1906, Jinja was a fishing village that benefited from being on long-distance trade routes. The origin of the name "Jinja" comes from the language of the two peoples (the Baganda and the Basoga) who lived in the area on either side of the River Nile. In both languages "Jinja" means "Rock."

In most of Africa, rivers like the Nile hindered migration. The area around Jinja was one place where the river could be crossed because of the large rocks near the Ripon Falls. Here, on both banks of the river, were large flat rocks where small boats could be launched. These rock formations also provided a natural moderator for the water flow out of Lake Victoria. For the original local inhabitants, the location was a crossing point for trade and migration as well as a fishing post. This might explain why, despite this water barrier, the two tribes have very similar languages. The more powerful Baganda had an enormous influence on the Basoga. They called the area the "Place of Rocks" or "The Place of Flat Rocks."

In pre-colonial times, Jinja had merely been a fishing village but it gained much recognition as the source of the Nile following the visit by the British explorer John H. Speke in 1859.

The development of the Ugandan Railway in 1901 and the opening of port services was another achievement for Jinja. This developed into the firm establishment of the town in 1907. Its rich agricultural land and coffee-processing and cotton-ginning enterprises stimulated the development of Jinja into a medium-sized trading center. They established more railroad lines in 1928 and 1931, further connecting strategic transportation avenues.

Thereafter, the natural endowments for hydroelectric power production led to the opening of Owen Falls Dam in 1954. Driven by Euro-Asiatic enterprise, the dam provided the abundant electricity which transformed Jinja into Uganda's top industrial town throughout the 1960s, 1970s and 1980s.

The bridge to the villages is heavily guarded. Destruction of it would bring much commerce to an abrupt halt and cripple defenses. In spite of its exceptional base of affluence, Jinja fell into sharp decline as a result of the exodus of Asians who followed Idi Amin's declaration of an "economic war'" in Uganda in 1972 and post-Amin civil wars. Also contributing to the decline has been the migration of many of the businesses to the capital city of Kampala.

I can see the British Colonial influence today in the housing permeating Jinja Town. Most of the homes have decayed, but their former extravagance is still being proclaimed. Their elegance, though diminished, speaks of an age gone by that was once powerful. With the independence of Uganda from colonial rule, many structures were destroyed, but the remaining buildings and houses are worth viewing to remember their former influence.

Along with homes, the city provides a small airport, a golf club, and a sailing club. Bruce enjoyed seeing baby monkeys frolic about as he golfed. At one time animals were abundant, but when hungry people hunted and ate crocodiles, hippos, and monkeys, the remaining animals were moved to protected areas where we now have safaris.

Nile Guest House

We always stay at the Nile Guest House, renamed The Nile Hotel a few years after we made it our Ugandan home. It has four levels and is always clean. You can't call it luxury but usually the water is hot and the electricity works. If not, a generator is used until the electricity comes back. Theft can be quite a problem because of poverty, so the armed guard and high wall that surrounds the spacious, well-cared-for garden are welcome. The stairs to the rooms are uneven, which takes an adjustment. Each room has a balcony with a couple of chairs to encourage us to enjoy the view.

On Bruce's first trip, we stayed on the first floor where geckos often visited. Bruce almost stepped on one during his first shower. The friendly little guy was just trying to welcome him to Uganda.

First Glimpse of the School

After unloading, we headed out to the village of Masese to visit the school. Coming closer and closer to Masese, Jean and I each had a sense of expectancy, wondering what we would see. When we left on the previous trip, we didn't know how they would hold classes or even if they would stay the course.

As we entered the compound, we heard the children reciting their lessons! Tears streamed down our faces. They were learning! The sound of their voices coming from their classrooms brought up a feeling in me I never felt before. I was overcome with gratitude. Awestruck that God was using me, little insignificant me, to impact these children's lives. I was incredibly proud of the work the teachers and students were doing and felt full of hope for these precious children.

When we left the village on our last trip, we couldn't imagine what this class would be like. And now, here it was in full swing. My heart burst with joy as I saw the kids in their school. They sang and clapped and welcomed us as only African children can. "We are very happy, we are very, very happy. We are happy to see you today." They proudly stood in a group singing. As they sang a single student would leave the others to come nearer to us to individually sing their welcome song. It went something like "My name is _____, the head girl of the school. Our nature is happiness whenever we look at you. Our visitors, you are welcome to this place where you are. We have waited for you coming from the bottom of our hearts."

I was so proud to be a part of what God was doing in this village. We were prepared for ninety students and found one hundred fifty! And ... we found Billy.

The teachers

Billy was a young man who volunteered to teach with Ben and Lydia. Billy's mother died just after her youngest child was born. The baby also died soon after. That left six boys and two girls. They lived with their father in Northern Uganda. When Billy had gone to school for a year, the war broke out in Northern Uganda. All schooling stopped.

When Billy was ten years old, people were running for their lives from the Lord's Resistance Army. None of his elder brothers and sisters ever went to school because of the war. They lost most of their relatives in that war. The war was not ending and young children Billy's age were being stolen and trained as soldiers. Billy's father took Billy to Jinja to live with his uncle and aunt.

There was no money for school fees for the next four years. Billy's father died, leaving him an orphan. In 2004, Billy fished by night so he could go to school during the day. This took him from Primary grade three up to Senior 3. Once again, he could not pay school fees and had to leave school. Billy was safe with his aunt but his aunt didn't have the means to send him to school.

Billy loved teaching at the Help School and was well-liked by the children; however, he didn't have the education to be a paid teacher for this fledgling school. We sent him to night school to complete his secondary schooling while he taught for us during the day. Susan Bruns, who sponsored Lydia, the second teacher, had a granddaughter who used her allowance to sponsor Billy. For years, this young girl and her parents made a difference in this young man's life and in the lives of the school children he was teaching.

Today Billy has not only completed his secondary schooling, but he has his teaching certificate and his diploma. It has been an extra-long haul, as a school he and Lydia were attending for their teaching certificates closed down suddenly, causing them to lose all their time there. He had to start over, but he was determined and has fully earned his success. Billy is also a superb coach for our school athletics program and teaches math in Primary 5 and Primary 6.

Once I overheard him talking to a class about addition, telling them that the plus sign could remind them of the cross that Jesus died on. He has a great big heart for the kids and loves God passionately, and I love him!

We met Lydia for the first time, too. She was perfect for our little school. She not only had a heart for the neediest, but she had lived that life herself. Lydia grew up with her grandmother in her early years and never met her father. She was "collected" from her grandmother by her mother and a new family when she was in grade four. That family welcomed her and still loves her. Her stepfather lost his job and couldn't pay her school fees. She worked for

teachers and sold dried fish and sugarcane up to high school to get her own money for the fees. When she could no longer afford the fees, she got married. She finished her schooling to become a certified teacher and taught until her school closed.

Her marriage didn't work out so well. She had to struggle to find a job so she could buy food and pay for rentx and medical services. Teaching in the Help school has changed her family's life, and she is proud of what she is doing. She can now care for her four children as a single parent.

I enjoyed getting to know Ben better on this trip, too. His parents died when he was two years old so his grandmother and aunt educated him. He completed his education in 2001. At that time, his grandmother and aunt passed away. Married to Rona, he had two young boys and one on the way. He previously taught at a high school until it closed due to lack of funding.

Teaching Conditions

Ben, Lydia, and Billy were gentle and patient as they worked with the kids. With very little to work with, they did amazingly well teaching over one hundred fifty children kindergarten age and younger in one small space with no walls!

The Baby Class, equivalent to nursery school in the U.S., starts at age three. The student then attends Middle Class, which would be like our preschool. Next, they go to Top Class, which is similar to our Kindergarten. Primary 1 begins their elementary school years. The Primary 1 class had less students than the younger classes and was much more manageable. Still, as a teacher myself, I knew there were entirely too many kids in each class. The government allows forty-five students on average. I would be more comfortable with less than thirty.

Further, imagine no sound barrier! Teachers relayed information, and the students loudly recited what they were to learn. Just imagine the cacophony of multiple classes! Planks of wood about shoulder high separated the classrooms. No ceiling existed. There was an uneven, rugged red dirt floor, and no walls to the outside. With so many distractions, it is a wonder anyone learned anything at all!

The goats loved coming into the school rooms. Like in the nursery rhyme about Mary and her little lamb, they "made the children laugh and play to see the 'goat' at school." Then the goats proceeded to eat the papers the teacher had displayed, right off the wall!

We were thrilled for the roof since there was a downpour one day. The kids laughed at me under my umbrella. They ran and played in the rain. We watched boys play soccer in the rain as if there weren't large puddles and torrential rain coming down like "cats and dogs." The boys were oblivious to Bruce as he videoed their game. As Bruce hid behind his camera, I wondered if he was comparing his own boyhood to that of these young guys. He mentioned that he admired how they were competitive, yet stopped to take care of a younger one who fell. The person was more important than the game. I could see the wheels of Bruce's heart turning as he experienced this foreign way of life.

The school grounds quickly became a lake since their drainage was poor. Red dirt became red mud with pools of red dirty water standing everywhere, until the rain stopped. All the puddles soaked into the ground in just minutes once the downpour stopped, leaving us with murky mud to navigate. Red dirt stained our shoes, so in future years we kept the same shoes to wear each time we visited.

Cleanliness is important, even though conditions are difficult. Soon after the rain stopped, there were women and students cleaning the veranda. This way, less mud would be tracked into the office rooms. Cleaning consisted of dumping buckets of water onto the concrete then vigorously sweeping the water and mud off to the dirt below the veranda. If it was the floor of an interior room, a bucket of water and a woman or child scrubbed with a brush on their hands and knees.

First Team—Vacation Bible School

Trissa, Sandy, Stephanie, and I decided to do a form of a Vacation Bible School for the kids in our area and in a neighboring village. I'm not sure how many came to the first one, but there were 800 kids in the second village—extremely challenging and rewarding. We taught them songs and explained that God had promises for their lives. We read Bible stories and did a craft.

The craft was simply a paper plate with their handprint on it in red paint. We wrote the words "Jesus loves me" on each child's plate. Working with kids who don't speak English and have never done a craft makes for much excitement and pandemonium. By God's grace, we persevered and felt like we got our message across that we loved them because of God's love for them. A group of kids took their plates and waved them over their heads, shouting "Jesus loves me" to everyone who passed.

First-time visitors to Uganda have different initial reactions. Many weep. One man was approached by a child who pointed to his pudgy tummy and said, "You must be rich." The man fell to the ground and sobbed. Some newcomers just shake their heads, not knowing where to start. Some play with the kids right away. Others sit in the safety of the van until they acclimate to the harsh surroundings. Bruce hid behind his camera. He took lots of video, knowing he could never tell the story of what he was seeing any other way.

We performed our second program in a nearby Karamojong village. This area was even poorer than the village of Masese where we had established the school. Life and the people were rougher. The nomadic Karamoja tribe is a warring tribe. They are IDPs (Internationally Displaced People), shunned by the locals like a leper colony without leprosy. Men are said to go around naked as a healthy sign that they are clean from disease and, therefore, desirable.

This tribe doesn't usually put down roots, so their sense of community is contentious at times. Rivulets of urine ran alongside the unpaved street, people stared in rather unfriendly ways, and kids pulled and pushed. The poverty was so overwhelming a few members of our team didn't want to leave the van. However, we smiled and sang to the kids, wanting them to feel God's love through us.

Kids at Karamojong

Everything was going well until we tried to give out bread. Bruce didn't know that white people will get mobbed if we give out anything ourselves. With Frank's help, Bruce began to distribute the food while we finished up the craft. But as they passed out chunks of bread, women grabbed it, hid it in their dresses, and grabbed for more. They even took from the children.

Bruce was getting mobbed until a couple of twelve to thirteen-year-old boys who had been following him around stepped up to help him. They took the bread and distributed it themselves. The boys knew their people and the language, so they could be fair. They helped to diffuse what had quickly become a riot. There was more bread in the car reserved for our village and the local women figured that out. They grabbed into the car for more bread. Jean got our team's attention and led them by foot across the village, perpendicular and away from the car. Bruce and Frank were able to get in the car.

As the car drove down the road, people ran alongside still trying to get more to eat. Again, Bruce was not sure he would make it out alive and didn't know where we women had gone. He looked at Frank and said sarcastically, "Well, that was fun! What's next?" With a smile Frank answered, "Don't be afraid, my brother." He drove away and soon we met up with the car and jumped in. All of us marveled at how quickly the people's desperation led to the little riot. I didn't return to this village for quite a while, but now I have good friends there. We learned lesson after lesson about cultures and tribes and expectations and hunger.

Feeding the School Children

Our team fed the children each school day. There was no kitchen at the school, so we bought fruit, raw carrots, roasted peanuts, boiled eggs, and slices of bread. I don't think the kids had ever eaten raw carrots. They would chew for a while and then spit out chewed bites. I expect it is safer for them to eat cooked food, anyway.

We learned as we went. In the last class to be served, we could see we would run out of eggs for each student. I was not sure what to do until I saw a girl take a bite out of her egg and pass it to her friend. I was touched. Ben said the kids come to school hungry and can't concentrate well. It became clear we needed to raise money for a feeding program.

Sandy's eight-year-old grandson Asher took his wagon around his neighborhood and raised money for her to bring to help the kids in Masese. The generous donations he received from his neighborhood and his family helped in several directions, but most of all, he was appreciated for his feeding of the children. Way to go, Asher!

Finding the money we need almost always presents a challenge, but introducing hungry kids to potential donors is not a problem. No one wants someone to be hungry, especially not children.

One dollar feeds ten kids a lunch. Or ten dollars feed those same ten children school lunches for two weeks.

We needed to feed 150 kids, five days a week, week in and week out, and couldn't stop for school holidays. We needed to purchase equipment and pay cooks. The school was growing, so we needed to account for growth. We couldn't feed the children without feeding the staff. The challenge was how to reach those with a heart for helping. Since this project was God's idea, I knew He would have a plan.

Looking back, it seems like just another multiplication story, I don't know exactly how we got the money at first. We kept feeding and somehow the money to cover our expenses just kept coming in. Eventually, we got donations specified for the feeding program, and as the school has grown, we have been able to continue feeding all involved.

This whole feeding program is a testimony to God's faithfulness.

I do not think it is His will that anyone should be hungry. He not only provided for their hunger, but He added good nutrition beyond anything they were consistently getting at home. When asked to describe the essence of the Christian message, Mother Teresa would often hold up a child's hand and recite Jesus' words in Matthew 25:40: "Whatever you did for one of the least of these brothers and sisters of mine, you did for me." She would then jiggle the child's fingers one by one, and repeat: "You. Did. It. To. Me." Mother Teresa saw Jesus in the face of every needy person she ministered to because she understood that "the least of these" referred to the poor.

Our students came from Masese, Soweto, and Walukaba. All of these areas are in the Jinja District, with Soweto being the poorest. Eighty percent of our students come from Soweto. About one third of our students were Muslim. The Muslims, Catholics and Born-agains live peacefully, respecting each other's beliefs. I recognize that a child is Muslim by his or her name. They are hard to say or spell.

The rest of the kids have both an African name and a Christian name like Betty or Ronny. All the children learn both their mother's tribal language and their father's, along with the country's common language of Lugandan. Children may know three languages when they start school. Educated parents also teach English (British style). This gives the child a fourth language and is a great boost to their learning. English is the country's national language since they were a colony of Britain for many years.

History of Masese

Masese was a squatter area in the Jinja District with an ethnically mixed population of 700 immigrant households from different parts of Uganda who were dependent on low and unreliable incomes. We learned that this portion of Masese was also called Danida, short for Danish International Development Agency.

The Danish became involved in the area at the invitation of the Ministry of Lands, Housing and Urban Development, and the project was managed by the African Housing fund.

Most of the households in Masese were led by the women so the project became known as a women's project. This project was to improve living conditions and to develop skills and employment opportunities for women.

The Danish funded this program with a combination of loans and grants from 1989 to 1994. Under the project, 300 houses were built, and water, sanitation, roads and drainage were provided. Loans were provided to the workers so they could purchase the homes they were constructing. At its height, 250 Masese men and women were employed as manufacturers and suppliers of high quality building materials.

The Masese Women's Association (MWA)

The Masese Women's Association had a president, secretary, and treasurer with offices on site. The pole barns where the school began were originally used for the building of roof tiles and blocks for houses. This was a showcase project, recognized and applauded by the Ugandan government. Unfortunately, after a few years, this project failed from a lack of oversight on the side of the Danish government and from corruption on the Ugandan side. The flow of work was spasmodic and limited to a few markets.

By 2006 business was at a standstill. The roads were still good, and the houses housed people who held loans now in default. The buildings serving the construction of the tiles were falling down and weeds had grown. There were rectangular concrete pits filled with water and sewage. We renamed them the mosquito pits.

The people became discouraged and lost hope. Many turned to the local distillery to drown their dashed dreams. No one used this area except for drug dealers, witch doctors, and a rather dubious video parlor. The MWA gave us permission to use their property when Jean was approached about helping the youth get vocational training. These "youth" were the grown sons of some of the MWA members. Somewhere along the way that permission was not given in the way we understood. Even though the earlier business project had been defunct for many years, a few of the members wanted to collect rent and control what we did on "their" property.

Water, Electricity, and Latrines

The school needed water for the kids to drink and wash their hands. There was no latrine, and students were being sent home (or wherever!) to relieve themselves. Electricity was a hit-or-miss proposition, as we relied on a rather tenuously spliced connection to a nearby shop providing air time and various other sundries to the local community. The computers we sent for vocational training and the sewing machines for tailoring classes could not be used until we had a building in which to house them.

Jean Kaye and Bruce set about meeting with the powers that be to get the permissions and blessings needed. This could not be a functional school, let alone an accredited school, without a latrine. During this first trip, Bruce realized he had some political clout. On this trip and every subsequent one, he was able to bring in different governmental groups, other NGOs and local businesses to further the good of the school and community. He started building these political muscles to get the latrine, water, and electricity on his very first trip. He became a political guru, getting anything done and done well.

We put in a water tap for the school children to use. A lock was put on it to keep the villagers from using the water we were funding. This didn't prevent the locals from stealing the copper piping, however, which created serious problems for the project.

In order to get electricity turned back on in the office buildings, we were required to pay back bills incurred by the previous group. God intervened and most of those old bills were waived. Quite miraculous! The wiring strung above the ceilings of the abandoned office buildings wasn't safe. When Sandy's husband, Bob, came on a subsequent trip he helped make the wiring a bit safer.

Once the electricity was on, we set up three computers. It thrilled me to see young faces in total amazement as they sat in front of a computer for the first time. I'd brought computer learning games for different ages. Older boys were learning keyboarding at the same time I introduced the computer to a few primary students. They had so much fun learning keyboarding you would have thought I had brought them a video game. I love this part of teaching.

Seeing kids awaken to what the world has out there for them to learn and having them be such eager learners was a true joy. They were excited to come to class. Before our school opened, these kids would watch their friends walk to the local school in their nice uniforms while they stayed at home, working in their rags with no hope of ever having anything better. Now they were proud to get a chance to learn and were grateful for each opportunity.

Meetings

More insidious than the issues with the latrines, electricity, and water, was our dealings with a small faction of the MWA who claimed we did not follow protocol when gaining permission to use the building and land for the school. According to our documents, we were not in any error. But that didn't ease the tension. It took three attempts to meet with all the persons in power in the village until a resolution was reached.

Meetings in Masese, and maybe in all of Uganda, don't start on any strictly enforced schedule. This is hard for Westerners who value schedules. The cultural difference was frustrating because we had a limited amount of time to get things accomplished. At times, it seemed like we were swimming in molasses. The final meeting was supposed to start at two on Sunday afternoon. As we waited and waited for anyone to show up, we wondered if they were coming at all. Almost two hours went by, and Jean and Bruce were getting disgusted. We wondered if these people even wanted our help. Maybe we should leave the area and look for a more welcoming location.

As I listened to their frustrations, I remembered all that had led us to this very place—the miracles and successes; hearing the students recite their lessons; and working with Ben, Lydia, and Billy. In my heart, I knew we were right where we were supposed to be. I had a peace I couldn't explain. I decided to say nothing and just watch.

A little boy, maybe three years old, all dirty and ragged, and with a runny nose, came up and tugged on Bruce's hand. He looked up at Bruce with big, pleading eyes, that seemed to say, "Are you going to leave me?" Bruce said he felt like he was looking into the eyes of Jesus. As Jean and Bruce took in this moment, they both knew, as I did, that we couldn't leave. There was no one else. God had plans for us here. We could see it in that face. This was a defining moment in our hearts, and right after that, people started arriving for the meeting.

This was my first time meeting the village chairman. He was older and wise in the ways of his people. We liked him from the start. He was a Muslim and was uncomfortable working with women. He didn't speak any English, and for a few years, wouldn't look me in the eye. From the beginning, though, he recognized that we were trying to do a good thing and told the MWA to work with us. He spoke to the small faction of people, "Why are you giving these people trouble when they are doing such good things for our children?"

After much discussion (in Lugandan), we had a groundbreaking at the site where we ended up digging our first latrine. Both Jean Kaye and Joyce, the president of the MWA, turned a shovel full of dirt. It was momentous!

Katie

Katie came to Uganda on a school break, during her senior year in 2007. She was a normal high school girl. Katie had a serious boyfriend, college plans, and a close-knit family. When she returned the following year, she never left. Barely beyond her teenage years, she adopted thirteen Ugandan girls—not one or two, but thirteen. She took them in to live with her permanently. Can you imagine?

We often warn people that Africa will ruin them. Well, that could probably be said a better way, but the warning is that you will be changed. Katie saw the opportunity to make a huge difference by being the hands and feet of Jesus to those who desperately needed her. I read her blog avidly, impressed that so many of her readers financially support her work. Maybe that is where the seed was planted for me to write this book. I know it encouraged me to write my own blogs to capture my experiences and feelings.

We met Katie and her girls in 2009. She worked in the Karamojong village right next to us, feeding 1500 kids every school day in a school just up the hill from ours. At this point we weren't feeding anyone, so it amazed me she could do so much. Katie says she felt like she was supposed to love Jesus and each one He put in front of her.

This young woman often brought the sick, dying, lost, or homeless into her home, along with her thirteen girls. Katie would nurse them along, share the love of Jesus, and send them away better in body and soul.

She wrote a book called *Kisses from Katie: A Story of Relentless Love and Redemption* (Howard Books 2012). Katie made Masese famous. Her village is called Masese 3, whereas ours is Masese 2. There is a Masese 1, a fishing village, by Lake Victoria.

Katie inspired me, and I've loved seeing what God is doing in Katie's life and in the lives of all she touches.

Changing Lives

In the early days, staying at Nile Guest House seemed like staying with Ugandan family. The owners, Alex and his wife, Florence, always talked with us. He worked at an office job at a large brewery in Jinja, and she ran the guest house. We found them both charming. He was tall and attractive and quite smart looking in his suit. He was a member of the Jinja Rotary Club and well respected around town. She was always professionally dressed and thorough in her administration.

There was a bar at this guest house where a person could get a Nile Special, a local brewery beer. I don't drink beer, but Bruce enjoyed one in the evenings after a stressful day in the village. The bartender, Bosco, became a friend we would see year after year.

One of our favorite parts of staying at this guest house in the early years was the morning worship time after breakfast. The Ugandan staff and the American guests stood together and sang to our God. We loved hearing the songs they taught us, and we loved singing with them songs we all knew. Somehow their worship seemed deeper than normal. One song that was (and is) meaningful was, "Somewhere Working for my Lord." That "somewhere" was right there in Uganda. We were working for our Lord, answering His call. A favorite memory is of Bruce singing this with all his heart, tears running down his face. I wasn't sure I knew this Bruce, but I knew I loved him more and more.

Other hearts were changing during this period, often accompanied by newfound relationships with the local schoolchildren. One by one, they won our hearts. They weren't exactly handpicked. God just wove them into the fabric of our hearts.

Hillary and Henry touched a tender place in Bruce's heart. Bruce talked about what a "stand-up guy" Hillary was as he helped distribute the bread in the Karamojong village. With Henry, it may have been his shy smile and eager eyes. We don't know what hooks us, but we know our hearts won't let go and many of the relationships continue to this day.

Stephanie, one of our team members, couldn't get Fauzie and Marian off her mind. These two followed her around like true groupies. They idolized her, told her their dreams and their challenges, and infused her with the overwhelming desire to give them hope.

Thus, we began our sponsorship program for older kids. If I remember correctly, we paid about $6-$10 a month to cover their primary school fees and supplies. It wasn't much of a stress for us to commit to that small amount. Our sponsorship program for these kids didn't support our fledgling school as these sponsored children were too old to attend the Help school.

Later trips brought Boo and Elvin together and Betty took on Cook Betty's girls. Cory watched two boys share a lunch and took Sam and Juma into her heart. One winter Joel impressed Lynda, and she committed to helping him finish school so his dream of becoming a lawyer might become a reality.

Jackie was distraught because she had just lost her school funding when she had just one more year until she could apply to the university. She dreamed that a white man, she could only define as Jesus or Jesus in someone, told her help was on the way for her schooling. Many of these kids sat out of school so much that they are way too old for the class they are in. That doesn't seem to matter. They are so very grateful to get to continue their education. We were grateful for the chance to give them hope in their future and be a part of their lives.

I was particularly involved with this group of kids. A few sponsors changed. Some kids are not still being sponsored for one reason or another. But most are years further along in their studies than when we first met them. I can't help but be proud of them. I am the lucky one. I got to meet with them and call them my friends. They have continued to mature.

We added Pricillar, Annette Peace, Michael, and Joel the artist, bringing the number up to more than a dozen that became part of the Help family. Five were in boarding school. This was more expensive, but in their circumstances, it was the only solution we could figure out. One was being strangled by a step parent, one was a street kid mortally afraid of his father, one was sleeping with animals and not eating unless he was at school, and one was sleeping in a church because he had been rejected by his mother.

They all won our hearts. As sponsors, we receive more than we give. It is vastly rewarding to give a kid a chance and make a real difference in a young life! It is heartwarming to receive a letter telling you they are praying for you and eternally grateful for your help. You become their heroes even though all you may be doing is giving up a small unimportant thing to be able to send the money they so desperately need.

In some cases, they would not still be alive today without this intervention. In all cases, they would not have the schooling and the promise of a future. God says in Jeremiah 29:11 that He has plans for us. Plans for good and not for evil. Plans to give us a future and a hope. We are getting to play a part in God's plan for these children. It is just wonderful if you ask me!

Big Changes

My friend Sandy, another member of the team, also experienced big changes on this trip. She brought her husband back, and their lives changed dramatically.

Bruce, who had been so "opposed to all this African stuff," was overwhelmed with this Africa experience. God captured his heart like He had mine and Jean's. My husband saw with eyes he never knew he had. He was shown part of himself that he didn't know existed. Bruce wondered why he had to go halfway around the world to find out who he truly was. He fell in love with a people very different from those he previously knew, yet very familiar.

Now he understood. Now we were walking in the same footsteps. Our love and respect for each other grew immeasurably. God has knitted us together from the inside out. It is easy to sing God's praises. He has been faithful to us as individuals and to us as a couple. We are truly blessed. It has been a process, and we are excited to see what the future holds as we know who holds the future!

The Shofar

Just before going to the airport for our return flight home, Frank, Jean, Bruce, and I went to Kampala for business. Frank drove us through a rough part of town populated by a large number of Somali refugees. Potholes and much needed road repairs slowed us down. Trucks, motorcycles, and cars were bumper to bumper.

People were everywhere, and they didn't seem friendly. We were afraid to roll our windows down because it would be easy for someone to reach in and take whatever they could get in their hands. It was hot, so we moved what we could away from the windows and rolled them down just a little.

Frank didn't seem concerned so the driver's side window was all the way down, relieving the cramped stuffiness. Jean had hand carried her shofar all the way from home. She had learned how the Jewish nation used a shofar for various reasons, including bringing victory over spiritual battles. A shofar, a ram's or kudu horn, has a piercing and distinctive sound.

Traffic stopped completely. We couldn't move the car an inch in any direction. We couldn't see what the problem was because a large truck sat directly in front of us. We didn't want to get out of the car to investigate.

A car coming the other direction tried to cut across our stream of traffic, right in front of us. There was no room. We didn't know what he was thinking. There was no place to go. His bumper touched ours. Traffic filled in behind him so he couldn't back up. We were crunched for time so, without warning, Jean took her shofar out of its cover, rolled down her window all the way, and blew with all her might. I was aghast. People looked at us like we were crazy. However, instead of the scary faces, they smiled and laughed. Miraculously, the car heading into us backed up and the truck in front of us started moving. We were on our way! I had a new respect for the shofar.

I didn't understand it, but it worked.

The whole carload started laughing hysterically. We rolled our windows down and started singing praise songs from sheer enjoyment and relief. When we stopped at an intersection, a uniformed soldier carrying a rifle came over to Frank asking what was going on. Their conversation was in Lugandan. Later Frank told us he had explained that we had just been to a tent meeting and were full of zeal. The soldier smiled and allowed us to pass. I think Frank might have said that we were just crazy Americans. We just laughed even harder as the spirit of joy carried the day.

Returning Home

Coming home from Uganda in November 2009 was entirely different this time. What could have ended our marriage turned out to knit us more closely together. What Satan meant for evil, God turned to good (Genesis 50:20). What could have destroyed us, instead strengthened us. The special memories of our time in Uganda often brought tears. Where there had been hardness of heart there was softness and openness, vulnerability and closeness. We had a common passion that went beyond ourselves. God's calling wrapped us up in a great big hug for each other and for the people of Masese.

We stayed busy through the year with our hearts still engulfed in Uganda. Bruce researched and found a brick-making machine we could use to add classrooms to our growing school. A British NGO, Haileyberry Youth Trust, (HYT), had an office in Jinja. They could get this machine for us and help us learn to use it.

In addition, HYT provided a supervisor and a foreman to lead a team for our upcoming building program. We were thrilled.

The bricks this manual machine would produce would be much better for the environment. They used less mortar and didn't need to be fired so less trees to cut down. These were Interlocking Soil Stabilized Blocks, (ISSB). The blocks interlock on the top, bottom and ends, like big Legos. They are made of inexpensive materials: soil, water, and quarry dust. They use much less cement than conventional bricks.

Done one at a time, pressing each block properly requires great strength and technical skill. Not everyone can do it. The pressed blocks dry in a shaded place for about a month. Experienced men could press an average of 400 blocks a day. Jean went to Uganda in June and introduced the community leaders to this innovative idea to prepare for our return that next fall.

Meanwhile, I directed our first fundraiser at home. My son's friend Brian heard me talk about the new school in Uganda and the need to feed the students lunch. I mentioned possibly getting cows so we could have milk for the kids, teach the kids how to care for the animals, and sell milk in an effort to make the school self-supporting.

Brian is into Hinduism and offered to do a fundraiser in LA to buy a cow for the school. He wanted to title the project "Holy Cow." Since he lives in California and this was the first fundraiser for the school, I decided to fly there to help Brian and his wife Sherry. I brought 8x10 photos of kids from Masese to display.

The day of the event I met the man who offered his yoga studio to host this event. As we talked about coming together from different worlds to bring help to this village, we were captured on video. It was like the East meeting the West. I was bringing the Christian perspective while they were tapping into the Eastern culture of Hindu/Buddhism. Together, we were both reaching out to help impoverished children. They sang Hare Krishna songs and played Eastern instruments in a performance. I wore my cross and was glad I didn't know the words to what they were singing. It was beautiful music being performed by talented people. I was out of my comfort zone, but still thought it was wonderful of them to help us.

Brian was nervous about what I would say when I got up to speak to the crowd. I expect he thought I might try to convert them or something. I didn't know exactly what I would say until I spoke. Sometimes I feel God speaks through me if I don't get in the way. I had no real idea how to address this diverse crowd, but He did. God led me to thank them for their support and then to speak a little about the poverty in this Ugandan village. I continued by saying that the God I love and serve has two commandments: To love God with all my heart and to love my neighbors as myself (Matthew 22:37-39). Loving the people in this Ugandan village was a way we could all love our neighbor together. Brian relaxed and so did I. The evening was a success.

We Love Our Students SO much!

2010

Container Hijacked

In 2010 I helped load another container to ship from the H.E.L.P. International warehouse to Masese. It was a labor of love from start to finish. I chose each piece of clothing, each book, and whatever teaching materials I could find. I delighted in cute little dresses and good functional shoes. Books that didn't seem too American made it through my edits. No Barbie doll stories or Halloween or Thanksgiving or Santa Claus.

We loaded some new equipment (like a welder) and some donated equipment (like a specialty saw). We included chairs, paper, and school supplies. The Croc Company sent us 154 pairs of Crocs to give away. A bike was donated and soccer uniforms. And we included computers! Not only did we send computers, but another NGO put computers in our container for their ministry in another part of Uganda.

I don't know if you can imagine how much space there is in a container but we packed a ton of stuff! I was told I was packing too much. They thought I would be disappointed when I couldn't get it all on. I was so determined to get all I could to this community I wouldn't say no to anything. God created space, and all I wanted to go went. Then we had to pay for it. Ugh. It was $15,000! Crazy, but we did it.

The container took months to get there. It made the port in Mombasa, Kenya, but then got stuck. Somehow the manifest was off. Our load weighed differently than we had recorded or some unexpected problem arose at the port. For years Jean had sent containers all over the world without a hitch, so this was a surprise to all of us. The container couldn't be released without another sizeable sum of money. We didn't have the money, so the container sat at the port racking up storage fees.

Finally, with some greased wheels, the container was taken to Kampala where they released the books and computers. The computers, however, were just shells. Somewhere along the way they had been gutted. We were sick. They wouldn't release anything else from the container, and we continued to be charged for storage. Jean tried unsuccessfully to get that load released for a year or two. We don't know if they just wanted bribes larger than we could manage or if they wanted the ingredients to resell. Whatever their motivation we never got that container. I am still heartsick when I think of it.

Little Things—Big Difference

From time to time I hear a song on the radio that gets me thinking. Recently I heard "Change" by Carrie Underwood. She sings about how little things can make a big difference, little things done in love. She sings about how foolish it seems to think we can change the world.

We often want to talk about our heart for this African village where God has placed us. People rarely come right out and say we are crazy or foolish. But we do experience the changes of topic, vacant looks, disinterest, and platitudes. We know there are few who will understand, and we remember when we didn't understand. I don't always get excited about the passions of others. Serving in the African village is my burden. My passion and joy. I don't need everyone to walk my path.

Sometimes I feel overwhelmed, though, and need to remind myself why I have involved myself with what seems to be such an impossible undertaking.

It may well be just that. Who am I to think I can help change a village? Much of Africa is poverty stricken, disease infested, corrupt and without hope. Sure, this can often seem disheartening, but I have good intentions, good motives. I am a true "well-wisher," but I want to go beyond wishing. It would be much easier to just send some money to those who are already successfully making a difference. Much easier! But praying for change and never acting on those prayers didn't feel right to me. I bless the intercessors for their prayers, but I am not wired that way. My desire is to do something— to make a difference, even in impossible situations. Maybe what I do makes me look like "just a fool" sometimes. Alone, we don't have the money we need. Without help, we don't have the spiritual, mental, or physical resources to accomplish what our hearts long to accomplish.

But ... when I see kids learning who formerly had no way to obtain an education, I am encouraged to stay the course. The clothes we supply get dirty and worn.

The food only gives nutrition for a time.

The medicines get used up way before the sickness is gone.

But the learning can change the future.

The love we offer in giving the clothes and medicines and food is felt and remembered when we are long gone. And best of all it is passed on. So I continue to give what I can and love as much as I can. If this project fails, we will still have made changes. It may not be a completely changed village, but we will have affected lives. Those lives will affect others and the ripples will continue. It is not a drop in the bucket but a drop in a huge pond where the ripples are ever widening. What a privilege and responsibility!

Back Home

Of course, we have lives to live at home along with our passion for Uganda. Our perspective has definitely been altered. We've spent time in Uganda with kids who have almost nothing but rarely cry or complain. We are now less compassionate with our grandchildren when they cry over relatively trivial matters.

Complaining, from anyone, hardly made a dent in the real-life problems we have come face-to-face with. Poverty in America is an issue, but there is help available. Opportunities to climb out of poverty. Agencies to aid those in need may not catch everyone but offer services to most.

We, who have been on the mission trips, marvel at the disparity between our homeland's poverty and that of Uganda. When I first got home, I sat in my garage and cried. Our cars are better housed than most of the people of the village. When Jean went to a grocery store after returning from Africa, she cried at our abundance versus the struggle and hunger she had seen. The clothes in our closets seem so excessive after seeing the rags and nakedness of the children in Masese.

Just for fun, my family spends some time at a cabin in the mountains. We all share one room for everyone and everything. We have beds, dining furniture, propane for our stove and lights—no electricity, running water, or indoor toilets. Outside, there's a fire pit with plenty of firewood already cut. Quite primitive, but our view from the windows on the front porch overlooks a beauty only found in the Rocky Mountains.

It was hard to clean without running water, but the water we had easy access to was clean. The kids sat in the dirt to play or got black from soot around the fire pit, but a little dirt didn't hurt them and there were showers near. The road to town was nice. There were usually eight or nine of us. We enjoyed each other's company most of the time. Of course, we all had to adjust at times, but we could always escape outside for a breather. Someone would bring a guitar and we'd sing around the campfire while we roasted marshmallows and made yummy s'mores. We had plenty to eat and drink, clean clothes to change into, and a nicely maintained outdoor latrine. The walls, ceiling, and floor were solid and secure. We did have a mosquito problem, but we could control the bites with spray or go inside the cabin for shelter.

I could not help but compare a few days at this cabin with what I know of living conditions in the Ugandan village of Masese. There are some houses, but most people live in mud huts. Inside there are sleeping mats on the floors with very little bedding. There is no cooking space or clothes for closets. They have a fire outside for cooking and sit on woven mats on the dirt. They have no running water, and the water they can get needs to be boiled before drinking. Some have latrines to use with holes in the floor, no seat. We call them "squatty-potties." It's hard to keep them clean with little water available. No showers anywhere. Not enough food and no way to store it. No electricity is available for the majority of the community. Without lighting, they go to bed when it gets dark and get up with the sun. There are few motor vehicles and roads are rough and filled with potholes. Many family members inhabit a small space. Firewood is scarce.

There really is no comparison. Our trek into the mountains to "rough it" at the cabin doesn't come close to the harsh conditions of village life in Masese. It doesn't seem fair.

Poverty is a problem in the United States. There are people in desperate circumstances. At one time, I might have said, "Why go so far to help? There is plenty of need right here at home!" That is true, and I sincerely hope the destitute in our country receive the help they need.

Sadly, there is great need all over the world. God brought our attention to Uganda in a big way. The villages appeared to be forgotten places. No one else was helping. We felt like we could make a difference in the lives of these people. We had been called. Jean Kaye, Bruce, and I all knew that God intended for us to do what we could. What we didn't know at that time was that He had bigger plans for us and for this village.

Prophecy

In March 2010, our church hosted a conference put on by Global Awakening. It sounded like something we might relate to, but it was actually centered on prophecy and healing. This didn't excite us, but we decided to attend at least a couple of the evening services. The first night we attended had a message for Bruce. God showed him some insights on why he was able to be more of who he was created to be in Uganda than at home. It was explained that Jesus was given no honor in his own hometown. It is harder to see God in or through those closest to us.

Bruce didn't want to go back a second night. He was expecting a lot of "hype" around healing and prophecy. Since I was going, regardless of his decision, my husband changed his mind and came with me. When we arrived at church, the auditorium was almost filled. We sat next to the wall. People traveled up and down an aisle in front of us, so it was hard to even enjoy the worship. I was not sure I was glad we had come. However, as we stood, a woman caught our eye. Dressed as a child of the sixties, with a long flowing skirt and peasant blouse, she wore a mash-up of styles. Her hair was almost punk, spiked and pink on top, white and short for the rest. And she was coming down that aisle toward us. Rather attractive and hard to miss, she came right up to us and stopped. This woman began to prophesy saying, "The anointing of the Lord is all over you."

I wanted to ask her how she knew that? Did we have a "glow" or did God highlight us somehow? What did anointing look like?

I kept quiet as she started saying "boatloads ... boatloads ... boatloads ... boatloads," looking us straight in the eyes. Boatloads of what? I wondered if she meant boatloads of anointing or blessings or trouble or what?

She stopped and asked, "Do you do something with containers?"

I know my eyes got big and my mouth dropped open. I didn't know how she could have known that unless God was actually talking through her. I wondered if she knew Jean, but Jean told us later that she had never talked to her.

This woman asked, "Do you have a ministry?"

We nodded our heads.

"There will be boatloads of provision for your ministry. Not only for your ministry but also for your own finances."

She put her hand on Bruce's chest and said, "Oh, man of God, God is going to expand your heart and give you His vision for the world."

I thought to myself, "Well, at least for Uganda."

Then she turned to me and said, "Words ... words ... words ... are you a singer or a politician or a teacher?"

"Yes, a teacher."

"Your words will drip like honey, like honey from a honeycomb. They will be sweet, sweet on the tongue." Then she added, "They will be like a two-edged sword, sharp and cutting. They will cut and bring freedom. You will think your words have been hard but others will walk away saying, 'I needed that!' and it will bring freedom to them."

As I wondered if I liked this particular word from God, she turned to both of us saying, "You will have many, many children." I thought about the 150 children in the school in Uganda along with our own kids and grandkids, but she went on to say, "Look at the stars in the sky and count the number. They will be as many as the stars and they will outshine you."

Then, as quickly as she had come, she turned and walked away.

My knees gave way, and I had to sit down. Overwhelmed with emotion, I cried. To think that God, the God of the whole Universe, would pick us out and send someone with such a powerful word for us. We who didn't even know if we believed in modern day prophecy. I was in awe with what all her words from God might mean.

I was so excited that our "children" would outshine us. What more could a mother want? I wondered if the number of stars meant that the children we were helping would pass the blessings on down to the next generation. Or would we be involved in a bigger ministry? Would this ministry grow supernaturally? How could that stars-in-the-sky number actually become a reality? I knew that Abraham had been promised children as many as the sands of the sea. That prophecy is still being fulfilled and Abraham is dead and gone. But it happened! Lots of prophecies happen down through time. I was good with that!

September

Diana and Bob and Corryn

Coming home after the first trip in 2009 where Jean and I proposed

Ben teach, I emailed Diana and Bob. These were the friends I met earlier on the medical mission in Kenya. After telling Diana about the school beginnings, I strongly encouraged her and Bob to come with us to Uganda. Bob's dental work was especially needed, and

I needed Diana. To my delight they came on our trip in September 2010 and brought their daughter, Corryn, who was in her mid-twenties.

Delia and Peter and Trish

Diana and Bob also brought their best friends, Delia and Peter and their daughter Trish, who was in her early twenties. Delia had recently retired as a school administrator having been a public-school educator for thirty-seven years. She served as a math teacher, a teacher of the gifted, mathematics department chairperson, curriculum supervisor, assistant principal, and assistant superintendent of schools. She had experience I never dreamed of. She even received the New York State Middle School Assistant Principal of the Year Award in 1996.

Dr. Garrity, or Peter—as we call him—taught Theories of Knowing and Learning Mathematics, as well as elementary and secondary mathematics and methods courses at the Teachers College at Columbia University. He is also a full-time professor at Molloy College where he teaches quantitative analysis in the Division of Business. As this story goes on, you will see how incredibly vital these people are and how they add important complementary colors to tapestry!

Sandy and Bob

Sandy and Bob came with Bruce and I for a month in September 2010. Sandy had been with us on Bruce's first trip in 2009. Her heart melted for these people as she visited Soweto and the Karamojong village. Tears flowed as she felt their struggles and pain. She held babies, encouraged mothers, loved on our teachers,  and raised money for food for the new school. When she and Bob talked about their hearts' desire for Kingdom work, they explained their plan to educate teenage girls who had never been to school. Since it is hard to incorporate a teenager into a Primary 1 class, they wanted to have a separate school for these girls. I thought this was a good idea!

We interviewed teachers and started the process for this new school to begin. In the meantime, Bob and Sandy both worked hard at the Help School. Bob is an electrician. What little electricity we had in the offices was scary. He straightened out what he could to keep things safer. They walked with us, supporting us in every way they could. Today they have graduated some of their girls! And ... Sandy and Bob sold their house in Colorado and moved to Jinja! They were all in!

Goodrue

Coming into a foreign airport not knowing the person picking you up is unnerving. What if they don't show up? What if they take you somewhere you don't want to go? What if the vehicle they are using is not acceptable? What if they didn't account for the amount of luggage you and your team have brought? What if they charge you more than you feel comfortable with (especially considering converting from dollars to shillings)? What if you don't like them? Or feel safe with them? Or can't communicate with them? Oh my! Faith is really tested here!

So far I have been able to put my faith in Jean Kaye, as the group leader, and she has provided the very best possible for us. I have loved the different men chosen to be our driver/translator/tour guide/caretaker/friend.

This trip our driver was Goodrue. Actually, his name is Badrue. When he did something that could be construed as naughty, we teased him about becoming Badrue again. Always making us laugh, he was Goodrue most of the time. We loved him. Every chance he got he would share words of wisdom from the Bible with us. In fact, he could pick up on a cue and turn the whole meeting into an opportunity to share about His Jesus.

Goodrue is confident and competent, with a smile and a laugh that draws people to him regardless of what he is saying. You should see him swagger as he describes haughty people he calls "cowboys" who act like they know it all but don't have a leg to stand on. He tells it like he sees it. He can sing and drum like a professional.

His greatest joy on our trip was Sandy's iPOD, loaded with hours and hours of Christian music. The only time Sandy ever saw it was when it needed a charge. It was always in Goodrue's ear. In addition to driving us, Goodrue translated for us when needed and helped his people understand what was meant by some of the concepts we taught. He was a student, a teacher, and a translator all at the same time.

Welcoming Celebration

Before we arrived, the students were admitted to a competition in their division. They competed in music, drama and debate. In June, Jean had purchased drums, flutes and grass skirts.

Remember that just a little over a year ago these children had zero opportunity to attend school. They had no opportunity to excel, no opportunity to feel proud, no opportunity at all. That fall, with the help of H.E.L.P. International and the amazing teachers at the Help Uganda School, thirty students prepared and performed their drama, dance, and debate, coming in second place in their division! Everyone was so proud!

Their drama addressed the fact that many stepchildren are treated badly. Sad, but true. Gives a new meaning to the stigma of stepparents. Whenever someone marries for a second time, the children from the former marriage are not accepted. Remember Hansel and Gretel? Too true to be funny!

The parents of the students wanted to thank us for what we are doing for their children. Since they have nothing to give us, they entertained us with their singing and dancing and a funny skit. We were touched at their obvious gratitude and desire to be a part of the good happening in their community. These are just impoverished women trying to manage, in rather unfriendly circumstances. They love their children and feel helpless to give them a good life. We give them hope that their children can have a better life than they are able to provide.

We want to empower them to not only survive, but to prosper. I am continually humbled at the task God has set before us. He is a big God and loves these people passionately. He brought us to this place, and the more I am here, the more I understand His love for these people.

I have a picture of Bruce watching this performance. He is standing back in the crowd with a little village girl on his shoulders. It reminds me of the song "You Raise Me Up" by Josh Groban where the singer sings about being strong when he is on someone's shoulders. That person has raised the singer up to more than he thought he could be.

SIGNIFICANCE

Some time ago I learned that one of our basic human needs is significance. I have pondered it over the years in terms of the legacy I want to leave behind, who I am and what I do. In this world, we crave and search for significance. We long to matter to those we care for. It runs deep in our being. Even to make a difference to those we don't know is important to us. Pride and power and fame and fortune are all subsets of a search for significance, as well as the need to be loved. We are alive to the extent that we are significant.

There are two areas I am concerned with in the area of significance, but they are intertwined. One is in the natural world and one is in the kingdom of heaven. We are rarely aware of this search. We may even reject our need for it. There are those who seem to retreat from any possibility of significance. I think that if we were to look into their lives, we would see how they compensate. Maybe they reject people but need to have an animal around or a garden to care for where they are needed and thus significant.

My husband and I have been surprised at how much we need to matter in this world. I have always known I wanted to be a positive force in my sphere of influence. I have poured myself into being a good mother and grandmother. I have worked in the church and in helping ministries. I have been as altruistic as I know how to be. However, ministering in Africa has ratcheted this up several notches. In Africa, I am able to help bring life to a level that would not have been possible had I hadn't been there. The position is humbling. Who am I that God would choose me? The ministry has literally rocked my world!

My husband is the same, except he was unaware of his need to help others. His significance primarily came from performing well at work and being liked by his family, friends, and co-workers. As he sees the difference he makes in this village in Africa, he melts into who God means for Him to be. He craves it. He blossoms through it. What he does matters! He can see it, up close and personal, through changed lives of formerly hopeless people.

In God's Kingdom, we are given significance because of Jesus. We are His beloved. He showed us our significance when He died for us. When I think that the God of heaven wants me to be His friend, I am brought to tears. He knows how really insignificant I truly am, yet He has exalted me to sit with Him in heavenly places (Ephesians 2:6), to reign with Him (2 Timothy 2:12), and to be His bride (2 Corinthians 11:2). He is creating a mansion for me (John 14:2), and I will walk on streets of pure gold (Revelation 21:21)

When I asked God to take my life and use it, His answer surprised and overwhelmed me.

The Bible tells us to be doers of the Word and not hearers only (James 1:22). We are also told that it is not by works of righteousness that we are saved, but by God's mercy (Titus 3:5). There is a fine line between these two. I believe that if we love God, we will do what He leads us to do. He says that faith without works is dead (James 2:14-17). However, we are cautioned to know that it is not by our deeds that we make it into heaven. We simply can't earn that.

September—Team Activities

Our September 2010 trip, Bruce's second time in Africa, was a complicated one. We took a large (twenty-six altogether), diverse team of men and women. Sandy and Bob and Bruce and I went over a week before the team arrived and stayed a week after, being in Uganda a total of a month. Jean and her husband, Don, came with the rest of the team. There were conservative Christians and those not Christian at all. There were medical people and educators, construction people, and a business woman named Chris.

Some women on the team worked hard cooking lunches for the team. After learning what food was available and what cooking methods they had to work with, they had to learn how to incorporate Ugandan women helpers with the different food options. This group took on a challenge the whole team appreciated!

Unfortunately, we also learned how upsetting it was to eat such bounty in front of the children. Each bite brought more conviction. After that we either ate out of the villagers' sight, went to town to eat, or just didn't eat lunch at all.

Team members Phil and Rob decided we needed a Western style bathroom. Getting total agreement from all of us, they navigated the supplies available in Jinja and had Ugandan guys dig a leach field where the liquid waste was channeled into a field, filtered through sediment and gravel, and became organic. Then the guys installed a stool and a sink with running water.

A young teacher from Kentucky came to teach math but chose to help the medical team for a part of the trip. Thanks to Bob, his daughter Corryn, Jean, Boo, and Tiffany, we were able to provide dental work and hold medical clinics.

The school had grown to 250 kids but had no school lunch program so some of us set about getting that started.

Diana secured a donation for supplying mosquito nets to our school children. She bought these and boots and passed them out. A sewing group in Colorado sent handmade pillowcase dresses for the girls and shorts for the boys. They put panties in the pockets of the girls' dresses and little cars in the pockets of the shorts for the boys. The kids looked very nice and really perked up.

Rosemary, a woman in her eighties who Bruce and I met in Wyoming, came along and took notes so she could write an article about the school. She was accompanied by a nice gentleman I never got to know well.

Chris taught business training classes. Goodrue interpreted for him and later became a business teacher himself. At that time, we decided to call him Badrue again so his friends would know who we were talking about.

A year later we interviewed those who started businesses after attending the class. Ninety percent of them were still in business. They told us they believed the most important thing they learned was to keep their business income separate from their personal business so they would have money to resupply their stock and grow their business. Because they are such relational people, when they saw a need in the family, they would be drawn to spend all their money to meet the need instead of saving some for the future of the business. This new information enabled them to stay in business while others failed.

The school team had their hands full with the primitive condition of the school. We had benches for kids to sit on and plywood to separate the space into four classrooms. Classes learn by rote, so the noise was nearly unbearable. There were too many kids in each classroom—250 students divided into four classrooms. Language was a barrier as the kids were just learning English. The teachers interpreted, but it still was less than optimal. With no outside walls, the kids were easily distracted and hard to keep contained. There were goats and a small herd of Ugandan longhorn cattle that walked through the middle of our compound daily, leaving behind them some rather smelly, unsanitary piles.

Diana brought the book *The Rainbow Fish* and a craft with glitter to illustrate the story. Both the story and the craft were a big hit, but they required patience because the kids had never done a craft of any sort before. While we were there, crafts were a part of each day at the school, thanks to the hard work of the Long Island, NY, team. Each night the education team members prepared for the next day. We cut out shapes and organized and planned how to teach kids who were still learning to sit still. Trish, Peter and Delia's daughter, taught the preschool's Top Class each day. She read to them, used flashcards to teach from and generally loved on them. She was a big hit!

Seeing Delia's dedication and fervor, her amazing ideas to improve learning, and her heart for these children, I wistfully said, "I wish you could come with us every year. I desperately need you. I am just a substitute teacher. I have never been an administrator nor taught for any length of time. Neither of us know how to manage a school in Africa, but at least you have experience in the States."

Her response excited me to the point of tears. She said, "Well, what am I retired for if not this?" With Peter's expertise in training teachers and his exuberant love for the kids, they were the perfect couple to help the Ugandans run this school. God provided "boatloads" of talent in these three Garritys and the Silons (Bob, Diana and Cory)! God was doing some fancy weaving with these strong threads.

Parents' Meetings

Encouraged by our Ugandan staff, I held a parents' meeting. Interestingly enough, I just about caused a riot when I told them we had forbidden the teachers to beat the children. Over three-fourths of them were adamant we could never teach without caning their kids. One man stood up and said, "It's well known that a black man

89

can't learn without stripes on his back." I thought I would be sick. I answered him and his supporters with, "You just watch!"

I hoped to show a better way proving that kids, black or any other color, can be taught and taught well, without being hit. From there I had to train teachers how to have a well-behaved class without using a stick. They had learned that kids get beaten when they disobey when they were attending school themselves. Nothing taught them any differently as they learned to teach themselves. They knew the fear of being hit with a stick was powerful and didn't have much faith in any other method. They were willing to try because we had threatened their jobs if they hit the students. I am quite sure they did what they wanted when we were not there, but slowly we were changing behaviors.

In a different parents meeting, I asked the parents if they could help us. We wanted to start a feeding program for the children. Could they contribute something to offset the cost? Maybe they could send firewood or a potato or some greens or maybe a cup of beans. The parents instantly began a heated discussion in Lugandan. I didn't know what they were saying and wondered what trouble I had stirred up. Finally, I asked Ben what was going on. He had a participant in the conversation stand up and tell me they didn't agree on contributing something toward lunches. One person might bring a big stick of firewood whereas another might just bring a twig. They proposed that each child bring a small amount of money from home to help us pay for our supplies. It dumbfounded me! I had no intention of asking them for money. I didn't think they could pay anything. They assured me each one could pay this small amount. There were some ladies who had multiple children in the school and insisted they could not afford to pay this. The other members scolded them and assured me again that everyone could pay this little amount. Two people in the crowd stood up and said they didn't even have any children at this school but they would help pay. I was truly impressed and encouraged.

Collecting these fees proved to be a problem though. We started as a free school, and some people, both in the village and back in the States, did not like changing that. Some refused to pay anything and others paid regularly. The leaders of the PTA put pressure on those not paying. Those paying didn't think it was fair for some to not pay when others did. What if a child turned up at school without money? We were told to send them home. This would put pressure on the parents to get them back in school. How were we supposed to teach them if they weren't allowed to come to school? Why should a child be punished for their parent's refusal to pay? Wasn't our school there to meet the needs of the poorest in the community? How could we keep those who could afford to pay from taking advantage of our generosity? How could we teach the kids to do the right thing as they watched their parents skirt their responsibility?

We settled part of the problem with our sponsorship program that identified the neediest in the school to be sponsored. Sponsorship pays the lunch fees they agreed was fair. To this day there are still problem areas. We stepped back and let the Ugandans decide how to best deal with the negligent parents, with the understanding that our goal was an education for all in our school. Whew! Helping can be complicated!

Cooking in Uganda

Swinging an ax is not something I can do. At least, not very effectively. I am quite sure I would slash my leg, or worse. I have never had to worry much about firewood, anyway. When we go camping, we find what we need lying around or some wonderful Ranger has already cut some for us. At home, I just turn on a switch to heat my oven.

Cooking in Uganda is quite another matter. The women there are "can do" people. I called Bruce and ask for help if I needed firewood. Not in the village where we were. The women take on that chore. As I first walked up to the cooking area for the school to check it out, I saw a woman off to the side. She was attacking a rather large felled tree trunk with her ax, expertly chunking out fuel for the pots used to cook lunch.

Jean and I were excited to be feeding the kids since it had been over a year since the school started, and we had not had funding until now. Our funding was still limited, but we had to begin. I asked for volunteers from the village to help. Three women brought their own pots and mixing sticks (and their own ax). They cut their wood, built their fires, and prepared vegetables for "spices" with a dull knife and no table or counter. They stood over pots in the hot, smoke-filled area, with babies strapped to their backs as they stirred. It seemed like they were there all morning.

At first, cooking was done under a big tree, but rain had required them to reconstruct their space under the roof where the classrooms were being held. The teachers didn't complain, but many students had burning eyes because of this (somewhat) indoor cooking arrangement. There were no barriers to keep the smoke contained.

But, no one complained. They were as excited as we were to be feeding their children.

Hunger is everywhere.

Distended bellies are common due to malnutrition. Obesity is not a problem. The children lick their plates to get every last bit of food. Thankfulness is in their eyes as they do a little curtsy when they see us. I am humbled. It is just maize meal and beans, but to them it is a sumptuous meal. A favorite in fact.

I was curious as to what was cooking in the delicious smelling beans, so I asked questions. I was concerned about nutrition and not just filling tummies, so I was pleasantly surprised to hear what they added. Depending on availability, they might add cabbages, tomatoes, onions, greens, beef spices, salt, and maybe a bit of garlic. The posho looks like cream of wheat cereal but thicker and a bit yellow. They serve them in the same bowl, the beans beside the posho.

Billy saw me snooping around and invited me to try a bowl. I answered with a big smile. We weren't supposed to eat the local food because we often get sick from the unfiltered water used to wash the dishes. I just trusted that the cooking had killed anything that might hurt me. Hospitality is second nature to these lovely people, so they found me a makeshift chair (an upside-down bucket) and sat me down with a large bowl of beans and posho.

Wondering how I could wash my grimy hands, I looked up and saw one cook with a pitcher of water ready to pour over my hands. Like Ugandans, I would eat with my fingers. With no napkins, sitting on a bucket on a dirt floor with a steaming bowl of unfamiliar food and no fork or spoon, I had to figure out how to get this concoction into my mouth without spilling it on my lap or having it dribble down my chin or run down my arm to my elbow. Laughing didn't help. I asked Billy to show me how to eat the Ugandan way. He took pity on me and brought another bucket over for me to use as a table and proceeded to show me how to use my fingers as a scoop. My audience was polite and didn't join me in my laughter, but there were smiles all around. That may have been some of the best beans I have ever eaten. It was a challenge that makes me laugh still today. It was a fun moment I got to share with new friends who happened to be a different culture and color than me. The next time I ate with them, they produced some utensils. These were much appreciated by the whole group of Americans, me especially!

Unrealistic Expectations with the Brickmaking

Bruce had purchased the brick-making machine for the interlocking soil stabilized bricks but needed a construction crew. We hoped community members would donate their labor, but we didn't yet understand the poverty they lived in. They refused to volunteer to help build the school and instead demanded we provide wages and food for lunches. These men desperately needed to eat and to feed their families. When Bruce said he expected them to volunteer their time and we would feed them their lunch in return, he thought he was in grave physical danger. The only white man around, he looked into the eyes of an angry mob of black Africans. Fortunately, some HYT (Haileybury Youth Trust) guys standing with him calmed the group down. Since Bruce was already convinced he would die in Uganda, he was now surer than ever!

Manasseh

Manasseh was an unexpected jewel. We found him, by accident, on a Sunday when the service was packed full. Ugandans dress nicely for their Sunday services, so I did too. When the service ended, I intended to change out of my heels before hiking that afternoon. I needed to hurry as Jean had made arrangements to meet with me. As I left, though, I found Teacher Ben waiting for me. My shoes were just short wedges, but they weren't for hiking! Teacher Ben saw me, grabbed my hand, and took me up; up the road some ways, down the hill, and off the path to his church near the Karamojong village.

I felt impolite since I had to leave almost as soon as I arrived, but I met Pastor Manasseh who warmly welcomed me to his church. We made plans to meet his wife, Rose, and then I hurried on to meet Jean.

Manasseh and Rose were special people. They were missionaries from Kenya to the Karamoja people. Their church wasn't large, but they had big plans. There was something about them that engendered a kinship and trust from us. They would help us in any way they could. Our greatest need, at that time, was to have someone we trusted to funnel funds through for the project needs. They had a bank account and could communicate with us through email. This worked well.

When we were ready to start our building program, using the ISSB bricks, Manasseh was the obvious one to manage that work. At least that was what we thought. We made as many plans as we could over the Internet. Bruce felt confident we could hit the road running as soon as we arrived. Manasseh showed up in his work clothes, ready to be our right-hand man, but our hopes backfired. The village of Danida (Masese) would have nothing to do with this Manasseh—an "outsider!" He wasn't from their village, or even from their country. They barred him from the property with strong and abusive arguments.

We tried to explain that he had management skills and was helping us. We trusted him, so they should. They would have none of that!

Philip and Yeko

Now what was Bruce to do for a manager? HYT stepped in and funneled funds for us. Their Ugandan supervisor, Phillip, agreed to oversee the building project and train Yeko to be the on-site manager. So our project moved forward.

Manasseh continued to help us as he could. He remained a friend even though his feelings were hurt by the rejection from the villagers. His daughter, Phyne, came to do her practice teaching at our preschool. Manasseh and Rose helped Sandy and Bob start their school and walked alongside of them for years.

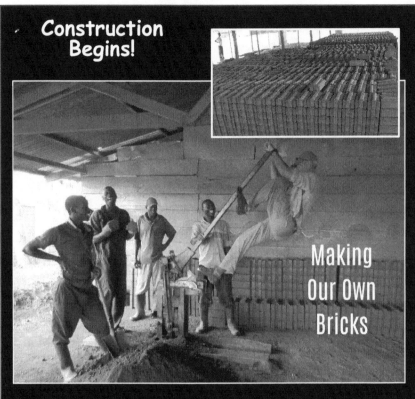

Construction Begins!

Making Our Own Bricks

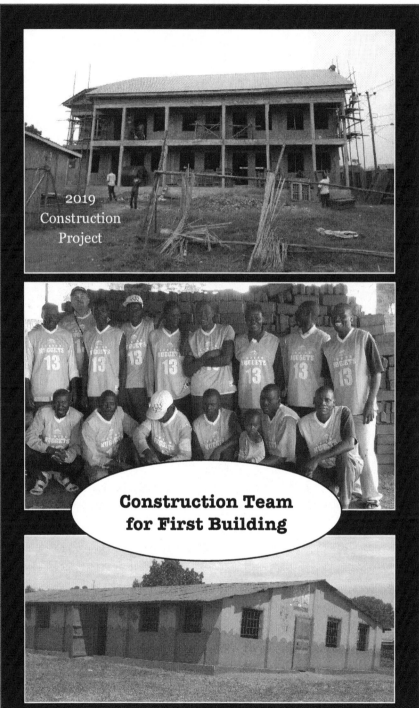

2019 Construction Project

Construction Team for First Building

We came to love both Phillip and Yeko. Philip was super cool. He rode a motorcycle with an air of confidence uncommon in our African friends. He'd learned English slang by watching American movies on television and talked with a swagger that made us smile. He was a Muslim but had some serious questions about the Christian faith. Badrue, being a preacher at heart, loved talking with Philip and Bruce.

Philip drew respect from the construction crew members, especially when he convinced us to pay the crew a small salary and buy them boots and gloves! He brought some men to Bruce to show their hands after working. Those poor hands were chewed up and bleeding. They dug with hoes in bare feet. Every time I saw a hoe dig into the ground, I worried about those bare feet. I was thankful Philip intervened for the men and Bruce willingly provided what they needed.

Yeko knew his construction skills and was willing to learn new things. He was a charming man everyone enjoyed. He became our maintenance man for years after this first project. When we needed a larger project, he would rehire his crew and get the job done. In the meantime, he kept the school in repair. Yeko was good with the kids and taught physical training groups for futball (the original name for soccer). He charmed me and most of the women around with his smile and warm personality (and good looks). We found out later he had a wife (we knew about) in another village, a wife in Masese, and a girlfriend (neither of which we knew about)! A few years later, much to our dismay, Yeko suffered from a serious bowel obstruction. A combination of a lousy surgery and taking herbs from the local witch doctor killed him. We were grief stricken! He was about the same age as Bruce's son, and Bruce thought of him as his African son. Not only were we sad, but we were angry this life was taken from us so needlessly.

Construction Lydia

Bruce, Philip, and Yeko interviewed men for the construction team. I was sitting on the porch when a Kenyan woman living in the village with her Ugandan husband came up to visit me. I knew Lydia and considered her a friend. Imagine my surprise when she stated that she wanted to be on the construction team. This was a team of all men, and my limited experience of construction team men made me question her sanity. However, I was quick to take up her cause. It seemed she should have the opportunity to interview and not be denied just because she was a woman. I brought her to Bruce who agreed she should be given a chance. He took her to Philip. Philip tried to talk her out of it. He told her the men were rough and they would not respect her. She would have to dress like a man in pants rather than a skirt like other women wore. He told her the work was physically challenging even for a man. She looked him in the eye and said, "I can do it." He hired her.

I was so impressed. She was the Ugandan version of Rosie the Riveter! We called her Construction Lydia. I took her picture when she showed up in her pants and boots. I loved her moxey!

The brickmaking machine was hard for anyone, and truly impossible for Lydia, but she gave it her all. If the guys had given her their secret, she might have been able to get it. Honestly, most of our own men couldn't do it, including my husband. There was a technique that took their whole body weight and some certain timing to get a brick pressed. Only one person at a time worked the lever so there was other work for the crew where Lydia could contribute. I cheered her on, as did Bruce. But after a while, she became the construction crew's cook and went back to her skirt.

Around a year later, Lydia and her family went to Kenya to see her relatives on a Christmas holiday. When they left, they took all their belongings out of their house and locked them in a storage. Their house only had a cloth as a door so their things weren't safe left there. While they were away, the storage caught fire and all their belongings burned. It was devastating. Neither of them had a job. They couldn't replace and start over. Lydia left her daughter Elizabeth with our school to finish her schooling and took the rest of her family back to Kenya to live with relatives. Our teacher Lydia took Elizabeth in. Elizabeth hasn't seen her mother or family since. We tried to find Lydia but failed. I would have helped Lydia get started again if she had given me a chance. I have always felt bad for Elizabeth. Sometimes we don't understand, but things have a way of turning out differently than we would expect. Elizabeth became the top girl in the school for years. She was an excellent student. We were glad to have her in our school.

Building Bricks

Once the construction crew was established, they dug to get the marram from the ground. Marram is the soil layer just under the topsoil. Once they had the soil they needed, they added a mixture of water, quarry dust, and a bit of cement. Then they pressed their blocks. The blocks had to cure for about a month, so they were stacked under the roof of the building we had prayer walked. This was the building we would finish and turn into six classrooms. We were excited we didn't need to fire the bricks since that destroys their already scarce trees and fills the air with smoke. The crew made around 400 blocks a day for months and months after we left. We had adequate blocks for our building and more. We found out later that cobra snakes had birthed their babies in those stored blocks. The guys had to be cautious when they retrieved the bricks to use. Yikes!

Cory—Sam and Juma

Corryn, Bob and Diana's daughter, had her heart broken for the children and Ugandans. I didn't get to know her well on this trip, but each time I saw her, it seemed she was hiding tears.

One day, she saw a young student share his lunch with a friend who wasn't a student. Since we knew they don't have enough to eat, it touched her that he cared enough about his friend to give up some of his own lunch. Cory asked if she could help both boys. She enrolled the friend into our school. Then she found out about each of their families. Both mothers have HIV and the fathers are not around. Neither mother worked and there were younger siblings in both households.

We all fell in love with these two boys. Sam was younger and smaller. He was quiet and shy, usually in the background. Juma was just the opposite. He was gregarious and charming and almost always in sight. Juma would wave at me from across the compound or from up in a tree. He smiled almost always. This young man was eager to please. And he was smart!

Over a few years, Cory helped both mothers set up a business to help support their families. She bought the house Sam lived in with his mother and siblings to prevent the possibility of the family taking possession in the event of the mother's death, ensuring a place for the boys to stay. She made sure the boys and their siblings had clothes and shoes.

When we were there, we often took them with us as a special treat, until one day we found both of them scared and in hiding. They said a teacher had beaten them for bragging. We investigated as best we could. They wouldn't tell who had hit them as they were frightened of repercussions after we left. We also found out other kids were mistreating them. The other kids were jealous and became mean. We had created a problem. Sam became remote and wouldn't acknowledge us. Our heart for giving to these boys actually made life harder for them. We had to change our ways. To this day we try to keep anything special for a child out of the awareness of the others. We try to be discreet and as fair as we can be. What a learning curve!

One year, Cory found that Juma had been kicked out of his house. He was sleeping in a church. We didn't know it at the time but this is common as the boys grow and are physically too big to stay in the house. As I know from raising boys myself, boys are always hungry and that is a burden on families struggling to feed many mouths. Once the boys are out of the house, they are on their own to find lodging and food. Often that is with a grandparent or uncle who has room. Just as often, there is no one and the boys have to make do as best they can. It is a harsh coming of age!

Cory and her parents took Juma to a boarding school. They researched and discovered that one of the best schools in Uganda was on the road from Kampala to Jinja in Mukono. Juma thrived there. He was always a good student, but our school wasn't nearly advanced enough at that time. Juma excelled in sports as well as academics. He also joined a church group at the school. We were sad to see him go but were very happy for these wonderful opportunities.

Sam missed Juma. He became more withdrawn and began failing at school. I wanted to hug him but that was the last thing he could accept. Cory kept trying to reach out to him, but he was hurt because he wasn't chosen for boarding school too. A wall formed between them. Fortunately, he turned around when he finally realized he would never have a chance at a boarding school if his grades were low. Sam also became involved in a church that helped him have faith and hope. Now he smiles at us and engages when we are around. Once, we were able to take him with us to visit Juma. Having never ridden in a car, Sam got carsick. After putting him in the front seat, he did better. He was all eyes as we traveled. Sam had never been out of his own area. That was a fun reunion for the boys. I am not sure what Cory's plans are for Sam, but I know for sure her love has never wavered.

School Uniforms

In the beginning, it was confusing as to which children were boys and which were girls. They all had shaved heads. Once in a while a young girl would have darling hair, usually in cornrows or in little clusters adorned with brightly colored beads. Once a girl was in school, her head was shaved. This mandate was in effect until they were through secondary school. There may be multiple reasons for this rule but I suspect it is the difficulty of cleanliness and the prevalence of skin diseases among the poor.

As grown women, they have a choice. The poorest still shave their heads or wear their hair cropped short. It is easier to care for and costs little. It isn't expensive to have their hair plaited with extensions added for style, so even many of the poor will splurge and get a new hairdo. Colorful scarves are used, wrapped in elaborate fashions, around their heads as well. Many times, I had trouble recognizing a bead woman from our co-op because she had dramatically changed her hairstyle.

We could soon differentiate the girls from the boys at school because the girls always wear a dress or skirt unless they are playing on a sports team. Even then, a skirt with shorts underneath is preferred by the elders. School uniforms are often a jumper and a blouse for younger girls. The older girls wear a button up blouse and a straight skirt, usually in their school colors.

From the start, Ben, Lydia, and Billy chose red and yellow to be the Help school colors. They called them "shouting colors." At first, the kids had to wear their own clothes to school. That could be a problem as some of the little boys had big rips in their shorts and no underwear. Both students and staff asked right from the start for uniforms, but it was difficult enough to pay teachers' salaries and get simple school supplies. I couldn't promise uniforms.

One day, I was surprised when Ben emailed me and thanked me for the uniforms. I had no idea what he was talking about. Come to find out, some boxes of yellow T-shirts from the first container shipment had been stored away. I think God had hidden those from us because we tried to give out all those shirts on our first trip. The kids were thrilled to have the beginnings of a uniform. It pleased me for them to be more properly dressed and to show off their school pride, without having to come up with funding.

Later we found the funds to have actual uniforms sewn for us. We started with yellow shorts for the boys because we had some new red sports shirts donated. With the natural activity of children and the copious amount of dirt in the village, the yellow shorts didn't remain viable. When we could, we switched to red shorts and a yellow shirt. At one point, we encouraged them to use three colors so we could have black shorts and use the red and yellow in their shirts. This was never approved. I think three colors are not the norm. And black is not a "shouting color," however practical.

The Library and Finding Richard

This trip, 2010, the president of the MWA, gave us the keys to use her old office. It was quite a big decision for these ladies to give up any of their territory. Grateful, we painted and put in a ceiling. Remember when we received all the books from the container that had been confiscated? At the time, we had nowhere to put them. This office was a godsend. We added rough-hewn shelves to make this room our library. There wasn't enough time on this trip to put the books on shelves. We left a big desk sitting in the middle of the room with boxes of books all around.

After we got home, a man named Richard emailed us and asked if he could put the books on shelves. He said he loved to read, so it was a joy for him to be around so many books. I asked if he wanted to be our volunteer librarian. He gave me an enthusiastic "Yes!"

I got to know Richard through email. He was an educated man with a degree in accounting. When he was in his early twenties, he contracted polio and was bedridden for three years. He was able to finish his schooling after that but was unable to get a job because he was on crutches and had limited mobility. Richard was considered a cripple. I think he speaks five, maybe six, languages and is resourceful. We were happy to have him with us. He had some guys that were his "legs" that we were also blessed to have around. We met Bonny and Robert and then the two Joels on the next trip when the library became the hub of the project. Every trip we take Richard a new book to read. Devouring it, he explains that his eyes are how he travels and experiences life beyond his infirmity.

Getting to Know Hillary

We got to know Hillary better during our 2010 trip. On our trip to Uganda in 2009, Bruce met a young man in the Karamojong village who impressed him. This young man helped with the food distribution that had become the riot on Bruce's first trip. Hillary was only about twelve but he was responsible and helpful, even to the point of giving away all he was entrusted with and keeping nothing for himself. Bruce remembered him after we returned home and wanted to make sure this young man was in school. Bruce sent a picture and Pastor Manasseh recognized him. We sent money for his schooling (only about $10 a month). Hillary was surprised and delighted that he had been remembered. His pastor also recognized him as an honest, upright boy.

This trip, we sought out Hillary to get to know him better. Our first Sunday we went to the church he attends. He proudly sat with us. My heart was touched as my husband sat with his arm around this young person who has no father or grandfather to embrace him. I could just feel him soaking up Bruce's affection. Hillary lives with his grandmother. I know little of his earlier

life, but since we were in the village next to his, he came to see us each day.

One day, Bruce was helping him understand how far away Colorado is from Uganda. They did a math problem together. Without paper, Hillary jumped up and took a stick, writing in the dirt, to help him do his figuring. We found paper for him to work with and he persevered until he got the right answer. Sharp kid. I saw this and gave him some little projects to work on each day he came: mazes, word searches, etc. He loved the challenge, along with the special attention. Hillary was always happy to see me, but he looked for Bruce most of all. We may never know what influence Bruce had on this boy's life. We pray that we reinforced his values, work ethic, and thirst for knowledge, and sowed seeds into his life that will one day help him to grow into a man of integrity.

As we packed to leave Uganda, I picked up my tennis shoes. They were dirty, but in good shape. I didn't want to bring them home and considered throwing them away. When Hillary came in to say goodbye, he showed me his shoes. They were falling apart! I was surprised I hadn't noticed before. Now there was no time to shop or I would have bought him a pair. On a hunch, I showed him the pair I'd worn. Lo-and-behold, they fit perfectly! Hillary was so happy. He put them in his backpack to save for school. What looked dirty and used up to me was a treasure for him!

Meeting My Namesake

We met again with Praise, our Compassion child, who was now a preteen. She and a Compassion chaperone traveled across Uganda to Jinja to see us. I loved giving Praise the chance to travel out of her village and see

more of the world. She wasn't quite as shy this time, but she was still quiet.

I love this Ugandan grandparenting thing.

I also met my namesake. Samson and Hellen had birthed a baby girl that year and named her Princess Shalom Pam Kaboko. I had already met their boy, Prince Angelo Kaboko. I was really honored. Both Angelo and Pam are adorable.

Bruce celebrated his birthday while we were there with a cake Samson and Hellen bought. Of course, we shared with Samson's kids. Can't have a party without the children!

Lots of Firsts

I had my first jackfruit that I still love to eat when I am there.

We were honored to have the mayor of Jinja visit the area we were transforming. We would get to know him better in future visits.

We went to the Source of the Nile for the first time with a team. The Nile River comes up from a spring under Lake Victoria and flows north, becoming the longest river in the world.

We also drove to Murchison Falls National Park for our first Ugandan safari. It was a long drive and expensive to stay at a lodge, but what is Africa without some wild animals?

Bruce's First Safari

I had been on a couple of safaris on previous trips, but this was Bruce's first. I loved getting to be with him as he experienced the wildness of Africa first hand. We saw amazing exotic birds, kobs, different species of antelope, elephants, lions, jackals, wild boar, crocs, hippos, cape buffalo, warthogs, and, best of all, the giraffes. Bruce loved watching them with their long legs and necks move with grace and beauty across the savannah. Each animal was a treasure as was the habitat in which they lived. No one should go to Africa without experiencing this visual delight. Nor should they go and just see this part of this amazing continent. Experiencing the people and their culture is richer by far. I recorded some of my conundrum in my blog.

"Sleeping under a mosquito net feels like elegant security. At least some nets do. Tonight, we are at the Paraa Lodge, near Murchison Falls, in Uganda. Some nets don't cover well, which makes me feel just the opposite of secure. Tonight, I love being inside my net, in my comfy bed, looking forward to a safari tomorrow. I can't help feeling guilty as I know too well those who sleep on the floor with no protection at all. They may not even have a door to their little living space, bedding, or a change of clothes, or a way to bathe, or even food in their stomachs. It is hard to reconcile their lack with my abundance. I hope they are rich in ways I am not. Jesus says the last shall be first and that the poor are blessed. I bless them in their lack and in their happiness, regardless of their circumstances."

Expanding the School Feeding

The first year we weren't able to feed the students. The kids only got one meal a day at home, so Ben had to send the kids home after a half day because he said they didn't have the energy to learn. Actually, we found out that there were many that only ate every third day. It was no wonder there were starvation bellies on so many of the kids and that they were susceptible to skin diseases, malaria, and multiple other preventable diseases. They were all very thin except for their protruding tummies.

When we were able to provide lunch of beans and maize meal, for posho, the physical changes in the students were amazing!

Their limbs filled out to a normal child's body. Their tummies became normal and their overall health improved dramatically. Their energy level and ability to learn improved along with their bodies.

The pots in our new kitchen are black iron, waist high and maybe three feet across. A "mixing stick" is used to stir the ingredients. The cooks have to carefully sort the beans because there is debris of all sorts to be cleaned out. Sometimes I join them and we visit while we work.

Kabagala, Million Fish, and Greens

A nice change in the students' diets is rice instead of the posho, but rice is a bit more expensive. Thanks to Diana and Bob's generosity, we added fish to the beans for school lunches on Fridays, and greens were added to the beans a few days a week. We chose to add million fish, otherwise known as guppies, because they were the least expensive of the fish options. This greatly improved the nutrition of our students and staff and added welcomed variety.

The Silons started a breakfast a few years after our feeding program got started. Breakfast alternated between Kabalagala, a banana based fried pancake, and a slice of bread with peanut paste spread on it. Most breakfasts in this community are either simple tea with sugar or a porridge of maize meal and sugar (a liquid posho with sugar).

We can feed a child a school lunch for about ten cents a day and adding breakfast only made the total fourteen cents per child. At least that was what it was when these programs started. As in all the world, food prices keep going up, so I am not sure exactly what our cost per day per child is currently. We also feed all the adults working for this project. The adults easily eat twice as much as the kids. Feeding people is one of the joys I get in life. I love to cook and I love to eat, so this feeding program is near and dear to my heart.

Mazungu Food Offerings—Restaurants

In town, there is a much larger menu available. When we first were in Jinja, there was only The Source Cafe where we could get somewhat familiar food. Now there are many good places to eat. Indian food is popular in Jinja since there are many people from India with businesses in the area. Whole tilapia, deep fried, is especially popular with the Ugandans, but their first favorite is fried chicken and chips (French fries). We have to be careful not to eat fresh food unless it has a thick skin or rind because the water there is hard on our stomachs. The service is slow in restaurants since they don't have the modern facilities we do in America. It is more difficult to get quality meats, but, more and more, we are enjoying dining in Uganda. We can now get smoothies, milkshakes, and lattes—quite a treat.

Some of the nicer places are located on lovely grounds, maybe overlooking the Nile or Lake Victoria. When I first saw a restaurant called "Two Friends," I thought I had walked onto a movie set. The setting was African cool with lush green plants all around, thatched roofs over our tables, and lights strung around for romantic ambiance.

Currently, my favorite place for atmosphere is called "The Black Lantern." We sit outside, high up on a patio that overlooks the Nile

River and watch monkeys playing in the trees. The sky is glorious through the greenery. Bright red flowers bloom on nearby trees. Lovely white flocks of birds fly through the air. The river is wide, and the interplay between the currents and the small fishing boats creates intricate patterns on the surface. For just a bit, peace permeates our beings. Ahhh! Africa! I never tire of that scene! We are often there when the sun is setting on the horizon of the Nile. The colors are spectacular.

On one of our earlier trips, Riley, an American teenage boy we had with us, was in withdrawal from pizza. On a subsequent trip, we discovered Surgio's Pizza, so even good pizza is now available.

Matoke

Chapati is another local favorite, both in the nice restaurants and in the villages. It is similar to a tortilla but not as thin. I actually like chapati a lot better. It is served fresh off the griddle. In the villages, they love matoke which is a cooked green banana. Matoke is cooked in a pot lined with large banana leaves then is mashed and sometimes served with a groundnut sauce. This is not my favorite. I avoid it when I can do so without being rude. Sweet potatoes and Irish (white) potatoes are also common in a traditional Ugandan meal.

Jackfruit

A surprise to me was the jackfruit. I had never heard of jackfruit before my time in Africa. It hangs heavy on the tree, bigger than watermelon. The skin is bumpy and the fruit pale yellow in color, sticky and chewy like tender meat. Recently I had some in a vegan restaurant in Colorado in a mock "pulled pork" sandwich which was delicious. The jackfruit is made up of hundreds or even thousands of individual flowers that are fused together. We eat the "fleshy petals" that surround the seed, which is the actual fruit.

The tree is in the fig, breadfruit family. Its fruit is the largest tree-borne fruit, growing as large as eighty pounds, thirty-five inches in length, and twenty inches in diameter. A mature jackfruit tree can produce about 100 to 200 fruits in a year (usually in two seasons).

The jackfruit is not your typical fruit. It has a distinctive, musky smell, and a flavor that some describe as like Juicy Fruit gum. Actually, the flavor changes when you cook it depending on whether you want savory or sweet. I like it fresh in Uganda but also really enjoyed the sandwich I had in Colorado.

Some herald it as miracle food since many parts of it can be used and it grows in tropical and subtropical climates, so no global warming worries. It is a source of protein, potassium, calcium, and iron, and is versatile—thus, a potential economic boon for countries that market it. Jackfruits can be dried, roasted, added to soups, used in chips, jams, juices, and even ice cream. The seeds can be boiled, roasted or ground into flour. Even the tree itself is valuable, providing high-quality rot-resistant timber for furniture and musical instruments. The tree requires relatively little care once it has been established. By contrast, popular crops like wheat, rice and corn need lots of irrigation and pesticides. And the jackfruit is a perennial so it doesn't require constant replanting. One word of caution though. I didn't like it from a jar, and it is expensive to buy fresh in an American grocery store.

Life Lessons

Some of my memories are more challenging to write about than others. Even so, they are part of the story. Actually, everyone involved in this amazing endeavor would write their experiences differently than I have. Each would see through different eyes with different perspectives. Each would be valid because it would be their own story. I am attempting to tell some of their stories but as I do, I see through my own lens.

Peter V. had been working with Jean and visiting Masese since before I became involved in the ministry. He lived about an hour away from us in Colorado. Peter's love and respect for the Ugandan people was true and heartfelt. His work involved mediating and bringing together dissenting people groups. The typically opposing groups existing in Masese were a thrill for him to encounter as they all got along and lived peacefully together.

I met Peter after Jean and I started the school. He helped Jean, Bruce and I develop our goals for this project. Peter's interest was in feeding the kids. I was also interested, since feeding people had been a way I have shown love for years. However, since there were so few of us at the beginning, I was more needed in our education endeavors. Bruce took on the construction responsibilities and Jean the management of the whole project while I took on the school and Peter the feeding. Peter traveled separately than the rest of us so we would meet after his trip to catch up. We would do what we could to help the feeding program when we were in Masese and Peter was not there. I liked this man. He was as passionate about Uganda as I was.

Peter and his future wife, Tawnya, raised money for the feeding program in a clever way. They attended events (ballets, theaters, etc.) offering shoe polishing before and during the breaks of the production. There was no charge for this service but the recipients were encouraged to tip. Their tips became a donation to the feeding project. Between this service and the donation match Tawnya received from her work, they were able to provide funds to feed the whole school. This was a huge boost. The kids were malnourished and desperately in need. I, personally, was extremely grateful to Peter and Tawnya because I had been brokenhearted over the abject poverty and hunger I had witnessed.

All was well for a while. Tawnya had Jean and I on her local TV program to talk about the project. Another time I was invited to do a show about the jewelry. Being on TV was pretty fun and good exposure. Tawnya traveled with Peter to do a segment about Masese and Uganda on her show. I think she won a prestigious award for her efforts. Peter managed the cooks and the ordering of the food supplies.

I was busy trying to build an interested community and donor base in the US. I set up social media and an email list to keep people updated and interested. Without being aware of what I was doing, I insulted Peter and Tawnya, and they left the ministry for a time.

I had a lot to learn. The experience reminded me of a picture I once saw. A giant God-hand held a chisel to a rough, ugly spot on a diamond that was being hewn out of the rock. Without chiseling away the unwanted parts, the diamond's beauty would forever be hidden. I valued God's chiseling in this situation, but it was sure uncomfortable.

After a few years Peter and Tawyna joined us again and are now working through H.E.L.P. to feed children on the islands, Kisama 1 and Kisama 2, just across the water from Masese 1. Our whole team praises God for these two and their commitment to feeding these children.

2011

The Library—March

In March 2011 Jean Kaye and I along with a friend from our school district, Linda, went to see what we could do to help at the developing school in Masese. Linda was especially interested in the library. There were books on shelves but no order. Students were not using the library since that was no check-out system in place.

We got to know our new teacher, Phyne. She is the daughter of Manassa, the missionary pastor from Kenya that Sandy and Bob work with. Phyne came to us through her school's practice teaching requirement. She taught the upper level preschool called Top Class, equivalent to our Kindergarten. Her class was smaller than the others so she could pay more attention to individual needs. Phyne loved when we brought teaching aids like flash cards. I have a photo of her in a dress of mine I had worn and decided to leave. It fit her and she loved it. I loved blessing her with it. This class increased our school to four classes. Everine was in the Baby class, Lydia taught Middle, Phyne in Top, and Ben taught First.

Blog—*Joys of a Library*

Unlocking the world through books might seem like a lost art in this time of movies, Internet and all the electronics available to much of the world. But how do you expand your world if none of that is possible? What if you don't have a TV or a computer or even electricity?

People have always told stories. Stories have been passed down from generation to generation throughout history. The storyteller and audience bond while remembering history, learning lessons, or enjoying entertainment. A good animated storyteller is a delight to encounter. We can sit transfixed as they invite us into a world we can imagine through their words and actions.

When authors and illustrators took the storytelling to the written page, books became the method of transformation. Whole worlds opened as books spread throughout the literate civilizations. As households enjoyed an abundance of books, libraries were formed for sharing of the wealth. Now the privileged and the less fortunate had access to books. If you couldn't read, you could at least look at the pictures and form your own story to match the illustrations. The pictures were a great incentive to learn to understand the words.

Today in the village of Masese in Eastern Uganda, there is a library. This is a place of great joy. The world has expanded for these people. Not all can read, but many are learning. For those who can read, this library is an oasis with lush, life-giving tales of other lives, in other worlds, and in different times and faraway places. For those just learning to read, the books offer amazement and delight as they unlock the words into sentences, sentences into paragraphs, and paragraphs into chapters. What a gift! What a wonderful way to learn!

The enchantment on the faces of children as I read a book to them and show each picture warms my soul and delights my heart.

Any class, anywhere, can relish a book being read. But in a Ugandan village, where books are rare, the amazement is unspeakable. Stories dear to the hearts of children in my part of the world are fresh and new to these eager listeners. *The Little Engine That Could* teaching the little ones that if they try, they can make it over the big hills of life, the silly fun of singing *Little Bunny Foo Foo*; the imagination of the Disney's Princess books; the vivid pictures and nature learning of *The Hungry Caterpillar*; and so many more to come. What a joy to share!

And then there are the adults! Grown men with too much time on their hands come and immerse themselves in reading, devouring books with starved minds. Many men in this village consume alcohol in their despair and boredom. How much better to consume books! Their formal education may be over or interrupted, but their desire for learning is still alive and well. Wow, a whole room of books can envelope them and take them away for a time!

The women don't seem to have found the library yet. I am sad about that. Young women, still in school, crowd in, eagerly reaching for what book they might find, but the older women aren't there. My guess is that they are too busy taking care of their families and have not had the chance to learn to read. Life in this village is hard, and the women get the brunt of the labor. I can't wait for the time I can sit a few women down in front of a computer and teach them to surf their questions on the Internet. Or I can put a book in their hands that helps them lighten their workload. Or read a story to them that helps them relate to women all over the world. Or show them how to improve their family's health through current educational opportunities found right there in their own library. Or, best of all, they can read God's Word and learn of Him, encountering His love and the grace of forgiveness and redemption.

The possibilities are endless now that there is a library right there in the village of Masese, Uganda, on the outskirts of Jinja, at the mouth of the famous Nile River. The world is being unlocked! Praise be to God who is the Giver of every good gift!

The Engineer—American Richard

In the summer of 2011, an engineer named Richard volunteered to go to Uganda to help us with our building program. We could see he was brilliant, but we hesitated at first as his involvement would require some additional funding, which was in short supply. The evening we met at our house in Loveland to discuss this possibility, the discussion wavered back and forth. I had to leave the room for a minute, and while I was away, I heard a voice in my head saying we were looking a gift horse in the mouth. I hurried back into the room and privately shared what I had heard with Bruce. This turned the tide, and Richard was soon on his way to Uganda.

On this trip, we introduced Richard to the community and helped him get set up to live there for a few months.

Richard was a provision from God! His team of Ugandans from Masese and the HYT guys became his pupils. They not only learned about building a classroom block, but they learned principles that would help them in construction wherever they went. He used the bricks that the construction team had been making the last few months and walled in the building Jean and I had prayer walked back in the beginning—the same one where the kids waited for their papaya treat. They formed six classrooms. We didn't have money for a proper floor, so he rigged up a device to pack down the dirt, and mixed it with a bit of concrete. The result was definitely a step up from the uneven dirt floors they replaced.

Next, he undertook a kitchen structure. Bruce had researched large energy efficient cooking pots for a kitchen, but he had to wait until there was a place for them. At this time, there was no fence around the property so everything was subject to being stolen or damaged. Even firewood. Richard designed an open-air kitchen with a roof that funneled smoke out the top. He was able to tap into the water line that supplied the western style bathroom so there would be water to clean dishes. The open-air design was amazing. All the kitchens we had seen at schools were in smoke filled rooms that were hot and dark.

Richard borrowed a brickmaking machine that made curved blocks to make a counter and waist-high walls around two-thirds of the cooking space. The same curved blocks were used to create two rainwater retention tanks. This was so innovative that HYT brought people to see it and featured it on their website. Richard added two rooms off the side of the cooking space for utility purposes and to store firewood. In one of them he designed a system for handwashing for the kids just outside the wall of the building. There was a locked closet to store food and cooking supplies. Our volunteer cooks were delighted!

Paper Bead Jewelry

Jean talked about jewelry with some women, parents, and grandparents of children in the school. They had been giving us gifts of their jewelry, but I didn't realize they created these lovely accessories themselves. After they told us they didn't have a market for their work, I asked some questions. Jean talked to them about partnering with us in a jewelry business. As a result of her encouragement, they put together a Co-op of around thirty women.

Each woman could make the jewelry, but sometimes, one would make the beads, another might preserve them in varnish and dry them, and another would fashion the designs.

Now, this isn't jewelry you would see here in the States. They made this jewelry from recycled paper. Paper! You would never know it unless they told you and then showed you what they do. They look like pretty beads.

First, they purchase a large paper sheet (usually recycled). It may previously have been a poster, but not one using stiff paper. Glossy and colorful and a certain weight are the main requirements. Then they have to get it cut into long triangular strips.

Pam McCormick

Once cut to their specifications, they take each strip and roll it around a pin, starting from the wide end and tightly rolling to the point of the triangle. They glue the small end point and string this bead onto a strand of other beads they rolled. Once their string is full, they hang it on a line in the sun and coat each bead with varnish.

I love walking around the village seeing these strings of beads drying. They bring color to a village that has very few flowers and is brown almost everywhere you look.

Once the drying is finished, the beads are durable. They unstring their beads and proceed to fashion their jewelry. Memory wire is used to string beads for a "wrap" bracelet, or they use a stretchy string to sew beads together to form a different style bracelet. The women string beads onto a thin cord like fishing line for necklaces. The color of the paper used decides the color and design of the bead. Each bead is different as the paper is not usually a solid color. Sometimes they purchase special paper in certain colors to meet requests from us to match fashion or seasonal colors. As they roll, the pattern emerges for each bead. The shape of the bead is decided when they have the paper cut. Their beads may be a simple oval maybe a half inch long or maybe a tiny oval. They might be large using a lot of paper in their roll and a thicker cut. There is a bead called a saucer bead that is forced into the shape of a disk as they roll. Difficult!

To display their work, the women spread a colorful cloth on the ground and sat on it beside their work. They were proud and hopeful. We were perplexed. How could we help each woman equally since at that time most of them made the same style? We chose a few from each lady, trying to make our selections fair.

Jean and I brought back a few pieces of jewelry to attempt to sell. We were test marketing to see if this would be a style women in America would purchase. It was popular! Everyone we showed it to wanted to buy it. I was even selling from the back of my car in parking lots after lunches with friends.

This trip was the beginning of an income venture benefitting both the Co-op of village women and those of us at H.E.L.P. who wanted to support the school. We paid the women what they would make for the beads in their tourist shops in Jinja town. Then we marked it up to sell back home. All the income from the markup is used to support the project.

Besides beginning the bead market on this trip and working in the library, we got to know some people better. There were Bonny and Robert who helped Richard in the library. We met the two Joels that year. Lynda put the older Joel back into secondary school. She was impressed that he aspired to be a lawyer. The younger Joel became our resident artist. Even without organization we enjoyed hanging out with the "library guys."

We also got to spend time with Marian and Sadat. Marian loved "styling" my hair and joking around. Sadat was affectionate and sweet. She would stand close by my side, holding my hand, and laying her head on my shoulder. She seemed to crave physical nurturing. Hillary was around too, ever curious. Juma and Sam were fun to interact with. They always were together. Juma loved to get our attention. Once he climbed a tree and after waving at us and smiling from  ear to ear, he threw fruit for us to catch. Sam had this sweet smile accenting his soft brown eyes that melted into my soul.

We brought the construction team some donated light blue, sleeveless Nugget's basketball shirts from Colorado that they wore proudly.

A Blog from this August 2011 Trip

Today was a day that will be difficult to put into words. God touched me and taught me. This afternoon Jean was talking with two Karamojong women, Alice and Sarah. Alice is the leader of the Karamojong bead Co-op and Sarah is the assistant leader. This village they live in is even more impoverished than the worst of ours, yet they present themselves with dignity and friendliness. Alice told Jean of two dreams she had. She didn't know what they meant, but she knew they were from God. Jean interpreted them both for her.

It is hard to describe my feelings as I listened. God had come to this woman in her dreams. The Almighty God, God of the Universe, and King of Kings visited this woman who lives in a hut in the midst of squalor. Beauty shown from her and a knowing that she is special and gifted by Him. Humbled, I realized my bias. I thought God only came to us in our dreams. Shame on me. God is deepening my understanding of who He is and what He cares about. I am grateful and love Him even more.

Embuzzies (Goats)

As a young man, before he was established in a job, Kaboko wanted money to buy goats and build a fence for them. I helped him get that going, thinking that might be the start of a moneymaking endeavor to help him become self-sufficient. It surprised me to learn he was not interested in milking goats. He wanted goats for meat. He found a job and left his goats to a family member, ending that endeavor.

As a birthday present for Praise, Compassion suggested a goat for her. I thought that was a good idea as it would help teach her how to care and be responsible for an animal. Traits she could use as she became an adult. Bruce and I sent money for the goat. She was delighted. The goat was starting to be a pet when it died. I didn't find out exactly what happened, but we sent money for another.

Goats are all over the place in Masese. They are cute at first. Especially the young ones. My niece in Missouri raises goats. She milks them, drinks the milk, and makes cheese and soap from their milk. I am not crazy about goat cheese but the milk is good. I have been there in the spring when the baby goats are playful and fun.

In Uganda the goats are pests. Hardly anyone keeps them fenced or tethered. We tried to have a garden at the school before we had a fence. The goats ate anything trying to grow. I have already mentioned how they would come right into the school and eat papers off the wall. I expect there are wars over goats eating other people's gardens. Hunger is too real in Masese. There is a law about keeping them tethered, but it is loosely enforced.

No one milks the goats or makes cheese from their milk, which I still think is strange; but they love to eat them. Goat meat is a favorite in Uganda.

The first Ugandan word I learned after hello (Oli otya) and thank you (webale nyu) was embuzi (goat). When Sandy was there on our first trip, she would see the young goats and lovingly cry "Embuzzy!" She couldn't believe they would kill and eat such a cute, lovable creature. I still don't order dishes with goat meat in them. I guess it is a good thing I don't think of cows or pigs as cute, and I am happy to go grocery shopping and buy my meat without having to think about the animal that gave its life for me to eat it. Two grandsons refuse to eat meat or meat products so they can live by the "do no harm" motto. I respect that but surely don't abide by it.

Rescuer by Nature

Sometimes we have to make sure we aren't doing more than our share. A definition of "rescue" I learned many years ago was doing something you didn't really want to do or doing more than fifty percent of the work. I tend to be a rescuer by nature. It is something I learned from my mother. I remember my dad saying, disgustedly, that if a bum came to our back door, Mother would give him the shirt off her back. I thought that was great of her.

Now I am older, and I can see parts of each of my parents being right. If that "bum" could work and was choosing to beg instead, then maybe Mom would do him a disservice to give him something he could provide for himself. There is a time when helping hurts. I am sure I have been guilty of that. However, I am trying to learn to listen to God's prompting rather than relying on my own impulses.

Rescuing Henry

Henry is an example of a time where a true rescue was needed. When Bruce first came to the village of Masese, he surprised me by bonding with two boys. He was drawn to several, but when he decided to help he narrowed it down to a couple, Hillary and Henry. We were already doing everything we could for the school, but these boys fell outside the parameters of the primary school.

Henry was a quiet boy I might never have noticed. I think God picked out this orphan boy for Bruce. We sent money for his schooling. Henry wasn't particularly visible and we almost lost track of him. He didn't come around and try to get our favor after that first visit. He was getting his schooling, but we weren't getting any relationship. I didn't understand his reticence as all the others clamored for our attention each time we would revisit. It made me wonder if we were doing the right thing. His brother, Dixson, was helping build the schoolrooms. We found out that Henry had been sent to live with a relative who did not value school or encourage education. Henry's grades were not good. The relative was also against Henry's Christianity. I worried about Henry! It looked like he was on the edge of a cliff and could easily fall. We might lose him, in more ways than one.

I forgot about my desire for a relationship and my frustration over his grades and prayed for him more earnestly. We hired a tutor and enrolled him in a Christian camp over the last school break, along with some other sponsored kids in the village. Bruce and I received a nice letter from him thanking us for the opportunity to attend the camp and asking if we would send him again next year.

After the camp, I found out he had moved in with a different relative and his grades had soared. He was twenty-six out of 144 students! He was thriving! He came up with his part in his well-being. We were happy to assist him and see God making Himself real to Henry.

It is not a rescue in the definition of doing more than fifty percent, but it was a true rescue from the edge of that cliff. God stepped in between him and the rocks below. We rejoice in seeing a young man apply himself and get to know his God. We had much hope for Henry. I know if you could ask him he now had hope for himself.

In our school, besides Juma and Sam, there were Elizabeth, Margaret and Betty, Ronald and Maureen and others that would vie for our attention or be shy and turn their eyes down as we came around.

Betty, the student, would stay after school and clean the classrooms. No one asked her nor did she get any recognition. It was just in her grateful nature.

Betty and Irene

Betty, the cook who helped me get the food program started, and Irene, the leader of the bead Co-op, became my friends. Betty helped me decide what amount of beans and maize flour would be needed to feed the school children. She would go to town on a boda, purchase the food supplies we needed, come back, and help cook it. She helped cut firewood with her own ax. I relied on her, and she loved being helpful. We laughed together as two women who shared a common purpose in developing this school.

Irene, a natural leader and businesswoman, was eager to learn. She took English lessons from Ben so she could "talk with Pam." At times, we grab an interpreter, but it is nice to communicate a little. I was chagrined once when she hadn't seen me for a time and in her delight said, "Oh, Pam, you are so fat!" Fat had a totally different meaning to her than it did to me!

Two Families

Because we visit Africa on a regular basis, we almost feel like we have two families. One in the villages and one at home in the States. Naturally, these are bound to conflict eventually. That happened during our March 2011 trip.

Bruce was in Tokyo attending a training class his company sent him to when the magnitude 9.1 earthquake and tsunami hit in Japan. I couldn't reach him to find out if he was even alive as I had no contact information. I was so scared, I thought I would be sick. My brain was in a fog.

Thankfully, Jean took over, trying to get some information for me. An hour later (the longest hour ever!) I received word that Bruce was okay but wouldn't be able to get back for a few days because the airport was closed. It was then, I cried. I couldn't imagine life without him, and this was way too close for comfort.

A couple of days later, I got word that my oldest son had had an emergency appendectomy. This mama needed to see her son, take care of her granddaughter, and help her daughter-in-law. I was heartsick that they had gone through so much pain alone and decided to fly home a few days early. The evening before I left, our little church in Soweto prayed fervently for my son and my safe trip. I could see this wonderful African worship flow into Adam's hospital room. Those spiritual eyes comforted me and gave me hope. A burst appendix is a serious matter—Adam could have died. I don't know which upset me more, the earthquake or the appendix!

2012

Summer

Jean, Bruce, a team of young adults from Colorado, and I saw our first glimpse of all the construction. Bob and Diana and their daughter, Cory, were there too.

The young adults focused on teaching at a pastor's conference and hosting a women's conference there in the village. They loved on the Ugandans in Masese and shared their love of God with them through prayers, testimonies, and service.

The team painted some of the newly constructed water retention tanks, played games with the kids, and slept in an orphanage rather than a hotel. The money saved went to buy beds and other supplies for the orphanage instead of profiting the hotel. These young adults were living out the Scripture from Isaiah 6:8 when the Lord said, "'Who will go for us?' And I [Isaiah] said, 'Here am I send me!'"

Worship Service in the Rain

One Sunday morning we were worshipping at a Ugandan church when one of those torrential rains descended on us. This little church had tin sheets as a roof which we were very thankful for even though there were definitely leaks! However, the sides were cloth or plastic sheets hung from the roof. The rain brought a wind with it that made those sheets worse than just not helpful.

The whole congregation moved toward the middle of the room to avoid leaks as best we could as the wind and rain showed us who was boss. No one could leave because the rain created a temporary but daunting "lake" all around us. We huddled close with our arms around the younger children who were shivering from the drop in temperature and the damp. And we sang and sang and sang! For at least a couple of hours we stood, singing worship and praises to our God. Intense and special, tiring and bonding. We will all remember that service as we remember no other.

Once the rain subsided, we still had to navigate the puddles and mud. We had to drive the van over a slippery steep hill where the railroad tracks were. The van kept sliding sideways and then back down to the start. Knowing how to drive in slippery conditions from living in Colorado with winter snows, Bruce took the driver's seat and drove the van right over that hill! That Musungu knew a thing or two.

The team of young adults were all friends from Colorado attending the same church. Two who were a couple when they began the trip were not a couple when the trip was over. Two others became a couple, got married, and have three or so children as of this writing. We always say Africa changes a person!

One Sunday evening the world melted away for a few hours. We were worshipping at Pastor Frederick's church in Sowetto where many of our students live. Even though Jean liked us to support a variety of congregations when we visited, I felt most at home at this church. The young adults performed a drama, then Jean and Badrue made us laugh as they talked to the church villagers from the pulpit.

During the lively worship, we danced in the back of the church with the African kids. Reverence came on us as we moved into a circle with the kids, still singing, but this time softly communing in our hearts with our Maker. As I sang and swayed to the music, I looked down to my left. A three-year-old boy held my hand. He had his eyes closed, his head slightly tilted, and his other hand on his heart. The look on his face was the purest worship I've ever seen. He worshipped for the longest time. Tears ran down my face as I felt the presence of Jesus. I lifted my hand in thanksgiving and praise to the loving God who allowed this grandmother to stand in His presence, led by a three-year-old Ugandan child. It took me away. Later I held this child on my lap, wrapped my arms around him and whispered in his ear blessings he couldn't understand. I hope I never forget the look of worship on Alex's sweet face with his liquid brown eyes and soft dark brown skin.

Babies

We found a headmaster for the school, elevated Richard from librarian to Project Director and met two new babies. Lydia had a baby as did our preschool teacher, Everine.

The previous year Ben had asked me to name his new baby boy. I had never been asked to name a child other than my own. I asked God to give me a name, and I know this name came from Him as I had never ever considered Ezra as a name for anyone. But Ezra it was. It was an honor given me as this baby didn't have grandparents to name him. So, I was the surrogate. I didn't know it at the time, but later I found out that Ezra means "Help is Here." I find that amazing as it was true that H.E.L.P. was there literally and help from God for the village was there too. This baby was the personification of our involvement in this village and it began through his dad, Ben.

One woman we loved had a baby out of wedlock. The church and community shunned her until she went to them on her knees and confessed her sin, repented, and begged forgiveness. Not all the community forgave her, but her church took her back in. Eventually, her status in the community was restored.

Reconnecting

Several of our teachers would bring their babies to work with them. We protested, but they had nowhere to take them on the days they brought them. They would rely on a neighbor or spouse (if there was one) to help while they worked, but neighbors and spouses weren't always available. Daycare was available in the town, but it was way too expensive for the villagers.

Bruce gave out certificates of completion to the construction crew to show our appreciation of all the work they had completed in our absence. By now, they were no longer angry with him. Instead, they valued his favor. We took them all baseball caps they wore with pride.

This was our first view of the newly constructed kitchen. Wow! What a lovely job American Richard had done with his Ugandan crew. The six-room school block was being used even though the walls weren't complete. Even with partial walls, it was a huge improvement over the earlier building. Instead of a small blackboard to teach from, each room had a wall featuring a large blackboard made from blackboard paint. I didn't know there was such a thing. I don't love it as it is hard to write on, chews up the chalk, and is hard to clean. The teachers were so thankful however, that I didn't express my concerns. Someday I hoped to provide them with an actual board or maybe even a fancy electronic board.

Once again, I cried as the school put on a performance for us. They acted out Bible stories and read aloud from the texts we had supplied from an American school. These kids were reading! I was overwhelmed with pride watching them show off their new skills. Reading is literacy. They were learning and were no longer illiterate. I was grateful to the core of my being for being able to participate in this miracle of education.

The First Bead Buy

We did our first bead buy on this trip. Having no hope is a difficult thing. You wonder if something is wrong with you. Did God forget you, or are you so unworthy that you don't deserve to even have hope?

Given hope for the first time, these industrious artisans had gone to work! Diana and Cory bought from them as did Jean Kaye and I. The women displayed their creations on colorful cloth spread on the ground in a field behind some buildings where they wouldn't be visible to others. Each woman sat with their creations, exuding pride and hopefulness. It was a beautiful sight! The women from the Co-op we were working with sat in their gaily colored dresses and headscarves displaying their brightly colored jewelry in a field with cows in the background curiously watching. If our purchasing had been visible, other ladies from the village would have come to try to sell us something.

As it was, Ben's wife came and offered purses. She wasn't a part of the group yet, but we loved her amazing purses. Rona had attached the paper beads to a purse form, lined it, added an interior pocket, and attached a wooden handle producing an unbelievable showpiece for an American woman to marvel at. The Co-op ladies were not happy to be invaded. We encouraged them to welcome such innovation.

But we were in trouble! We only had enough money to purchase a few items from each lady. They had worked so hard and created so many beautiful pieces it was heartbreaking to leave so much work in their hands. Instead of this being a happy time, it became sad. We had dashed their hopes and rejected their hard work. It seemed like a slap in the face. What we had meant for good had not turned out so well. There were so many women attempting to sell their jewelry that we had an abundance to bring home even though Jean and I only bought three items from each seller. It wasn't much income per woman, but it was a start. The purchasing took longer than we expected, so dark came upon us before we completed our buying. Electricity would have been helpful along with a masseuse for our sore backs. In later years we were able to move into a classroom with the goods displayed on tables. This helped our backs and kept the women off the ground.

Marketing the Jewelry

Once home, we created a brochure about the project and the jewelry. The brochure name "Jewelry with A Cause," with the byline of "Feel the Spirit of the Ugandan Woman," portrayed our mission. We described the jewelry as "Unique, Creative, ECO Friendly and Life Giving." Since the women

use recycled paper to create their beads, we felt good about the eco-friendly portion of our advertising. Once people find out the lovely beads are created from paper, they are intrigued, and once they hear the story of the women creating the jewelry, they buy for themselves and for unique gifts. The customers can help as well as have a fun piece of jewelry to wear.

Opportunity (according to Webster) is defined as "an advantageous circumstance or combination of circumstances." A few months after we came home from this trip, an "opportunity came knocking" when we were invited to an event in California. It was a "golden opportunity" and a "window of opportunity." We "leaped at the opportunity."

Supplier's Summit

HELP International, meaning Jean Kaye and I in this instance, attended a Supplier's Summit. We were invited by Full Circle Exchange, an innovative nonprofit social enterprise that aims to "exponentially increase the reach of women artisans, farmers and social entrepreneurs who are dedicated to the development of more just economies and social systems as it pertains to the empowerment of women."

Are you impressed yet? Let me continue...

They invited us to bring the Ugandan jewelry we so proudly market for our Masese village women to present to ... Are you ready? ... Walmart.com!

Walmart.com was seeking to empower women in the United States and abroad! Through increased sourcing from women, to training, to enhancing women's economic empowerment and increasing philanthropic giving toward women's economic empowerment, Walmart.com was bringing "Shopping for Good" to the public. And we were in on the ground floor! Now you know what I mean by "opportunity!" It came knocking, and we enthusiastically said, "Hello!"

We found ourselves having conversations with incredible women from Peru, Holland, Malaysia, Kenya, Rwanda, China, Palestine (living in Florida), and Canada. The talent was supremely superb, incredibly inspiring, and a bit intimidating.

Let me tell you the best part. These women were all working with the underprivileged in some way. For instance, the woman from Kenya has a home for special needs children. It is their mothers who make the goods she sells. Some work with the blind or the victims of rape, and others represent those working to help victims of sex trafficking. All have a cause beyond themselves. Isn't that just like a woman!

It is hard to comprehend the entire scope of the vision of the Full Circle gang. The Walmart.com women are forward thinking, powerful, compassionate and encouraging. And we got to play in this sandbox! Is God good or what?

We came away with more orders than we originally thought would be ordered and hoped to replicate this model with some other big players. Just think how many marginalized women worldwide will reap the benefits of such programs!

Women shape the world. This group wanted to empower them and see the good that happens. What a legacy!

They ordered one hundred each of three necklaces and earrings to match. And then we panicked. How on earth were we going to replicate the specific color ordered? How were we going to get a mass order created? Not knowing how much they would pay us, we weren't sure if it was even worth all the effort. If it did sell well, would we be able to get the Co-op of women to fill ongoing orders? How would they ship them? The more we thought about it, the more concerned we became. It seemed like an amazing opportunity for the women. Not so much for us as there would be little markup to benefit from, but we were committed to our group of women. We took it on.

May—Unannounced Arrival

To bring this new opportunity about for our ladies, Jean and I took a trip to Uganda by ourselves to see what we could accomplish.

The Day We Arrived Blog:

Mar 7, 2012 9:20 AM

First day back in Jinja. We were driven two and a half hours from the airport to our guest house last night. I wish we could have seen the scenery but it was too dark. We are so tired with all the travel and having our days and nights mixed up that even today we are not hitting on all cylinders. Our car and room are more expensive than before. Hopefully, we can sort that out before we leave.

The rains have begun. It's damp out and the dust level is down. My asthma kicks in with the dust, so I was grateful. Going to sleep and then awakening to the sounds of African life makes me smile. I do love it here.

We slipped into the village unannounced for a surprise visit. It was hard to keep the day of our arrival a secret, but we wanted to see what life at the H.E.L.P. project was like on a normal day. Once we arrive from the States, things are never normal.

As we approached the school, we were happy to hear the sound of learning. This was the first time we have been here since the school building was completed. The classrooms were overflowing and the teachers were busy. Kids either crowded on benches or sat on the dirt floor. There were very few tables and not nearly enough chairs or benches. We had ordered furniture but only had funding for half of what we need. The need is always so great here. I have to remind myself of what it was like before we started so I don't get discouraged with what still needs to be done.

After greeting the school and all the little ones who appear to hold our hands and touch us, we prayer-walked the school grounds. Almost four years ago we prayer walked the building that is now our classrooms. It was a crumbling structure, desolate, empty, and surrounded with weeds—reminiscent of former days and the hope that had been brought to the village. When that showcase endeavor of the Danish failed, the people became discouraged and lost hope in the village.

This area is now our school grounds and the hub of the village empowerment program H.E.L.P. is assisting in. Prayer-walking seemed more than appropriate. Looking at the changes encouraged us. We not only saw a six-classroom building crowded with formerly unschooled kids, but we saw a school garden, the school cow, her new calf and their new two-stall shelter, new latrines where none existed, a playground with swings, a kitchen with cooks busy cooking lunch for 300 students, and the well-stocked library open for kids from all the schools around. God is good to let us see His love for the people here.

Accomplishing the Walmart.com Order

Day One Blog

After our walk, we met with leaders of the two Co-ops who would make the jewelry we were marketing. They were surprised and happy to see us. One leader, Irene, touched me as she not only greeted me with a hug but said a heartfelt prayer, blessing us and thanking God for His favor through us. I am learning much about gratefulness from these people. I think that may have been my most special moment of the day.

The women were excited to see the marketing materials we use with their pictures in them and to see how lovely their beads look when displayed professionally. They were all business as we explained the important buyer and the large order that may well be their ticket out of the extreme poverty in which they currently suffer. Tomorrow we will travel with them to the country's capital city of Kampala to find just the right supplies to help them be successful. It should be a fun day shopping. Women are women the world over, and this is exciting for us all!

One more important part of this tiring day was our meeting with the mayor of Jinja town. A pastor named Frederick has been helping facilitate the acquisition of the land where the school and project hub for H.E.L.P. is located. Because of H.E.L.P.'s commitment and improvements, the mayor is doing all he can to turn that land over to us. He assures us it will be complete before we leave. We are imbued with hope but reserved in our expectations as everything seems to move exceedingly slow here.

The moon was full as I wrote on our balcony here at the Nile Guest House. The day was pretty warm, but the night was lovely. I indulged in a two-hour nap, hopeful I could still get a good night's sleep!

The next morning's blog entry was the last blog entry that trip. Our time was chock-full. At night, we fell into bed exhausted, planning the next day's push.

Day Two

So many times, I have felt in over my head since we began this project. Today that old familiar feeling returned. My faith grows by leaps and bounds when I consider that success in this project will not be achieved through any of my expertise. The enormity of delivering on our jewelry order is just plain overwhelming. We are challenged to set up a business in a simple village with limited access to supplies and little experience. With poverty prevalent everywhere we look, the opportunity to help these women and the school their children attend is a powerful motivator. I think I am learning as much, or more, than the village women.

Correct Color Paper

Our first challenge was to find the exact color of paper to replicate our order. We needed orange, turquoise and black. Since the ladies had originally just used what they had, there was no way we could just go buy more. And we needed volumes more. Jinja would not have what we needed, so we pulled together some Co-op women and went to Kampala to the big Owino Market. This market is for the Africans and not tourists. Seeing our white skin was not a common occurrence, and we felt very much in the minority. But there was no time to worry as we had a lot of ground to cover. Our African women went before us and behind us and watched out for us as best they could. I am sure if Bruce had been there, we would not have been in this tenuous situation.

After trying several paper vendors, we were discouraged. There was a lot of paper for sale but never enough to make a quantity of the same color. We finally went to a paper printing company and found we could order a specific color. It would cost more but we didn't have much choice. We didn't order at that time but kept it in mind. The women tried to paint paper the correct color. That proved useless too as they couldn't keep dirt out of the paint as it dried. We ended up sending Badrue back to get our paper from the printing company. He didn't understand how much we needed so we had to send him twice, but we had the paper problem solved.

The Cutting Machine

Next the women needed a cutting machine. I did not understand what a cutting machine was. They had been taking their paper to a man who had a cutting machine and paying him to cut their paper. They often had to wait for other groups to get their paper cut before getting theirs cut. We asked them to take us to this man. He was simply sitting on the floor of his little house with a paper cutter like I used when I was teaching school. A simple device but not available in Jinja.

There is an art to cutting the paper. If it is not cut correctly the shape of the bead will be different. We hired this guy to cut for us. Unfortunately, he didn't have the urgency we did. With help from some friends that live in Kampala, we found a paper cutter. Once purchased and delivered by boda, our women went to work learning how to cut properly.

The Pin

After the paper was cut, it had to be rolled. Jean and I were getting frustrated because the women were just sitting rather than rolling. We thought they just didn't understand the time crunch we were under. As it was finally explained to us, they only had one pin to roll around. They were all using just one pin! Jean and I sent Badrue to Jinja town to get a bunch of pins. It was unbelievable to us that they couldn't provide themselves with more than one pin among thirty of them.

We could work at Irene's house. She has a nicer place than most with running water, a kitchen, living room and TV. Her porch was concrete, so we had a place to sit out of the dirt. Since the porch had a small roof, the ladies could sit in the shade and lean against the wall of her house as they tired. Some fun started as they tried to teach me to roll beads. The concept is simple but making a "good" bead is not so simple, at least not for me. My beads were loose or an uneven shape or otherwise ugly. We all laughed at my attempts. I gave up the bead-making to the artisans who knew what they were doing.

Interviewing the Bead Makers

While the women rolled the beads, I interviewed each one of them and took their pictures. This was a personal bonding time for us. I asked a few leading questions and then let them tell me their story. Ritah had a good understanding of our language so she interpreted. She was pregnant. I felt sorry that she had to sit on the ground giving me the one available chair. She wouldn't take a chair from me and assured me she was okay. I am sure it exhausted her and her back hurt by the end of each day.

As I watched each woman's face and listened to her words, I became more and more aware that I cannot begin to comprehend their lives. They are just women, like all other women, but their experiences and challenges differ greatly from anyone I know. Smiles still light up their faces, and the hope they feel from the prospects of money for their jewelry overshadows the reality of the words I heard. We simply had to make this work! These lovely ladies deserved more than they have been given.

I took notes on a small notepad, trying to record the challenges each woman had faced in their lives. It was heart-wrenching. One had been raped when she was three years old. Another was pushed into a fire losing an arm and her sanity. Another's stepmother had poisoned her whole family. She was the only one to escape as her cousin warned her to stay away. No one even told the authorities because of their fear of this woman.

Bead Maker #1

Twenty-five-years old, she was married three years ago. They were expecting their first baby. Her husband was a pastor in a small church in Masese. His profession was accounting, but he sold onions in the market. He taught accounting part time. She had just graduated in Social Work and Administration but was not yet employed. She had to look after her HIV positive mother. Her father was married to another woman when her mother conceived, so he tried to get her to abort their baby. With the grandfather's help, her mother kept her. Her maternal grandfather paid for her schooling until he died. This girl was one of seven children but was the only one with her father. After the grandfather died, her mother paid for her schooling by selling greens. She also contributed to her schooling fees by winning competitions. She sang and danced her way through school from age thirteen to sixteen. Fortunately, she got an American sponsor for her three years at the university.

When she was three years old, she was raped while her mother was at work. She suffered multiple physical problems from the invasion to her little body. A three-year-old's body is not meant for such abuse! Her uterus had been damaged. At age twelve she was hospitalized for three months with chest pain from a cough that was a side effect of the rape. At fifteen, she found a lump in her breast that the doctors said was a result of the damage to her body. She was happy she had not contracted HIV from the rape.

After being married for three years and not being able to conceive, she felt like she was disappointing her husband. Because of the abuse she'd experience, it was a miracle she became pregnant. She expected a difficult birth but was thrilled to be carrying this child.

Bead Maker #2

She was only twenty-eight years old. She was happily married for thirteen years with six children. Her husband was not employed but helped preach at a local church. Both she and her husband were born in Masese. Although her husband was semi-literate she was completely illiterate. She volunteered at the Help School as a cook, from early morning to late afternoon, helping feed the students and the staff. Looking for school fees for her children who did not attend the Help School, and money for food, rent, medical and other expenses she joined the group making beads. Hoping to make income to keep her going, the scarcity in the Ugandan jewelry market had disappointed her. She was excited about the possibilities since Help International has agreed to sell in the United States.

Bead Maker #3

She was a forty-two-year-old widow. She lost her husband to AIDS. Because of him she was infected with the virus as were some of her younger children. The TASO (The AIDS Support Organization) helped her adjust to her circumstances. She had five children and three grandchildren, all living in one room. She attempted to make ends meet by digging other people's gardens, selling water at a water tap and sometimes selling charcoal. This income had failed to meet her expenses, so she joined the group to have another way to make money.

Bead Maker #4

Fifty-four years old, she had been a widow for many years. She had four children but buried one boy. She now had a boy and two girls. Along with her own children, she was looking after her four orphaned grandchildren. She had come to Masese five years ago because it was cheaper to live there than other areas. She joined the bead group to supplement what little she made digging other people's gardens and selling charcoal. Like the other women in this group, her kids were sometimes chased from school for not paying school fees, and feeding them was a problem. Since she had to rent because she was a newcomer to the village and wasn't able to own her own home, the cost of rent added to her problems.

Bead Maker #5

She was fifty-eight, but she looked much older. She wasn't born in Masese but grew up there. Her paternal grandmother brought her to Masese after the death of her parents. She has been widowed twice, leaving her with seven kids to raise along with her five grandchildren. She lives in a mud and wattle house on a small plot of land she shares with her extended family. Because she wasn't going to school, she got married at an early age. At thirteen, she was already a married woman. This marriage was cut short when her husband died from malaria fifteen years later, leaving her with three kids to fend for. She was not a widow for long. Like property, she was inherited by her late husband's younger brother. She didn't stay married for long as once more, her new husband, after fathering four kids,

> Inheriting wives is a practice in some African societies. In fact, in some instances, a son might inherit his father's wives, too.

succumbed to hypertension, leaving her twice widowed. To make ends meet she sells foodstuffs outside her house. To some extent this has helped her bring up her children, however it is not enough to ensure they are educated.

So, what happened to her long ago, also happened to two of her daughters. They got married at ages fourteen and sixteen. Both of her daughter's marriages were shaky at best, so her grandkids were staying with her. Her daughters have no skills, so they stay with her as dependents, along with their children. One of her sons is married while the other is at home, dependent like his sister. For the last three years this woman has not been well. She was paralyzed and bedridden for four months. Even though she got back on her feet, she still has a painful limp resulting from foot drop. Another reminder of her paralysis is incontinence, which she has not been able to cure. This unfortunate woman also complains of arthritis and other aches and pains that come with age.

* * *

Many of the women were sick and couldn't get help. Most had lost a man to either infidelity, AIDs, or an accident. Many were caring for their grandchildren with the parents off somewhere giving no support. Several had AIDs themselves. Each story tugged at my heart. I thought I would never complain again. Nothing in my life compared with the struggles they lived with. I loved these brave, lively, laughing women who had overcome hardships I couldn't even imagine.

As they worked, some varnished the strings of beads and hung them in the African sun to dry. This was a messy job and hard on their hands. They didn't have gloves to protect them or lotion to repair their skin. They took handfuls of varnish and coated each bead on the string. Even buying enough varnish was a challenge as Jinja only sold varnish in small cans. Kampala wasn't close enough to run to every day, so we had some large cans brought to us via boda bodas. Once the beads were rolled and varnished, the necklaces and earrings came together more quickly. We actually got our whole order accomplished. I thought I would never want to see an orange, turquoise, or black bead again.

I was proud of the women and of ourselves. This was an overwhelming undertaking. Jean drove it all. She would power-walk through the large village to get the paper cut. She drove hard bargains and pushed everyone. She was tireless and relentless, and we loved her for it. It was what we all needed. I was the encourager and friend. She was the Mama fiercely taking care of her family.

Witch Doctor Scare

One day as I was sitting outside Irene's house listening to the women while they worked, Jean and Badrue drove up. In a voice I knew meant business, Jean told me to get in the car. I quickly apologized to the women for leaving so abruptly and got in the car. As we drove off, Jean said there was a dangerous situation we were avoiding by going to town for a while. We could see a large mob of Ugandans heading somewhere. Their anger was boiling over. Someone was in trouble! The Ugandan police were with the mob, but I couldn't see them. We found out three children were missing from nearby villages. The story goes that witch doctors sometimes kidnap children and sacrifice them. This crowd, with the help of the police, were looking for these children and destroying witch doctor shrines. Wow, we weren't in Kansas anymore! Eventually the children were found alive. Thank goodness! How awful to live with the ever-present danger of child sacrifice.

Only one other time had we run into a threat from what I call the "black arts." Bruce had made a Ugandan man mad by not hiring him for a construction job. That angry man said he would go burn Bruce's picture. That sounded a lot like sticking pins in a voodoo doll to bring harm to whoever the doll represented. No real harm came to Bruce, but these instances made us aware of the presence of dark spiritual realities we don't see so readily in the United States. The spiritual world is more familiar to the Africans. We don't recognize demonic influences so much, but the reality of spirits either working for you or against you is better known in African villages. We Americans focus on the visible and forget there is an invisible enemy. The Ugandans are very aware.

Stepparents

As I interviewed the women of the bead group to get their stories, I saw a pattern that disturbed me. Many grandmothers are raising their children's children. The parents are nowhere to be found and don't provide support for their own children. Many women have left their children in order to remarry. They have had to make a choice between their children and their new spouse since often men reject the children of the former husband. Many of the women feel like they need a husband to take care of them, so they leave their children with their mothers. At the same time, a new wife can reject her husband's children from his former marriage. The stepmother stories I hear make the wicked stepmother of the fairy tales very real. Living with stepparents was often scarier than being abandoned.

Once abandoned or driven off, the street children have it rough. Living on the streets carries a barrage of health risks. Malnutrition is widespread. Many children develop skin diseases and scabies because of sleeping in dirty conditions. Finding adequate, safe shelter for sleeping is an ordeal these children deal with every night. Nighttime is when the violence happens. You can see children sleeping on a sidewalk in town during the early morning hours when it is light out. Not too many tourists are around, nor are the businesses open that earn money from them.

A significant number of kids receive a small wage for collecting and recycling scrap metal. Others may carry out domestic duties for individuals or businesses. Others try to earn money from begging. Substance abuse is a big problem among Jinja's street children. Glue and jet fuel are cheap and readily available. Many children turn to solvent abuse to escape the hunger, cold, and danger that are the daily realities of their lives. They band together in groups similar to our gangs. The older boys take money from the younger ones and beat them if they don't give them their money or if they are playing instead of working the street. Life on the streets carries far greater risks for girls. So, while many girls make their living on the streets during the day, they return to some sort of accommodation at night.

Concrete is not very friendly to a good night's rest, nor are the chilly nights without blankets. Rain adds to the challenge. There are organizations that help feed street children. Some even offer medical help. But many of the street kids prefer the streets to more restrictive or abusive environments, and the danger can be deadly. It is tough to know which to fear most: the homes you ran away from or fending for yourself. One little kid showed us where a tip had been cut off his finger. He said his dad had cut it off because he had misbehaved one day.

It looks like the children can't win! Mothers won't keep them. Stepmothers don't want them and abuse them or push them out. Fathers are abusive. The streets are dangerous and orphanages are few since the AIDs epidemic has left so many parentless kids. And then there are the witch doctors who steal children and sacrifice them. Ugh!

Street Kids—Michael and Stanley

At times, Jean and I would take a break from the jewelry order and go to town to have an African tea or a soda and maybe a bite of lunch. We liked to sit outside at Ozzie's. Ozzie's is a small breakfast/lunch place right on Main Street. The older lady who owns and runs Ozzie's is Australian and is a great cook. I always enjoy her homemade breads and soups.

There are street boys hanging out on Main Street, back in the shadows, who look for Westerners to beg from. A little one named Michael kept finding us that year. He was about eight years old and full of personality. He could speak incredible English, just like an American. Most Ugandans have a British accent, but not Michael. He had learned American English while begging on the streets of Jinja. He was fun for us to talk with but we were careful to not encourage him or give him anything since we didn't want to promote street activity.

There are organizations working to assist street children. Giving a street child money just entices other kids to beg for cash handouts. A time or two some authorities would come around looking for the street boys, and Michael would run to hide until they passed. Then he would be back sitting at our table being charming. He would tell us outlandish stories in such an engaging way we couldn't help but smile. He was sitting with us one afternoon when he got a mischievous look in his eyes. As his eyes danced, he bounced up and said, "Watch this." He ran over to a tourist asking for a handout. Within just a minute or two he was back with us, money in hand.

One day Jean asked Michael if he would like to go to our school. He wasn't too sure. He asked where it was. When Jean said "Masese," he turned us down flat. Michael said his dad lived in Masese and this boy was terrified of his dad. Our heart went out to him and his embodiment of all the abused children who find the streets safer than their own families. We talked him into going in the car with us to see the school. He agreed but was still scared that his dad would hear that someone had seen him and he would be in danger. As we got near Masese, he ducked down in the car so no one could see him. He was truly frightened.

We knew of a boarding school in a more remote area. We offered to get him into it if he felt safer there. Michael said he would think about it. The next day we met him in town. He was limping and had a big knot on his head. The bigger boys had beaten him. The timing of that incident was excellent to prompt Michael to say he would go with us if we would take his friend, too. He brought Stanley to us.

Stanley was older, twelve or thirteen, and had championed Michael against some of the older boys. Stanley said he had been in the Watoto choir and had toured America. I had heard that choir and had even kept two members in my home when they toured our area. The Watoto Church in Uganda finds orphans and gives them Ugandan families to live with. To raise money for that mission and to educate some of their children, they teach them songs, dress them in colorful African costumes, and send them on tours in the United States and across six continents for a few months of the year. If you ever get a chance to hear them, be sure not to miss out. They are quite entertaining.

Jean was enchanted with Michael, and I lost my heart to Stanley. He told me how his mother didn't want him and his stepmother kicked him out. I knew others who had those same stories, so I believed him. I wept that a mother would not want her child, thinking how that must feel to this child. Jean and I kept these boys with us, providing bathing for them, treating each for scabies, feeding them, buying new clothes, taking them to church, and enjoying their company. Our Ugandan friends warned us that street boys steal from you and run back to the streets. We took our chances. We could hardly get them out of the bathtub. Since they were boys, we couldn't go in after them. They loved it so much they wanted to take a bath every time they were at our hotel. They had never been in a multi-level building and were a little frightened at first.

As it got near time for us to leave for home, we took Michael to the boarding school he had agreed to attend. Unfortunately, Stanley couldn't attend with him as was the original plan because his father and stepmother lived very near that school. It was scary for Michael to stay by himself in an unknown place far from his friends, but he stayed.

Michael was a wild child and could hardly stay in class. His teachers had to work hard to keep him interested. He has a brilliant mind and was easily bored. From time to time he would run away, back to the streets, but when they found him, he would happily return to his school. He just wanted to visit his friends. This school was in a remote place, so his ability to get back to Jinja when he chose to go surprised us.

The headmaster of that school kept Michael on holidays when the other children would go to their homes. This gave Michael a father figure and a place of acceptance he desperately needed. Jean and I would visit him when we could. He was always delightful to see. That headmaster became a temporary headmaster of the H.E.L.P. school for a while, so Michael ended up at our school after all. Jean cleared it with his father so there were no issues, except that our school was not structured enough for Michael.

Jean decided she needed to put him into a boarding school. We had another student, Juma, at a boarding school about halfway between Jinja and Kampala. It was expensive, so another sponsor helped pay Michael's schooling in addition to what Jean paid. Today he is one of the top students in his class. He is popular with the other students and regularly makes his Mama Jean quite proud. She saw something in him that, if channeled, could make him an influential person in his world. He is doing his part to become the man God intends for him to be.

Stanley was given the chance to be a part of another family. They loved Stanley and took him into their home. We sent money to get him into school and help pay for his care. Stanley was treated like a son. He broke all our hearts when he stole a sizeable amount of money from this family and ran away.

I was worried about him along with being extremely angry. We learned he had returned to the streets in Jinja, but any time he saw us, he ran. He thought we would turn him into the police. We found him and asked him why he had spurned the kind family's love and care. His answer was that the devil got into him. Stanley still tries to convince Michael to get help from us again as he is still on the streets all these years later. He threw away all we had offered him. All the future he could have had.

My blog for that heartbroken time:

Thirty Pieces of Silver or A Million Ugandan Shillings or $400

Have you ever wanted to ask Judas what he was thinking? We surmise different motives, but I would just like to talk with him and see what on earth he was thinking.

I often look at babies and wonder what they are thinking.

Well, Judas is dead and babies can't tell you what they are thinking, so I should just give it up.

However, certain situations make me wonder. Stanley, the thirteen-year-old street boy I wrote about, stole money and ran away from the loving home he was invited into. For a little bit of money, he left safety, love, provision, education, opportunity, family, and maybe a future. Now he is back on the streets and in a more dangerous city. Why would he do that? Is it immature thinking? Is there something about the illusion of freedom of the streets I don't understand? Is there a spiritual struggle going on here? Are drugs involved? I simply can't imagine what would take a seemingly fine young man who had just been given a chance in life back to a way of life that was so very hard. Did he think money would buy him better than what he was leaving? Did Judas want the money? Or was he trying to prove some unimaginable something? Look what he left behind?

The Lover of our souls. The One who offers eternity with God the Father. Goodness, mercy, forgiveness, power, and restoration were traded for a bit of money. Is that what Stanley walked away from, too? It is said that the love of money is the root of all evil. I can sure see that in this instance. What a shame. Makes me want to throw up! I would like to know what he was thinking. Then I'd like to shake him until his teeth rattled. I pray someday he returns to his Father as the prodigal son, repentant, and ready to live the life his heavenly Father yearns for him to live. Then we will rejoice. For now, I am worried sick.

Bead Buy—1,800 Pounds of Jewelry

Even though the main reason for Jean and I to be in Masese this trip was the order we needed to make happen, we still felt we should buy jewelry from the groups. We knew they were relying on us. A bead buy is intensive for everyone. The women set up their display for us to see and sit with it, waiting for us to get there and for their turn. At this time, they were sitting on the ground. In later bead buys we have a place in classrooms for them out of the blazing sun and off the ground. This year they were patiently waiting, sitting on the ground, crowded in a space near Irene's house. It was getting late as we processed through each woman's wares, buying what we could. It took a long time as we were also training them as to what is good quality and sellable in the States.

It was getting dark and we were losing our light. I felt badly about having to turn women away after they had waited for us. They needed desperately to sell to us. Irene came to Jean and I and said the women would like for us to take all of their items. I told her there was no way we could afford to pay for it all. She proposed we take it and pay them as we sell it. I was reluctant as I thought getting the women paid fairly could be quite a feat. We wouldn't know which woman had given us what items. Irene assured us she could keep it all straight and would distribute money fairly. She said it wouldn't do them any good to keep their creations in their huts as they had no market without us. Jean said, "Okay." I agreed to do my best to sell everything but secretly I thought it might take years!

Sometimes we don't have good sense. This was a crazy thing to do! The Ugandan women filled our bags after their jewelry was counted and recorded. We had to purchase several more duffels. We knew we would have to pay for extra bags at the airport. What we didn't know was how much jewelry there really was. It was hard to look at displays on the ground and visualize it packed into luggage. We had no way of weighing each bag to check for the airline fifty-pound limit per bag. Necklaces were laid in bags orderly but there was nothing to keep them in order. Earrings were just put in loose. I took months to sort out all the earrings and untangle the necklaces. But I am getting ahead of myself. We didn't know the volume of bags until we were loading to go to the airport. There were fourteen loaded bags!

At the Entebbe airport, there is a scale for weighing. Goodrue and Stanley (the street kid) helped us make each bag an even weight. Jean carefully packed each bag with thirty-two kilos of weight. We then had to load them onto a conveyor belt for an initial inspection before checking in. Our guys helped lift the bags onto the conveyor and I drug them off the moving belt on the other side of the screening. I laughed to myself when the scanner operator looked at me with raised eyebrows and asked "Jewelry?" It must have looked like a bunch of snakes all wound together. He let all the bags through, and thanks to gravity, I could get the bags off the conveyor.

Jean came through the people scanner to meet me on my side of the conveyor and helped with the last bags. Then we each grabbed a side of a bag and heaved it onto a rolling cart. We loaded too many onto each cart causing both of them to fall over as soon as we tried to push them. At this point we were still in good spirits and fell into a laughing spree. We reloaded, gave a great big push using all our strength, and proceeded on to the check-in counter. Between us, we were pushing almost 900 pounds. Our funds were limited so we were nervous about the number of bags we were taking. We didn't know the cost of extra bags.

Before we could even cross that bridge, we found out we had transposed the numbers. The bags were only allowed twenty-three kilos. Not thirty-two! We were seriously overweight as well as trying to check considerably more than normally allowed. What on earth were we going to do? There was nothing the check-in employees could do to help us. They would lose their jobs. So Jean asked to speak to the General Manager. She left me with the pile of bags and told me to pray. She didn't have to ask twice. This was an impossible situation! I must have been a sight sitting with all those bags crying and praying. Soon Jean came back, talked a minute with the check-in clerk, and began putting the bags up to be checked in. She hadn't been able to get everything waived, but she got a much-reduced price than we should have been on the hook for. I asked her what she said to get favor. She gave me a funny little smile and said she cried.

We were relieved to get the bags checked all the way to Denver. We weren't sure how to handle customs upon arriving, though. Each of us had to declare a value of what we were bringing in. This jewelry had no value if we couldn't sell it, and we had no idea if we could sell it. We had paid nothing for it and any money we received would be all nonprofit money used for charity. On our customs form we put the maximum amount allowed and crossed our fingers. By the time we got to Denver we were two tired travelers. It is a grueling trip even without the emotional and physical stress of all those bags.

Once in the customs area of the Denver airport, we had to again drag the bags off the conveyor. This time it was a carousel with an edge we had to drag the bags over. It was tricky, but with both of us grasping the same bag and pulling together we got them off and loaded onto rolling carts. We were able to get all the bags onto three carts, but there were only two of us to push the carts. As we moved bags toward the exit a cart broke. Again, we fell into maniacal laughter. It was laugh or cry! After reloading onto a cart that held up, we had to figure a way to get out the door. The bags we bought in Uganda were inferior quality. Seams were ripping out and necklaces were escaping. It was obvious what we were bringing through customs. We held our breaths.

We knew our husbands were just on the other side of the door, but they weren't allowed to come help us. Jean and I had to get all three carts across a certain line manned by customs officials without going back over the line ourselves. I pushed my cart of over 300 pounds across the line while Jean got one cart behind the other and pushed both carts to where I could reach and pull from my side while she pushed from her side. We made it! The customs guys didn't seem to have a problem with the bags of jewelry as long as we could get it across the line and out the door. Boy were we happy to see our husbands! They took our picture leaning on the bags looking as tired as could be. They took over from there and marveled that we had hauled all those sixty-pound bags ourselves.

This was so crazy and really fun!

Just an update on that endeavor. It was too hard to keep what we owed the bead women straight, so we ended up paying them for everything before we could get it all sold. We collected the money we made and paid our debt off as soon as we could. When we paid the ladies, there were tears and rejoicing. Most of them had never had so much money at one time. They told us how they paid off debts and bought new supplies and started new businesses to help them survive in between our visits. It was a major boost to the Masese/Jinja economy and elevated these women above the poverty they had been burdened with.

As of this writing, we have three Co-ops making jewelry for us (about 120 women). Their offerings have gotten much better in quality and design. It is still amazing to me what lovely creations they make from recycled paper. Delia and her team on Long Island, along with me and a few dedicated helpers, sell jewelry every chance we get. Without it we would not have been able to fund this project. We have no funding source other than individuals and an occasional grant. This marketing has been a blessing on both sides of the ocean. I didn't know boatloads would mean this, but I was certain this was a part of the fulfilling of the prophecy.

Fair Trade Certification

Another update from this time. Walmart's legal department got involved with the Walmart.com endeavor, slowing things down considerably. First, we had to get our Fair Trade certification. On the first pass, the women were asked if their children helped make the beads. They said yes since they are teaching the girls to be bead makers too. We had created an area we called the "factory" so women weren't using their own homes to create the jewelry. It wasn't anything fancy but there was a roof where they could be out of the sun and rain and a place to lock their supplies and products. It gave them a place to gather. This was a requirement for our certification, but we were not granted approval because it looked like we were using child labor.

A year or so later we passed our certification, but by this time many things had changed and our order was not valid. Since we had already paid our artisans, Full Circle Exchange took a portion of the order from us and sold it on their website. It still left us with quite an excess. Eventually a lot of it sold. Some of the United States team were happy the Walmart plan fell through for us. It would have been difficult to fill ongoing orders, and our project would not have made much money to cover our own expenses or to help with the school's financial needs. It would have been a steady income stream for the bead ladies if they could have pulled off the shipping and order fulfillment, but it wasn't meant to be. Also, the jewelry would have been sold at Walmart prices which would have been difficult competition for the boutiques and fairs and our online store where we sold the jewelry.

July
Garrity's Math Workshop

Delia and Peter, along with one of Peter's students from Columbia University, brought the first teacher's workshop. They offered this workshop to our Primary 5, 6 and 7 teachers as well as other schools in Jinja interested in sending their teachers. The workshop taught the teachers to use math manipulatives. Ugandan teaching depended on rote memorization. Hands on manipulatives were an exciting and daunting concept. With classes containing forty-five plus students, it is easier to teach to the group rather than individualized learning. Peter and Delia have held multiple trainings throughout the years in the States. To go to one of these workshops in America would cost a pretty penny. Our school is really blessed to have these two and their university students committed to its success.

Ugandan Children

Children play! No matter where I am, I see children play. It is a joy to see them happy. When they are playing, they are happy.

Soccer
(called football in Africa)
is everywhere!

These young beings forget their hardships and just enjoy their game and each other. I see hand designed dolls from whatever scraps they can find (sugar cane stalks, corn cobs, sticks and leaves, etc.); elaborate miniature living spaces from dirt, sticks, tree roots and rocks; and soccer balls made from rags wound into a ball. It is great fun to take a bicycle tire or a tire rim and roll it with a stick or to pull an empty water bottle cut out in the form of a taxi. Fancy cars can be made from bending wire to form the car and then adding a string for pulling or a stick for pushing. All kinds of games can be played from small rocks as you sit in a circle on the ground and figure out your rules. Girls all over the world play hand games and games with rope. Jump rope is common, but there are many versions of skills with ropes. If no rope is available, they can tie rags into a rope. Uganda seems to have no shortage of rags in their poorer villages. If a tree is down or there is a pile of logs, you will see children climbing all over them. That even looks like fun to me, though I worry they will hurt themselves with an unstable step.

Team sports are great fun for all. I don't see America's kind of football or basketball, but soccer (called football in Africa) is everywhere. Volleyball and a girl's game of netball are popular. Netball is similar to basketball but the ball is passed from player to player as they travel down the court. No dribbling is allowed. Baseball is becoming more common and older guys might play golf. Usually that game is for men, though, and not children. Once we dumped a pile of sawdust for a project we were going to do. Before we got to it the kids made a makeshift gym. They were impressive doing flips and such. I don't see dress-up or make believe very often.

Circumcision Ceremony

I did see a parade of young boys pretending they were in a procession for circumcision. There is quite an occasion when a teen boy goes through a circumcision ceremony. I haven't witnessed one, but I have heard stories of a dead chicken being carried on a stick as the candidates parade with white faces (from being smeared with millet paste), getting their courage up to have their foreskins publicly cut.

The circumcision ceremony is a time-honored rite of passage required of all boys in certain tribes of Eastern Uganda. During the ritual, villagers come together and celebrate for days, slaughtering goats, dressing their young candidates in ceremonial cloth, and smearing them in millet paste to prepare them for the event. It must be an incredibly painful episode, but as they goad the young man on with cheering, teasing, and applause, he's expected to maintain a stone-faced demeanor, with even his slightest reactions scrutinized. If all goes well, they will declare he is fit for the duties and privileges of manhood. And if all goes well, these same boys won't show up at the clinic the next day looking to stop infections.

While the Ugandan government has cracked down on female

genital mutilation, Ugandan president Yoweri Museveni himself has given the Imbalu practice for the young men his stamp of approval. This ceremony is only practiced every two years by one certain tribe in East Africa.

When I first heard about this custom a friend was telling me about her trip with Jean Kaye to Uganda preceding my first visit. She said she was in a car and saw these boys with white faces and a chicken impaled on a stick coming toward their car. She frantically rolled up the windows, saying, "Drive! They don't like us here!" Today we laugh, but at the time she was truly scared.

REI Shoes

Also in 2012, I took good quality shoes and sandals donated from REI, a retail store selling sports equipment and accessories, to give to the older sponsored students. The two Joels, Marian, Hillary, Hillary's aunt, Jackie, Henry, Priscilla, and Bonny. Robert and Richard received shoes as did the cooks. At first some of the best shoes were being rejected by the girls since they are not accustomed to sturdy shoes. Many Ugandans wear flip flops that have no support and wear out quickly. Or they are accustomed to no shoes at all. If they have school shoes, their shoes have more substance, but they are far from "pretty." I insisted that a couple of the girls take the sturdy sandals. I promised them they wouldn't be sorry. Henry was delighted I had sandals to fit him. He has large feet. I think God knew what sizes I would need because I just brought what they had donated. Each young person got a good pair of shoes that fit. Five years later I noticed several of these shoes were still being worn. They had worn these shoes every day for years and they were still trucking. REI could use this as an advertisement for durability!

Henry—Sleeping with Animals

Henry had people stealing his things and selling them for money. To protect his new REI shoes, Henry left them at Hillary's grandmother's house in the Karamojong village on his way home from school and then he walked the rest of the way barefoot. In the morning, he would leave the place he slept barefoot and pick up his shoes on the way to school. Before the year was out his shoes still disappeared.

Hillary, upset about the conditions where Henry was sleeping, insisted we visit where Henry was sleeping. It was a small shelter for animals. Henry only ate at school and was doing his best to avoid any family he had when he wasn't in school. This was a problem when school was on break. Sometimes a grandmother would feed him or an uncle, but most of the time, they were not nice to him. We put him under Ben's care and helped with expenses. Eventually, we took him to a boarding school. Ben and his wife, Rona, visited Henry on visiting days and kept him at their house on school breaks.

I appreciated them taking him in as family. The Ugandans do this more than I was accustomed to. I love that about them!

When we visited Henry, he was so starved for affection he wouldn't let go of my hand. He hugged us over and over. He needed a mother! I felt for him and was glad we could provide for him as much as we could. He received good fatherly attention from Bruce. Sometimes that meant Bruce had to be stern with him to encourage him to make good choices.

Once Henry finished primary school, we had to decide his next step. He wanted to go on to secondary school, but we were not too sure. This young man was bigger and older than the other kids. He had begun to get into trouble. We predicted Henry might feel like he needed to get a job to provide for himself before he finished his secondary schooling. Finally, we decided to send him to a vocational school. After conferring with our Ugandan staff, he was enrolled into an electrical installation training school. Henry was not happy about this. Whereas this young man was usually extremely grateful, he became sullen and withdrawn. Hillary had gone to secondary. Henry wanted to go to secondary, too. We held our ground and left for home. The next time we saw him, he was a different person. He loved his vocational school and was doing well with his studies. He walked with an air of confidence we had never seen from him. He was eager to please and back to his grateful self. We were proud of who he had become. No one could steal this from him!

Pricilla and Sadat

Priscilla was a sweet girl, quiet and pretty. We were paying her schooling along with other students (children of our staff) who were too old for the Help School. This was before we changed our policy about helping staff beyond paying them a salary. We decided that since they now had income to cover school fees, we would sponsor other students whose families didn't have a steady source of income.

However, all three girls lost their school fee funding because they were not passing their classes. Several times we warned both the girls and their parents before making the difficult decision to stop paying for their schooling. And we had standards for sponsoring that required children to maintain passing grades. Though I hated leaving those girls behind, it seemed more prudent to invest in those who put forth more effort.

Sadat was another story. Her school fees had been paid since our first trip. We would see her each time we visited. She was a very affectionate girl. One trip, though, Sadat kept a hoodie over her head and face. It was strange. She would come to hug us and then leave quickly. This was not normal for her at all. Finally, Jean got her alone and took off her hood. She found multiple bruises on her face and strangle marks on her neck. Sadat tried to make excuses for her bruises. Jean persisted in questioning her until Sadat admitted someone had beaten her and tried to kill her. I know teenagers can be difficult and hard to put up with, but this treatment was extreme and dangerous for Sadat.

Sadat was frightened. She didn't want to tell us for fear of getting in worse trouble. We decided to remove her from the danger by putting her in a boarding school. Her parents agreed as having a child in a boarding school is a privilege not everyone can afford. Sadat was thrilled.

Unfortunately, Sadat could not maintain good behavior. She started getting STDs and leaving school for periods of time. Her grades suffered. No amount of warnings or admonitions seemed to help. I expect she needed more counseling than we provided to deal with her childhood problems. An affectionate girl lacking in love can be drawn to get love any way she can find it. She graduated from primary school, but we were not willing to send her on to secondary.

We gave her a chance to prove she would take her studies seriously by saying if she could get someone to pay her school fees and could show us she was applying herself we would help her again. She got herself into school but never paid any fees. We wouldn't help her without proof of her grades, and she couldn't get her grades without paying her fees. Sad, but she had caused much of her own misery. There are just too many kids needing help and too few of us to help. We had to draw some difficult lines.

We didn't hear from Sadat for quite some time. Then one day she showed up at our office asking for help to go to a vocational school. She had birthed a baby, receiving no help from the father. She came back home and wanted to provide for herself and her baby. I contacted her former sponsor asking what she wanted to do. Now there was a baby involved. Her sponsor said she would like to help her get through culinary school, and that is the path they are on as I write this. I haven't seen her myself, but it feels good to be helping get her a start in her adult life as a single mom.

Marian and Sadat were the "groupies" I talked about on our first team trip. Stephanie was their first sponsor. Through the years, Marian kept in close contact with us when we visited. I thought for sure she would grow up to become a hairdresser since she always wanted to "style" my hair. She was a little sassy most of the time, but endearingly. We watched her grow into a young woman. She went through some difficult times.

Ugandan men, before Christianity and those who don't embrace Christianity today, may engage in multiple marriages. A man might have several wives and many children. Providing for all these people is very difficult; often, the women and children must try to provide for themselves. Alcoholism is often a problem when the men feel the pressure of all this responsibility, and beating wives and children frequently results.

Marian's dad lived in town with his family there, so Marian's family—living in the village—needed to rely on an uncle to help them when their father didn't have rent money. Life was hard. And tenuous.

One time Marian ran away from home. She had been beaten. It worried me sick as there was a sex slave trade in Jinja from the truckers whose route travels through there. She was vulnerable trying to live on the streets. Our staff finally found her and talked her into returning home, promising to smooth the way with her parents. I was relieved!

Not long after that we enrolled her in a boarding school. Our staff thought it would help her stay away from the wrong crowd. I think they were seeing signs of pending trouble. When I first saw her after she had been living at this boarding school, I was amazed and really happy.

Blog: Delightful Marian

Marian is a sixteen-year-old leader in the making. This young woman talks with confidence about her convictions and her newfound desire to be an entrepreneur. She is figuring out ways to make money with just what she has in her hand. She had mangoes, so she made juice and sold it to her classmates. Her dad owns a refrigerator (something rare in the village), so she will chill water and other drinks and then up-price them. She has been studying current fashion and offers to fix hairstyles for her friends for a small fee. Marian actually won an award in a contest where the contestants had to design something from materials available in a fifteen-minute timed event. Using banana leaves she fashioned a dress in five minutes modeling it to win the contest.

Not only is her business sense and creativity emerging, but her standards are impressive. She wants nothing to do with her former friends who experiment with makeup, party with boys, and skip classes. She has goals beyond that behavior. When I asked her what her favorite Scripture was, she didn't hesitate in quoting two with a fervor that told me she took them to heart.

Best of all is the impact she is having on those around her. She feels that since she is being helped, she wants to help others so they will help others, too. One of her most cherished successes is her own father. Since she has been doing so well in school, and H.E.L.P. has made sure she had a new sponsor when her original sponsor needed to stop her sponsorship, her dad is seeing her as someone important to listen to. Since others value her, he is seeing her in a different light. She has been telling him it is wrong for men to fail to pay bills or to beat their wives and drink alcohol. She tells him people don't respect such men. He is listening to her and changing!

So, we throw pebbles into the water to watch the ripples. We sponsor the Marians to see them change their world. We lose some, it's true; but it just takes one spark to light a big bonfire. That bonfire may just light up a whole nation. You just never know!

Unfortunately, that is not the end of Marian's story. She disappeared again. No one seemed to know anything about her, and we couldn't find her. She was not at school or anywhere to be found. In 2016, almost a year later, she showed up with a baby. What a mess she had made of her life. The baby's father was not good to her, and her dad said she was living like an adult now and could not live at home.

Our team gave her baby clothes and clothes for herself, but we couldn't help her further at this point. She and I talked and planned a business for her to support herself and her child, but she would have to leave her baby's father. We couldn't go against her dad who told her to go home to her "husband." I counseled Marian to go back to her baby's father and be the best wife she could be. Her best future would be to make that relationship work, even though she claimed he was tired of her and was with another woman.

I left and worried about her all year. I decided I would help her get set up in a business if we could convince her dad to let her live with her mother. I would see she paid rent to her dad like an adult, through her sponsor at first. Marian would take over this responsibility as soon as she could, within a year or less. So on our trip in 2017, she came up with a business plan and got her dad's permission. At least I think she did. I had to leave before we had everything in place. I passed her off to another team member just coming in. This team member helped Marian until she had to leave as well. Marian was trying to set up a small kiosk to sell food. I left money to help her get set up and then sent more for her to buy supplies. Our staff there gave it to her instead of purchasing her supplies with her. She told them she had help and didn't need theirs. We haven't seen her since. I am not sure whether her guy found out and forced her to take our money and give it to him or whether she just played us. Like it or not, she was gone with my money. I loved that girl and was sick at heart. I thought she was a true success story for our efforts and this was a great disappointment.

Asthma

My body has always been susceptible to breathing problems. It wasn't until I was in my 40s that I learned about my asthma. This is only a problem for me when I have irritation to my lungs like a chest cold or exertion above my normal routine. Unfortunately, I found out I am sensitive to dust as well. My trips to Africa have shown me more frailty than I would like to admit. My mother's motto in high school was "find a way or make one." I've adopted her motto as my own, proceeding to let very few things stop me from doing what or going where I wanted. I must admit this asthma thing was making me stop and think.

"Am I going to keep making trips to Africa with all its dust?" Regardless of how much I want to go and how I thought it was the right thing to do, I coughed and coughed and coughed some more. I coughed for weeks. I tried an inhaler for a trip and thought I had found the answer. That trip was the only one where I didn't have this persistent, lingering cough. That formula didn't work the next year. I tried keeping the windows in the car rolled up to keep the dust out. That would have helped except it was too hot with no ventilation. Very few of the cars we used had air conditioning. I scrambled to cover my mouth and nose with something while we drove through smog infused Kampala. The same goes when trucks would kick up dust or I was breathing the exhaust when we followed or passed them. I felt ridiculous wearing surgical masks, so I just held something to my face like a scarf or the fabric of my skirt.

Maybe my problem is staying too long in this environment. Maybe I go down too many dusty roads when I am there. Whatever, I realized that my body isn't as strong as I would like for it to be. What was I going to do with this realization? God said in 2 Corinthians 12:9: "My grace is sufficient for thee: for my strength is made perfect in weakness. Most gladly therefore will I rather glory in my infirmities, that the power of Christ may rest upon me" (KJV). Was I going to be able to "glory in my infirmities?" I wanted the power of Christ to rest upon me. Looking at this Scripture and seeing the word "rest," I wondered if I was too focused on the doing and not enough on the resting. I was looking for the power, not the infirmities. I wanted the strength, not the weakness. What I needed to understand is that it was His strength, His grace, His power. Being a "can do" person all my life may work against my accepting of this truth. Like the motto said, I've been making a way when I couldn't find one. Now I was learning that I need to acknowledge that He is the way. As I age, this will be more and more important. Maybe I am becoming wise versus able. I wish I could be both!

Sponsorship Program

Ritah had a story all her own.

I discovered she had a degree in social work. We needed a social worker at the school but didn't have funding for one. Much to her husband's dismay, she agreed to volunteer for us until I could get her funding. Ritah was forward thinking, trusting that her willingness to help us would be rewarded. It didn't take long to convince the H.E.L.P. Uganda Board of her value, and a woman in the States wanted to help us pay Ritah's salary. She was worth her weight in gold, but since our gold was in short supply, we were happy for the additional financial support that enabled us to hire her onto our staff.

Claire's story highlights the value of our sponsorship program and the need for someone like Ritah to oversee it.

> I first saw Claire sitting alone on a mattress in an unkempt room she and her grandmother called home. Claire had missed a few days of school and no one knew why. She was sick, as was her grandmother. Actually, this might be her great-grandmother since she is quite elderly. They both had malaria and an awful condition called "jiggers." Jiggers burrow into your feet and eat the flesh. It is gruesome. The jiggers live in dirt, and if a place is not kept "clean," they can infest it. With a dirt floor, you can just imagine ... We cleaned the place and cleared it of all infestation and then treated them both for malaria. Since then, Claire has been sponsored by a family in the United States.

> Part of the money helping Claire provides weekend food for her and her grandmother. It upset us to find she had had nothing to eat the first weekend, even though we had provided rice and beans. Her grandmother didn't have any charcoal or wood to cook with. Can you imagine being

hungry, having food, but staying hungry because the food can't be prepared? Argh! Now her sponsorship money includes charcoal, too.

The layers of poverty astound us.

When we returned that summer, Claire was sick again. Diana took her straight to a clinic to get a full medical checkup. Despite our having provided a treated malaria net for sleeping, Claire had malaria again. She was so sick she may not have lived had we not been there to intervene. Life is so precarious, especially with no provisions. We are truly thankful for this girl's generous American friend.

Ritah looks out for all our sponsored children as well as the children in the orphanage we opened later. Without her, we likely would not have been made aware of Claire's dire situation.

My Dichotomy About Money

As I pondered some of these issues, I wrote this about money and me:

> What a lovely choice to have, to be able to choose to spend money. Spending money is such a privilege! Maybe more to the point, having money to spend is the privilege. I am ashamed to admit that I take it for granted most of the time. For most of my life I have had money to spend. Sometimes I didn't have so very much. But I have always had enough. Even in college, when my husband and I were both on loans and only working part time, we had enough if we scrimped.
>
> My parents were raised in the Great Depression. That difficult time shaped their thinking in many ways, especially in the area of money. They knew what it was to do without. They knew how to be frugal. I learned much from their experience just by living with them. Not living in those desperate times, I learned

vicariously. My parents made sure I had enough even if they didn't. I, in turn, made sure my children had enough—maybe even more than enough, if I am honest. We always want better for our children than we had. Of course, the definition of "better" is the question. Is it better to have plenty or even an excess of plenty or to learn from having to be frugal?

Some people think it is good to be poor so we have to depend on God. I am all for depending on God. At least until it comes to not having enough to pay my bills or, worse yet, not having enough to eat. That kind of dependence is scary! I don't believe in giving everything to the poor if it means I am not taking care of my basic needs ... unless God tells me to. I am really glad He hasn't told me to. I am sure I would argue with Him and even seek a second opinion. I expect I would grow in my faith if I had to rely on Him to that extent. Part of me would like to be that close to Him that I depended on Him to provide my very existence. Just thinking about it makes me so thankful that I am not in such a place, even though I seek to be closer. A dichotomy!

That is a good word for me—dichotomy. I am a bit jealous of those who have more than me. I have neighbors who just got their backyard all done up nice enough to be recognized on TV. It is lovely! My home is a lovely home, and I would like to make it even lovelier. My closet is full of clothes, but I would always enjoy more. I have been able to travel to wonderful locations around the world but still wish to go more. (My husband is on his way to Japan for work, and I would like to go with him). However, I can't stand myself if I live in such a myopic way.

I am too familiar with a world that doesn't have money to choose how they spend. A world where children are truly hungry! Where frugality is not a virtue but a necessity that enables you to keep living.

I know the joy of buying a new piece of clothing or a sumptuous dinner. But I also know the joy of providing a much-needed piece of clothing to a person who wears rags. Seeing the pleasure on the face of the one receiving even a used item they need is way more rewarding than having a new item for myself. It can be argued that everything is selfish. Either I am selfish in getting for myself or I am selfish in the joy I receive in giving something to someone else.

We are interesting creatures. What I can say is that for now I get a greater pleasure in spending what I need on necessities and helping however I can to relieve the suffering I have encountered. I pray that brings me closer to my God. I think it will. I choose to focus on Him rather than on spending or not spending. The song says money makes "the world go round." My world has been spinning ever since I went to Africa the first time. When I came home and sat in my garage and cried because we house our cars better than most people are housed over there, I knew my world had been irrevocably rocked!

The truth is: Giving is a heart issue, not a money issue.

Children are the ones who really bless me. A classroom of school children studying poverty and education invited me to give a presentation. I brought some Ugandan jewelry for them to see since they were planning on selling this jewelry to help raise funds for awareness about poverty and education. It was near Mother's Day so some kids eagerly picked out a piece of jewelry to buy for their mothers. Their teacher picked up a bracelet that cost $15 and said, "Purchasing this bracelet for $15 will buy a pair of shoes for a school child." A boy listening to her asked, "I picked out a $10 bracelet. Can I pay $15 for it?"

I was touched! If we all had the heart of children, what a world it would be! Where does that heart of compassion go as we get older? I guess the pressures of life and the difficulty of obtaining money plays into it. I expect we all have that childlike heart in us somewhere. Those kids raised $800 with their sale!

You may want to know that a sponsorship is only $30 a month. With that, you not only get to know you are saving a life, bringing education and hope to the poorest of the poor in this impoverished village, and truly making a difference in this world, but you will build a relationship that will be dear to your heart.

Maybe you can't go with us (or maybe you *can* go and meet your child!), but your money can reach clear across the ocean into a life of a young child like Claire to change his or her life forever. We keep none of the money on this side of the world. It all goes to help this child.

This sponsorship helps fund their education and provide breakfast and lunch during the week, weekend food for their whole family, medical care, clothing, bedding, and a lifesaving mosquito net. Last, but not least, you are able to provide them hope for a brighter tomorrow, and the knowledge that someone cares and is praying for them. I believe if we could truly see what a difference this giving makes, most of us would do whatever it takes to help.

One of the endearing parts of this program is an exchange of letters. The kids really, really love getting letters. When photos are included, they are cherished. Often, each letter is kept in a safe place as a valuable item they read over and over. The kids not receiving a letter are jealous and sad. They want to know their sponsor and let them know how much they value them.

Whether or not a child receives a letter, each child writes his or her benefactor. Ben, who is no longer teaching but serves as Ritah's assistant, helps each child write his or her letter. The younger children can't yet write, so an adult helper is needed to write for them. Then the young child draws a picture for the letter.

It is fun to see how the pictures mature as the children grow. Soon they can sign their names themselves, and before long, they are writing their own letters.

We started a new communication I am excited about. We are doing videos. How fun is that? Christmas 2017 was our first Christmas video. It thrilled the sponsors. There will still be handwritten letters, but the videos are taking the communication to a whole different level.

Some hesitation to sending money to an organization could be a trust issue. I get that! Some organizations are not trustworthy. Your money may or may not get where you want it. Charity Navigator is one of the watchdogs to help you know how the organization rates. I doubt if H.E.L.P. International is on one of those lists since it is so small, but I can tell you, and you can see for yourself first hand, H.E.L.P. does not keep your money.

July 2012 was full of activities in our developing school.

A classroom of kids in the United States sent letters. The corresponding grade level in the H.E.L.P. School put a lot of effort into answering these letters. This was their first time to correspond with kids from American. As the students worked, they giggled. One photo attached to the letters was of an African American girl. Our Ugandan students did not know there were black people in the US!

We saw baby chicks colored pink and green and blue. It wasn't Easter! This was confusing until our Ugandan friends told us they dye the chicks because this different color confuses the chicks' predators. Smart!

Kisima Island

We took our first excursion to Kisima Island on this trip. There are three villages named Masese. Masese 1 is a fishing village located by Lake Victoria. The boat we took from their village to a nearby island was not much more than a large carved out wooden canoe sporting a small motor. Some transport boats have a partial roof to protect from the sun and rain. These boats bring officials, teachers, and trade people in the fishing industry across the water daily.

The water was a lovely blue. In the big, awesome sky the birds swoop and glide as they find their food, seeming to enjoy their airborne life. The horizon reflected silhouettes of fishermen casting their nets from smaller boats. Most Ugandans don't know how to swim and are deathly afraid to be on the water. We had to encourage our Ugandan friends to travel to this island with us. Getting into the boat was an experience for both the men and the women in our group. Instead of walking through the water, Ugandan men picked up each woman and deposited her into the boat. They hauled the men on their backs to board them. I secretly enjoyed being carried, but none of the men appreciated the experience. This procedure was entertaining to watch after we were secure in the boat.

The process was different when we reached the village. Once we arrived, there was a boat tied between our boat and the shore. We stepped out of our boat into this boat, then onto a rock, and then the shore. I was always glad for someone standing near to steady me by taking my hand.

The village was struggling to get clean water. They had a well a previous group had provided, but it had broken. We were able to fix it, but it broke repeatedly in subsequent years. The church we attended consisted of few congregants that day, mainly children. We were invited to dinner after church so maybe the women who would have been in church were busy cooking for visitors. Food is scarce for them, so we hate to eat it. But hospitality was very important to them, so we obliged. Jean always leaves a donation to help replace what we have consumed, and we pray we don't get sick because the water they use to wash their dishes comes from the lake and is not so safe.

Agricultural Fair

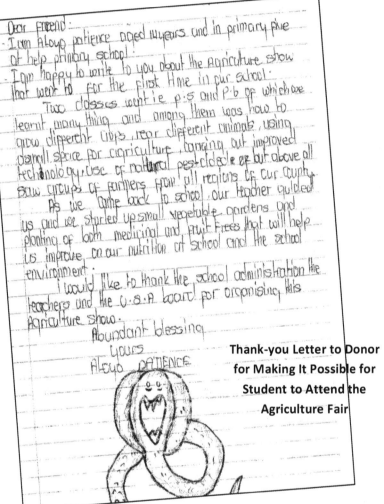

Thank-you Letter to Donor for Making It Possible for Student to Attend the Agriculture Fair

Back in Jinja, there was an agricultural fair with a small entrance fee. We rented buses and attended the fair with the kids and their teachers. We visited a display of a new farm technique—a cow pulling a plow. Most Ugandans till with their strong backs and a hoe. It was so different than back in the States where such a display would have included the latest version of a tractor or large machine to do the work. The Wildlife Education Center displayed different species of snakes. Other displays included prized cattle and a variety of crops. And then there were the inevitable fair rides. One fun one was a chance to ride a camel. Our kids loved the mechanized rides swinging their riders around in a circle high in the air!

I looked at the structure and shuddered. It didn't look safe to this mother's eyes. As with all fairs, there were some questionable guys lurking about looking for a chance to vandalize or worse. We had plenty of adults watching out for our students, and unknown to us, there were students looking out for us. Fifth-grade Patrick and a couple of friends alerted us when they saw a man trying to sneak into Bruce's backpack while he was walking ahead of them. Patrick and his friends had hung back to watch for that very type of attempt. I love how safe I feel because I have so many Ugandan friends watching out for me wherever I am.

Renee, Jon, and Riley

This was the first year Renee, Jon, and their son, Riley, traveled with us. Renee owns an upscale young adult used clothing store in Colorado. From that store H.E.L.P. receives a major influx of fashionable clothing to sell at their thrift store or to ship to those in need around the world. Renee wanted to take her thirteen-year-old son to experience another culture. However, she was concerned she would cry when she witnessed the poverty. I assured her she would cry. It is difficult to experience the living conditions of this struggling community without becoming emotional. Getting up her courage, they came with us.

It was a joy to see Riley interact with the Ugandan kids. He would run while the little ones chased him, all of them laughing with delight. He loved to drum and there is plenty of drumming going on in Masese! If older boys from the village tried to harass him, the school kids would step in. He was everyone's friend but especially the friend of a younger boy named Jared. Jared wasn't in our school, but Riley, Renee, and Jon loved him. They decided to sponsor him and his family to get them into our school.

Breasts in Uganda are not as sexualized as they are in America. It is very common to see mothers unabashedly reveal their breasts to nurse their babies. Bras are seldom worn. Breasts are functional and accepted rather than hidden or accentuated. Bringing a young adolescent, like Riley, to this culture must have been quite eye opening. I have seen several adult men team members' jaws drop when they first experience this openness. Conversely, hips are the emphasized part of African women's bodies. They are especially featured in their dances. However, Ugandan village women are careful to cover their bottom and hips, never showing more than a loose skirt allows. Modesty seems lax when it comes to breasts but quite in place around the hips. More and more young African women are now wearing Western styles, especially the ones in the cities. These go against their culture and are not welcomed in the villages. Pants (locally called trousers) are for the guys, but the young women are wearing them more and more. I wonder if Riley had a different perspective coming home from this village culture?

Stanley—Sickle Cell

One afternoon Renee was watching kids play on our playground. She noticed a little boy sitting away from the fun, acting lethargic. She asked about him and found he was sick. Renee asked if we could help him. We found his mother and took him to a nearby clinic. The clinic workers were familiar with this child. All he needed to be fine was medicine for sickle cell anemia. His mother didn't have the money for this medicine and without it, the child was suffering and dying. We were shocked to find out the cost of this life-saving medicine was only $3.00. Can you even imagine your child suffering and dying from the lack of $3.00 a month? We spend $3.00 on a coffee! Daily! Renee paid for the boy's medicine. Once she returned to Colorado, she put a donation box in her store telling people about Stanley and his need. Once they heard his story, her customers were happy to help with some coins or a dollar or two each time they purchased something from her store. Those small donations added up. Stanley is only one of many needing life-saving medicines in this and other developing countries. He is one of the fortunate ones because he was in the right place at the right time and someone noticed him.

Eve's Son

Another day Renee, Ritah, and I were at the compound talking when a young bead woman, Eve, came running up, crying, "Help me! My baby is sick!" Her face was frantic! Urgency coursed through her and spread to us. We sent her home to bring the sick child. She came running back with a young boy lying lifeless in her arms. Her face pleaded, urging us to save him. We ran to get Jean. She sent for our driver and yelled for him to run! We piled into the car and sped to the nearest clinic that had facilities. With panicked eyes, Eve held her son and wept softly. The clinic knew what was wrong. This child had cerebral malaria. Malaria of the brain!

"Most of the time malaria causes a bad fever and body aches. But in rare cases—often in children—the parasite gets stuck in the capillaries of the brain. The child has a seizure, goes into a coma, and possibly dies. This all happens in only two or three days," says Dr. Terrie Taylor of Michigan State University. "These are bright, happy children who are suddenly felled by a disease that quickly renders them unconscious. And quickly kills them."

This time God had other plans. Because the boy was treated quickly, he was running around playing in a few days, as if nothing had ever happened. Each time I saw Eve on this trip, and in following years, I would ask about her child. Her eyes would dance while I received a grateful smile of reassurance telling me he was still fine. Life and death! We get to see what a difference we make in very real measures. It is forever humbling.

Stone Soup Performance

Renee and Jon loved to encourage children in the arts. They had a program for guitar students at their elementary school in Wyoming that focused on kids who could not afford to learn guitar. They brought costumes for the Ugandan students—think dragons, princesses, crowns, angel wings, lions, etc. After outfitting the kids, Renee and Jon encouraged creative expression. I had to smile when we were trying to get the little Ugandan princesses to turn and twirl their pretty dresses in a dance. The young girls followed our suggestions and moved their hips in the traditional African way. Not exactly what we had in mind, but very appropriate for their culture.

Jon, Renee, and Riley also taught the students to perform the Folktale "Stone Soup." This is a story of hungry strangers who convince the people of a town to each share a small amount of their food in order to make a meal for everyone to enjoy. The strangers receive a meal and teach the value of sharing. The student actors in the play were given simple lines and were directed by Jon. One girl hammed up her lines, and another made us laugh at her funny antics. Maybe they will be famous actors someday. The parents and school community all enjoyed the kids' performance of the play.

After the kids finished their skit, some Ugandan women who excel in traditional dance performances jumped up and danced for us. Appreciative onlookers would run out to a dancer to hand her a few shillings. Not only did these ladies dance, but they brought Jean and I out to join them. That was embarrassing because I don't have the rhythm they do and feel like I look silly compared to them. It is all in good fun though, so we laugh and let them laugh at us. We are a community together and I love that!

Michael Jackson

We got to see Michael for a short visit at his boarding school. He entertained Jean and I along with Renee, Jon and Riley with his antics. Michael has a fun personality that delights us each time we visit. He makes us and his classmates laugh as he impersonates Michael Jackson.

Knickers, Sticky Fingers, and Forgiveness

One of the girls in our school came up to me one day telling me she needed knickers. I didn't understand at first. I came to realize she and a few others had started their menstrual periods. They didn't have underwear. I hadn't thought about this normal growth situation since our school was for younger grades. However, even though they were in earlier levels of school, the older girls that had signed up to be educated were now at this level of maturity. We bought them panties and then searched for solutions. Normally, a menstruating girl had to sit home on rags, missing school. After I got home from this trip, I researched and found some reusable pads, manufactured in Uganda, we could purchase for our girls and the female staff. Ritah held a meeting and explained how to use them and properly clean them. We passed them out to the eligible women and girls that year. In later years, we had to change because this style didn't stay in place while the girls played their sports. It always amazes me to see the challenges in this village we don't even think about in our cushy Americanized life.

This same girl had been getting in trouble with her caretakers. They said she had "sticky fingers." I experienced this myself when she and two of her friends came into the office and helped themselves to the stock of panties. I was frustrated and angry that these girls would take advantage of us this way. I set up a meeting with Richard, Ritah, this girl, and her friends. I addressed the culprit sternly, since she was the instigator, making sure her friends heard me, too. I told her she was special to me and that I was expecting big things from her, but I was disappointed. This behavior would lead to failure instead of success. I talked about lying and taking things that weren't hers. About being impatient and expecting others to just give her what she wanted. I talked about being grateful to her caretakers who didn't have to take care of her. I lectured long enough for her to let her reserves down and cry. When I saw her remorse, I changed. I began to talk about forgiveness and moving forward. She cried harder so I stood up and gave her a long, heartfelt hug. She clung to me. This girl did not have a mother. For this minute, I was her mother, loving her enough to confront her bad behavior while showing her how God teaches us to forgive and be reconciled.

A Short Reconnection

We were happy to spend time with Kaboko and his young family at a restaurant in Kampala on our way to the airport. Shalom Pam was full of giggles and fun snuggles. Angelo was full of energy and competed for some of our attention. They are easy to love.

And the Ministry Goes On . . .

After we returned home in 2012, Bonny supervised as the school staff painted the school and buildings red and yellow to match the uniforms. Everything looked "smart" as the Ugandans say. Young Joel painted a logo picture on the outside of one of the buildings. The logo included a lighthouse since the H.E.L.P. International logo features a lighthouse. I doubt many of the Ugandans knew what a lighthouse was since they are a long way from an ocean where lighthouses provide their services. H.E.L.P. uses this as a symbol of the Light of God that shines on the people being provided humanitarian aid through H.E.L.P.'s efforts. That Light is full of hope and safety.

The students were invited to other schools' Sports Day in the Walukuba School District. They did well in the competitions. Among numerous competitions, soccer, volleyball, netball, and various foot races were main events. I would have loved to have been there to cheer them on. We have some very talented athletes in the Help school. Our students also participated in debate, music, and drama competitions. Their dramas won awards that year, too.

Through our Ugandan staff, we were able to give away three hundred mosquito nets to pregnant moms in the community as well as to our students and staff. Bidco (a large local business near our school) gave a generous donation of treated nets for us to distribute. These nets are lifesaving, especially for those at greater risk like pregnant women and their newborn babies. Without the nets, malaria is rampant and often deadly.

Our teacher Simon Peter received a bike from his sponsor because he was traveling quite a distance to get to the school. A team member had also given Billy a bike because he was struggling to get to his own school in Jinja town and back to Masese where he slept and taught in our school. They were both willing to walk, but it took so much time that sponsors and visitors from the US saw their difficulty and pitched in to help.

A radio personality, Big Daddy, was a member of our PTA, so some students were able to tour and visit a radio station in Jinja.

Working through our Ugandan staff, Renee and Jon found a house in Masese in October 2012 to use for their dream of having a small family orphanage. It needed completing, so they sent money ahead to do the work, planning on it being finished by the time they returned the next year.

Renee also advocated for the bead women by encouraging other Plato Closet owners to sell the jewelry. She not only convinced them to sell the jewelry but to give all the proceeds to the Help Uganda project. This was a huge boost all the way around!

Bigger than Beads Branding

Renee also had talent and access to talented people for marketing. She made classy looking support materials for us to use creating a "brand." We all called the bead project "Bigger Than Beads" instead of our New York friends calling it "Mothers of Masese" and the Colorado group calling it "Jewelry with A Cause." Renee and her staff put together a web store to sell the jewelry online. Because she was designing this site, it was upscale and current in style. Renee received and filled the orders. Marketing on social media also ramped up. I still use the video she made telling the story of the bead project and the school. You can see the video and shop at the store by going to www.biggerthanbeads.com.

Help Uganda Board

Missing: the Silons & Kate

We asked Renee and Jon to be board members of the Help Uganda project. We already had Jean and Don, Bruce and me, Delia and Peter, Bob and Diana, Cory (Bob and Diana's daughter) and Patricia (Delia and Peter's daughter). The board does everything this side of the ocean. We all raise money, give oversight to projects, travel to the project, etc. We are separated by locale so our meetings are via phone conferencing.

It is a challenging board as we not only have the cultural differences in the United States and Uganda, but we have New York's culture verses Colorado's culture and Wyoming's. There are also age differences to take into account. We divided up into committees so our meetings didn't last into the night. Everyone brings something to the table. We are diverse in many ways but united in our desire to have this project be as good as it can be.

2013

Zendia's House Rescue Home

In late January and early February 2013, Renee and her family went back to Masese to start the small orphanage. Riley had a dream his family had adopted a girl named Zendia. Riley's dream resulted in a newly formed family in Uganda. It was quite a  process. They had found a house on the October trip and arranged for construction to be completed before they arrived in February. In the proverbial "African time," we should have known it would be far from finished. In fact, it was just a shell when we arrived. In return for almost a year's rent, Renee and Jon paid for the house to be completed while they were there to help and supervise.

While the house was being finished, we set about finding the right children to be a part of the orphanage. Jean, Renee, and Jon visited with the village chief to get his input. Orphans aren't just given that description because they have no parents. They might also be considered orphans if they don't have responsible adults to care for them.

Ten-year-old Rosie was recommended because she was the daughter of a woman who had mental and physical issues and wasn't able to care for her children. No one knew who the dad was. Rosie was the product of rape, apparently a common occurrence for this woman.

Pattie's mother had died in childbirth and her father died soon after. She was bounced from home to home, ending up on the streets until she was taken in as a sex slave. By the time we found her, she was staying with a pastor and his wife, working as a maid. She had syphilis so severely she had a terrible odor so the couple would no longer keep her. Because she had this infection as long as she had, her brain hadn't developed normally. She had trouble doing schoolwork. Pattie had a sweet personality and blossomed at Zendia's House after they treated her for her various diseases. Love is a powerful healer.

Two of the children, Faizol and Fahad, had been left with the Help school. Their mother left them with her landlady, but never returned. The landlady tired of caring for them and dropped them off at the school. Our staff found them sleeping on the school grounds. The brothers were eight and ten years old when we took them.

Janet, age eleven, and Andrew, age five, were cousins. They were abandoned by their parents to the care of their grandmother who struggled to care for them. When this grandmother heard about Zendia's House, she claimed the children were orphans. There were many dependents at her house already. Since there was abuse and the children needed rehabilitation, they were accepted. Andrew was shy and frightened. There was alcoholism and abuse in his home. The mother had absconded. It took a while to earn Andrew's trust, but soon he responded to affection and positive attention. His big smiles were especially rewarding.

Speaking of big smiles, Daniel could melt your heart with his. It was a good thing since Daniel had an ornery streak that could exasperate us. We met Daniel at the age of ten. He was living on the streets, not attending school, and only eating when he could collect scraps and sell them to earn money for food. One of our employees, Paul, found him and brought him to meet us. This street kid was a good candidate for Renee's rescue home.

Caroline stayed with her older brother after their mother died. The brother was too young, but there were no relatives to take them in. This became one of many child-headed families in Masese. At eleven years of age, Caroline was running wild before Zendia's House opened.

Renee chose a single woman, Winifred, to be the house mom. She had to get special schooling to qualify for this job. Winifred took classes and became a social worker. Working closely with Ritah, she raised these wounded kids as her own. It was no small task to bring these children into a family setting. They had been pretty wild, with little to no supervision or an adult to care for them. With a house tailored to fit them, food to eat regularly, clothes and gifts from America, and an American family with which to connect, their lives changed dramatically. Now they had schooling, other siblings to bond with, and a house mom to love and guide them, these children's lives changed dramatically. We were privileged to visit them in their new home. The older ones helped Winifred prepare a delicious meal for our team. After we ate together, they gave us a Scripture lesson and sang and danced for us. It was quite a celebration!

Uganda in the Eyes of an American Teenager

Riley—14 Years Old

When I traveled to Uganda for the first time, it changed everything. I view things completely different now. The first thing I noticed was that almost none of the kids had shoes. I decided to make a difference. As soon as I got back, I started planning. For my Eagle Scout project, I collected and delivered over 450 pairs of shoes. When we traveled to Uganda the second time, we brought eleven checked bags that were all packed with shoes for the children of Masese, Uganda. I set up in the school building and gave out shoes to kids one by one. Many of the kids had never had shoes before.

I feel like I have a great connection with the kids. I love going there because I feel so much love and attention from all the kids. It is the part of our trips that make me feel a little selfish, we are supposed to be going there to help them, but I receive so much love it is overwhelming. When I arrive to the school it's like a giant swarm of children, all trying to grab and hold my hands. They are all very curious of me, since they are not used to seeing "Mzungus" (their word for white people) my age. They were all fascinated with my braces and they would point and laugh.

When we went on our first trip, I met my friend Gerald on the first day. We immediately became best friends. I found out that he and his brothers could not afford to go to school anymore. I decided to sponsor Gerald and his brothers, and I send them money every month so that they can attend school.

The thing that had the biggest impact on me was my gift from my fri3nd Henry. On our last day in Uganda, as we were leaving, Henry handed me a small box, wrapped in pink and red foil. He told me not to open it until I had gone over the bridge. I did as he told. I unwrapped it and inside was a set of glasses with flowers on them, a bracelet, and a letter. I can imagine him taking the little bit of money that he had and going to a store and picking out the nicest thing there. It was so meaningful and touching getting a gift like that from someone who had nothing.

Our project over our last trip was a small orphanage, Zendia's House. On our first trip, I had a dream that our family adopted a little girl named Zendia. When we thought of starting this project, we figured that that was the perfect name for it. We had the shell of the house built when we arrived but we had to finish everything else. We bought furniture and set everything up. Then we selected children to be moved in. We brought in seven kids to the house. We took them all to the local clinic to be checked out. Then we moved them in. I am amazed that we are able to do something this important.

I am still a normal teenager with normal American teenage issues, but I am different now. I know another world, and I am so thankful to be able to help change it for the better.

Mayor Kezaala's Visit to Colorado—May

In May 2013 we had visitors at home. The mayor of Jinja, Kezaala, and his wife Hadassah came to Colorado to visit H.E.L.P. International after a conference they attended in California. We had been nurturing a friendship with this mayor since early in the project. He was a powerful person in the Jinja area and a valuable contact for us. He and Bruce enjoyed each other's company and Hadassah was fun for me to take shopping.

Jean, Bruce, and I took them up into the mountains. The town of Estes Park, Rocky Mountain National Park, and Trail Ridge Road was quite an experience for them. Jean set up a meeting for the mayor with Estes Park's mayor. They were both interested in tourist traffic as tourism is a valuable source of income. Jinja is drawing more and more tourists each year.

Hadassah was frightened on the drive over Trail Ridge Road. She would look how close the road was to the side where the mountain dropped down and away and crawl over to my side of the car so she couldn't see. She experienced snow for the first time when we reached a level where it had not melted. Her husband had seen it once before in Africa on Mt. Kilimanjaro. He threw a snowball at her, but she was too cold to play. The wind was cold. Even with coats on they were both shivering. She probably preferred shopping!

We also took them to see an aquaponics facility in Denver. They were very interested in learning this method of farming. Meeting the mayor of Denver was a treat for all of us. He promised a dinner at his house the next time our Ugandan visitors came for a visit. They made their television debut when they were interviewed on Channel 9. Jean made sure their days were both fun and educational. Bruce and I enjoyed sharing our part of the world with them.

Team from Colorado and Their Contributions

In July 2013 we brought a diverse team with us to Uganda. Ally had been connecting with H.E.L.P. International for about a year. She had been a volunteer for her church and was expanding her experiences as she looked for a fit for her passion for Uganda. Jean and I mentored her, and she became an intern. She brought her brother Brad and her boyfriend. Her boyfriend had volunteered in

Uganda at a project near Jinja called Musana. Visiting Musana with them made me see what having the backing of a church with serious funding could accomplish.

This project was started the year before our school but was fortunate to get the support of a large church. Not only did they have nice school buildings and dorms, a small medical clinic, a computer center and a library, a lovely church, a home for their leaders and housing for their staff, bedrooms for volunteers, a lunchroom and a big kitchen, but they had land. They raised farm fish, cattle, pigs, and chickens and grew crops. They ran a bar and restaurant on the main street of their town. Empowering men and women in their community and educating 1200 children in their school was impressive. They were becoming self-supporting! I was truly impressed. And more than a little envious.

In the beginning, it was a different story. Andrea, their founder, discovered 162 children living at an orphanage in the worst conditions imaginable. These children, ages four to fourteen, were sleeping in three tiny rooms on a rocky dirt floor without beds or blankets. Rats climbed over them as they slept, and their bedrooms turned to mud when it rained. Their bodies were covered in rashes, and many suffered from bacterial infections from the unsanitary latrines. Day to day, these children were hungry, bored, uneducated, unloved, and completely hopeless.

In September 2008, Musana Children's Home was established and moved eighty of the 162 children into a place they could finally call home. They began to receive three meals a day, proper medical care, a good education, and most importantly ... love.

Andrea and her Ugandan husband, Haril, were welcoming and inspiring. I am thankful to Ally for taking us to see this amazing work. I learned so much and my dreams expanded.

In the month of June, April, the accountant and bookkeeper (and so much more) for H.E.L.P. International, came on this trip to teach

Richard how to keep track of expenditures for our bookkeeping program. She is integral to the workings of this project, so it was helpful to show her what was happening on-site. Working from her office in Colorado, she now knows the children and adults we interface with on almost a day-to-day basis. Having Richard understand what we needed and in what format has made the transferring and accounting of funds manageable.

Remember Susan Bruns? She sponsored Lydia, our second teacher, and Susan's granddaughter Susannah sponsored Billy (along with her dad's help). Susannah was a teenager now and came with us to meet Billy and experience Uganda. She was a lovely young girl, and like most teenagers, she was searching for what she believes. At this point in her life she was not buying the Christian beliefs. We loved on her and prayed that she would find her way to God.

Erik worked for H.E.L.P. International at the thrift store. He was organized, dedicated, and a great help to the store. He loves to work with his hands so he went right to work in Uganda, digging and doing whatever physical work he could find. All three of the guys with us put their backs into it this time. One major project was to dig a culvert alongside our property so water could drain under the new, safer (less trafficked) entrance we were establishing. The three guys also put in a small tire playground.

If you take a tire, stand it on its edge, and bury the bottom half, you create an arch that kids can jump from. The guys put five tires in to jump between and fashioned a small sandbox with some other tires.

They also put up a tire swing the kids all loved. Actually, they loved it too much. The rope wasn't strong enough and broke after a while. The kids both big and small played on those five tires endlessly. Sometimes one would straddle two tires while others would scramble under his legs. And then another kid would stand straddling with the two of them back to back and the others in the game traveling under, between and around them. Sometimes one child would get on each tire and try to push the other off. Sometimes they would just leap back and forth from one to the other. Sometimes it was part of a bigger obstacle course. All in all, it was an inexpensive way to create hours of fun.

Our guys pitched in and helped the carpenters build benches for our classrooms. We were teaching carpentry to some construction workers to help expand their base of knowledge and get some work done for the school. The guys brought supplies to teach the men a craft. We often heard complaints that we helped the women with their jewelry but hadn't helped the men. So, Brad and Ally's boyfriend taught them how to make paracord survival bracelets popular in the States. Several Ugandan men learned to make them, but they didn't see the opportunity of making them to sell. They just wanted one for themselves.

Lynn offers ongoing help to eight boys in Haiti and a few children in a couple of other countries she sponsors. She and I met at a jewelry sale and now she helps me work jewelry events. Lynn brought a good perspective to our trip and went home with three more children to sponsor. Wase was a teenage girl from Kenya who attended our school. Her brother had not yet been brought from Kenya, but Lynn left money to transport him. We found later that Wase was going blind. We tried to get her help, but no doctor could do anything. One time we had loaded up the van and were driving back to our guesthouse when we saw Lynn running behind us. We had forgotten her. She seldom sat around with the other Americans but hung out with the children and teachers. I didn't let that happen again. It was funny, but concerning at the same time.

This team focused on teaching and encouraging anti-bullying. They prepared a song and dance and talks teaching against bullying. It seems all cultures have that problem in common. Our students used to carry sticks to school to either defend themselves or to bully and show power. I was forever taking sticks away and throwing them far from the school, knowing full well they would be retrieved as soon as I turned my back.

Bruce and I, and Bob and his daughter, Cory, did some exploring around the Jinja area. We visited some lovely resorts and looked at housing for Cory who wanted to move to Uganda for a time and for Ally who planned to return to stay a few months. We visited an island that had an exclusive resort as its claim to fame. On the mainland, there are several resorts I would love to stay at some time. They are true resorts with swimming pools, nice restaurants, gift stores, and luxury bedrooms—much more expensive than the Nile Hotel we frequent. When we venture out of Masese and the surrounding area, we find places where we could live and be pretty happy. The thought crosses our minds. We could live like kings without needing a king's purse to fund it.

Our school hosted a sports day while we were visiting. They invited another school to the challenge, making it even more fun. The events were many, ranging from preschool relays to foot races and exciting volleyball and soccer games. We watched a gunny sack race, a race where they blindfolded the contestants, tug of war, and dance team contests. For one event two older boys stood on chairs holding a long stick between them. A papaya hung on a string from the stick. Older primary kids competed with their hands tied behind them to see who could capture the fruit with their mouth.

There is an amazing amount of activities that require little or no supplies and are good fun for body and soul.

Politics

Politics has never been my thing. Not on any level. But politics has always been Bruce's "thing." He reads the newspaper avidly, watches the news every night, and has strong opinions. In the sixties he marched for changes he felt strongly needed to be made.

In Uganda, he became a politician for our project. He wasn't running for any office but was engaging with other leaders and politicians. He and Jean together were a force! She needed a man to have the respect of the male dominated Ugandan government. Bruce was her counterpart. He could speak to these men and get the respect both he and Jean deserved. She would set up meetings. The two of them would strategize. They would go together, with Bruce doing the talking. Jean would take the lead if Bruce was unavailable, slowly gaining the respect due her. From the local village leadership to Parliament, H.E.L.P. was engaged. These two gained favor (by the grace of God) but it was often a struggle. Pastor Frederick was instrumental in this process, helping open doors and giving his guidance as an insider. Ronny also helped guide us with legalities even before he was an official member of the H.E.L.P. staff.

Memorandum of Understanding (MOU)

Acquiring a needed Memorandum of Understanding was a challenge, for sure. Before I arrived on the scene, Help Uganda (mirroring and affiliating with the American H.E.L.P. International) had been formed as an NGO by the Ugandan Youth.

We were scheduled to meet with the commissioner at the Ministry of Lands, Housing and Urban Development in Uganda's national government, the Masese Women's Association (MWA), and H.E.L.P. International. Our goal was to get a Memorandum of Understanding (MOU) signed that would give us the right to operate on the land formally given to the MWA at an earlier time. Bruce and Jean fasted in preparation because we knew this meeting would be critical to the future plans for our ministry.

Unbeknown to us, several members of the community met in the village the night before the meeting to discuss issues we were not even aware of at the time.

As a result of his time of fasting, Bruce's sensitivities were on high alert going into the meeting. Normally, he would have been a leading presence, but at this meeting, he sat back, listened, and watched. This seemed to stir the commissioner's curiosity.

At the formal meeting with all agencies involved, a leader in this small dissatisfied faction introduced an agenda that would take our ministry backward instead of forward. Their ideas undermined the aims and objectives of H.E.L.P. International. Although we knew the leader of this group well, we'd never heard these ideas from him.

Jean and Bruce, Pastor Frederick (our project's Spiritual Overseer), and Richard (our Project Director) were astounded at what they heard.

Understanding what was transpiring when he heard this man speak, the commissioner looked Bruce directly in the eyes and asked, "Are you in agreement with this?"

Bruce spoke for the first time in the meeting, saying, "No sir, I am not!"

From there the meeting resolved in our favor.

Although the majority of the MWA supports our ministry in many ways, we discovered that a few controversial members were behind this agenda to get rid of our ministry and keep control of the land. Money was involved, and a hurtful and frustrating legal process ensued, setting back the signing of the MOU.

But God is still on the throne! Three months later, after multiple meetings and re-writings, the MOU was signed by the Jinja Municipal Council; the Ministry of Lands, Housing, and Urban Development; the MWA; and H.E.L.P. International. This document gave H.E.L.P International rights to the land for forty-nine years. We were free to move forward with improvements, knowing our investments would be protected. It was now time to celebrate!

The villagers and the Help school threw a big party. Just Jean, Bruce, and I were there to celebrate with them. Our American team members had left for home while we stayed to finish some work. There were throngs of Africans celebrating as only Africans do with dancing, singing, drums, speeches, and more speeches, food, and gaiety of spirit. We were tremendously honored to be guests at this momentous event. I think God orchestrated the three of us to be there. It seemed like an exclamation point ending the beginning phase of this project that only the three of us could completely comprehend even though it was, and is, incomprehensible in man's eyes. We felt like grasshoppers in our own minds when compared to the giant God had put in our path.

It has been said that God changes caterpillars into butterflies, coal into diamonds, and sand into pearls, using time and pressure. We weren't sure of the end result, but we had experienced the time and pressure. At this point, only God could foresee the diamonds and pearls. We had to rely on faith, which is "the substance of things hoped for, and the evidence of things not seen" (Hebrews 11:1 KJV). What an incredible ride we were on!

Tailoring School

July 2013 was our official beginning of the Tailoring School taught by Rehema. We owned a few treadle machines in cabinets and a tiny, poorly lit room in which to store and use them. Rehema reached out to women in the community that wanted to learn to sew.

Rehema learned to support her family after she and her husband parted ways years ago. She married at age twenty and birthed her first baby in 1994. When she was in the hospital having her second child in 2000, she had a leakage problem. Her husband left! Her problem was cured with prayer, but for thirteen years she survived on her own with two children. Interestingly enough, her husband came back a changed man after his long absence. Five years later, after he proved he was truly changed and after their son graduated from university, Rehema and her husband were happily reunited in Holy Matrimony at a beautiful wedding.

Rehema was the seamstress who sewed most of the uniforms for our school and did a great job. We knew her from Pastor Frederick's church where she was an energetic and inspiring worship leader. She was also the house mom for the orphanage where Jean and the ministry team of young adults stayed in 2011.

Rehema designed a year-long course for the tailoring classes. Around ten women, give or take a few, commit to this course each year. We have a sponsor who pays Rehema's salary and helps fund supplies (Thank you, Jim and Janie!). Rehema moves to an unused preschool classroom to teach theory and planning once the preschool classes are finished for the day. When she can, she moves the class outside under a tree, so there is room to move about to mark and cut their patterns. The machines stay in the small room as there is less chance of damaging a machine while moving it. Lighting is a problem, but they manage. Once in a while the machines are moved outside to the porch to take advantage of the light and cooler air. Rehema also teaches her students how to begin a business before they have any funding to purchase their own sewing machine and supplies. Each one who graduates can become self-supporting even if she can't read or write.

School Certification

A not so fun part of our trip centered on applying for government certification for our school. I held a terrible attitude about all of this. I believed the Ugandans should just be beholden to us for providing this school. After all, they weren't taking care of business in this area. How dare they come in and try to control us. I felt they should just be grateful and help us any way they could. We were the good guys. You know, the knights on white horses! I resented having to jump through hoops to dance to the Ugandan government's tune. There were fees to be paid. I resented paying them as I thought that money should be going directly to the kids and their school. We didn't have a lot of money to throw around. Fortunately, Jean saw a bigger picture than me. She and Ally set the certification in motion. Some teachers needed to complete their education. Some were just required to turn in their papers.

Blog entry: Headmaster Struggles

Headmasters have been an ongoing blessing and problem. First, it was difficult to pay for one. In fact, we didn't. We upped Ben's salary a little and told him he was head teacher. He was not equipped to be both head teacher and teacher of a classroom. One didn't seem to leave room for the other. This began our troubles with headmasters.

Unfortunately, position sometimes leads to power issues. There were serious troubles between one headmaster and the cooks, so much so, the cooks refused to heat water for the teachers' tea. Sounds funny to us, but things were bitter between him and the cooks. I think he didn't have much regard for them and treated them harshly. We worked on bringing the two groups together and it helped.

Every time we came, the teachers presented a list of things they wanted from us. Never before had they been so discontent. This headmaster would advocate for them, which seemed like a good thing, except I felt he was stirring them up in the first place. We were running on such a shoestring budget we could hardly do the basics, let alone everything he was pushing for.

After we were gone from one of our trips, we got reports that this same headmaster was having an affair and all the village knew about it. He had moved his wife and family to a nearby village and was blatantly involved with this other woman. As a professed Christian leading a Christian school, this was not acceptable. Jean told him that if he wanted to keep his job, he must stop his affair, apologize to his family and get counseling. It surprised me she let him stay, but she decided it was best to salvage his marriage and help a man redeem himself. I couldn't fault that.

The next time we saw him, he was back with his wife and getting counseling. His wife seemed okay, and he seemed contrite. I was suspicious, as was Jean, but we gave him the benefit of the doubt. Fortunately, we found out he didn't have the requirements we needed for a headmaster.

It is really difficult to monitor someone from so far away. No one in the community will reveal trouble if they fear repercussions or if they feel a kinship with the person we need information about. More than one headmaster has found a way to bring extra funds into their own pockets. One said he just borrowed the money and planned on paying it back. We let him pay it back, with a strong warning these funds were not for personal use. He didn't cross that line again. Another set up a fee for school attendance unbeknown to us and pocketed the money. Aargh!

I think some of the village people have the impression we are rich Americans and have so much they can keep some for themselves. Really, they are stealing from their own people, but there seems to be no shame if you can get away with it. In their opinion, if the opportunity presents itself, who wouldn't take from the rich. Well, their perception isn't exactly accurate. We are very limited in our resources and try our best to do all we can with very little.

When we were just starting this project, we were told by a man who lived in Colorado part of the year and in Africa the majority of the year that our school would never work unless we resided in country. A Ugandan told us our most important task was to find people of integrity. Trying to accomplish this endeavor while still living in the US has definitely been a challenge.

Fortunately, we finally have a trusted Ugandan team and many checks and monitoring practices in place to protect our resources and our reputation, as well as our underlying mission.

Fence Project

After returning from our 2013 trip, we had our first big fundraising effort using a Go Fund Me type page. We needed a fence! The property is five or six acres. Without a fence, we were stymied in several directions. Everything was constantly being vandalized and destroyed. The students couldn't be kept on the school grounds, nor could we keep predators off. Nothing was safe. A barrier was needed both to keep kids in and keep trouble out. The night security guard had been attacked and almost killed. Our school needed safety and security.

This wasn't a glamorous project to raise money for, but we needed this so we could move forward. We knew how to make the soil stabilized blocks so Yeko and his construction team went to work making bricks while we went to work raising money. We needed $30,000. It seemed impossible, but with God all things are possible (Matthew 19:26).

A middle school in Colorado gave us our first donation. The World Affairs class, under the direction

of their teacher Mrs. Easton, raised $400. Bidco, a large Indian owned company near our project, generously donated $10,000 for our fence. They had previously given us hundreds of mosquito nets since the Masese community is where much of their labor force comes from. The rest of our money came in bits and pieces from generous individuals. We needed to supplement some from bead sales, but we made it.

Watching the fence go up was thrilling. It was a huge project. At first, I didn't want a fence because I enjoyed having the community flow through in their day-to-day living. I didn't want to partition them off. However, by the time we started the fence I was totally on board. Yeko was being watched by us from afar, but he was confident with what he was doing. We had two young long-term visitors there while he was building, Ally and Bryan.

2014

Ally and Bryan

In my Spring 2014 newsletter to my ever-growing email list, I introduced Ally and Bryan and the fence project.

Two Colorado young people are in Uganda now. They are living in Jinja and helping at the Help School. Yea!

Ally will be there four months. She has been to this project twice before in the last year. Ally is already well known and much loved. She plans to give extra help to students who are struggling with their schoolwork. As she always does, she will spread God's love everywhere she goes.

Bryan is new to our project but has been in Uganda with another school and orphanage. His experience and zeal make him valuable to this village empowerment effort. He plans to be in Masese for at least six months. His big mandate is to help get the fence project done. He is working with our Help guys and with our partner, Haileybury Youth Trust (HYT), based in Jinja but with UK roots. We will make our own bricks through HYT's technology of soil stabilized interlocking blocks. These blocks need not be fired so we won't have to cut down trees to fire them. Because they are interlocking, we use much less concrete.

Full of love for the villagers and their children, Ally and Bryan wove themselves into the hearts of Masese. They were young and full of good ideas. Most of us involved with this project have quite a few years on us. We need the youth to bring about needed changes, but this is a hard thing sometimes. Demands and expectations from both generations can be divisive. In the end, both young people left unhappy. Some of our board members were glad to see them go. I saw it as a lost opportunity to move forward with fresh ideas and a chance to mentor those just starting out from our experience.

Founders Syndrome

Very early on Bruce and I were confronted with having "founder's syndrome." I had never heard of that, but I understood what we were being accused of. It was true. We felt like we owned this project. We had ideas we expected to bring about and were glad for the company and help, but underneath, we felt like we were in charge (along with Jean who was actually in charge all along).

Founder's syndrome is often a natural part of an organization's life cycle. The start-up or growth phase of any initiative requires a strong, passionate personality—someone who can make fast decisions and motivate people to action. We were the only ones making decisions at first, and it was hard to give that up. We knew the ministry wasn't ours because we gave God ownership, but we felt like He had entrusted it to us. Those confronting us were more capable and equipped to lead in many areas than we were. It was a relief since I was never comfortable making some of the decisions I was required to make. But our egos still took a hit. I expect those same people who confronted us know now how we felt as new people with new ideas continue to come along, wanting recognition. All the Board members of Help Uganda are strong committed people, passionate about this project. We don't always see eye to eye, but we always want God's best for Masese.

One of the big things Ally wanted was to empower the Ugandans. She saw us all as too controlling. Even before reading the book *When Helping Hurts*, we knew we wanted to give the Ugandans a hand up and not a hand out. We planned to empower them, rather than impose ourselves, our culture, and our ideas on them. That is a harder task than we imagined.

My first mindset was that I was there to teach and lead in the ways I knew best. I was always aware that the Ugandans were intelligent, but I figured I had more knowledge and knew what was best for them—kind of like a parent with a child. I now realize I was pretty arrogant, but there is still the push-pull of knowing more in some ways while being ignorant in others. I was educated in the United States and have more training than most villagers. And I benefit from a bigger worldview than the villagers. I have been exposed to different things and had more access to the Internet.

I am not superior in intelligence, faith, dedication, cleverness, or love of my fellow man. Ugandan women are as loving of their babies as I ever was, even though they don't benefit from the resources I am blessed with to care for them. They are more industrious since they have had to survive, whereas I have had an easy life. I think of myself as relational, but their culture is much more relational than mine. I have never been desperate or hungry or without hope. It is hard to relate and truly understand that reality. My self-concept has been nurtured, whereas many of the Ugandans I know hold low self-esteem.

When we go into a meeting with the Ugandans, our ideas are given deference. Only some of the leaders will speak their mind after we have spoken ours. At first, we just ran with this. We implemented whatever we thought was right and pushed everyone to comply. Sometimes they only followed our wishes when we were there and went back to their own ways when we left. Who can blame them? They had their own set of rules and traditions. We had our own vision for what we were hoping for and our own timeline.

One of our first challenges was our sense of time. The villagers just don't recognize the urgency or see the necessity of arriving on time for a meeting. You come when you can, and if you miss something, you miss it. They don't consider it to be what we Westerners would call "late." I have wondered if we weren't the ones with a lack of respect for their lifestyles. I don't know what it is like to walk everywhere, cook everything over a fire pit, wash myself and my family and our clothes from a small basin, and all the other rigors of daily life in the village.

Rarely does anyone own a watch or clock, except those who keep cell phones. If I lived in these circumstances, I might not worry about being to a meeting at a specific time either.

There were times we absolutely needed to get the community together, and they seemed to value and enjoy these meetings. We just had to acclimate to their straggling in at various times. Those who had worked with Westerners understood our need for punctuality, but the rest of the crowd didn't. We might start a meeting with thirty attendees and end with three hundred. It was frustrating to those of us who felt like we needed to accomplish much in a short amount of time! They might not have a specific time crunch but we did. We had planes to catch. Everything moves slower in Africa. We were told that, but over the years we experienced this phenomenon time and time again. Painfully, we are learning patience.

Another example of hurting while helping came from the Danish government. The Danish came in with great ideas. They taught a skill of building tiles for roofs and building houses. They didn't teach adaptation, so when the style of roofs changed, the Ugandans were at a loss as how to move forward. This was part of the reason the whole project failed. On top of that, the Danish set up what seemed to be a great practice, to grant those who did the actual work to be the owners of the homes built. If you physically helped build a house, you were given the title to the house (along with the repayment responsibilities).

In this culture, the women do the work concerning the home. If the men are working, they are in a factory, in construction, or working for someone else. When the women were given deeds to the homes the balance of power shifted. The men resented this power change and many left. What seemed like a fair and equitable decision proved detrimental.

We made mistake after mistake, especially in the beginning. We tried to bring in an outsider, Manasseh, to run the show. The community resented that and ran him off that outsider with threats and total rejection. They welcomed us as we were the donors, but they had their own potential leaders and their own ideas of how things should be done. Just like a parent thinks they know best and sets the rules accordingly, we thought we knew best. A two-year-old can change the course of a well-intentioned parent and a teenager can absolutely mix things up. These were independent adults with their own wisdom, and independence and they didn't like our superior attitudes. It took us some time to see what we were doing and frankly, we still err on the side of being controlling. One of the people who has helped us greatly is a man named Ronny Sitanga.

Ronny Sitanga

We learned of Ronny when we needed legal help. He lived in Kampala and had trained in company law. Being related to Pastor Frederick, he was happy to help us in any way he could. Ronny was highly educated and had the experience of working for other NGOs. He was invaluable as we navigated through difficult legal procedures. Ronny was a younger man with a working wife and the beginnings of a family, living in Kampala. He grew up in Masese, so he understood the people and their ways well.

His parents were very poor and growing up was a serious challenge. There were eight children born in his family, but three died. Ronny told us about the details.

> Two brothers, a five-year-old and a one-year-old, died of malaria. This could have been avoided if they had been able to use mosquito nets and receive immediate medication.

> But they were taken late after receiving self-medication at home. The situation worsened. One died on the way to hospital and the other at home. The third child was a girl who missed immunization and got polio. She died when she was three years old. We could hardly afford basic needs and scholastic materials and attended average schools. From the onset, I decided to work hard and change my future.

"There were particular years I missed school, but I refused to give up and reached a time when my parents could no longer completely afford my school fees. At this point, God directly intervened to rescue the situation and brought me a sponsor. The sponsor met my school needs and enabled me to complete my bachelor's degree in development studies. I thank God that through all these challenges, He was and has always been with me and made me the best student in class at all levels regardless of how long I missed school."

Jean offered Ronny the position of Country Director for our project. Ronny responded.

This job is a total fulfilment of the deal I made with God to help children I meet every day who are going through my experiences. God equipped me through experience and education with the necessary skills to counsel and advise these children, and I can, with great joy, say I am living my dream of helping children become better people. This is my calling and as long as I continue doing this, I regard it as true success in my life.

Ronny saw our donor hearts and understood the conflict we were experiencing. We wanted to help but acted with superiority. He gently and firmly taught us to stand back and let the Ugandans take charge, with our oversight.

One time Bruce decided to hire someone he thought was important without including anyone else in the decision. Bruce thought that if he was willing to pay this person's salary, he had the right to put him on staff. Now, Bruce is one of the outspoken proponents to let the Ugandans be empowered. He didn't see he was overstepping their authority until Ronny confronted him. I wish you could have seen Bruce's face when he realized he had overstepped and was being publicly confronted. A big sheepish smile spread across his face. He physically stepped back and admitted that this was not the procedure he needed to follow and changed, on the spot, to recommending that his guy be hired. I was proud of both Ronny and of Bruce. This conversation set the precedent for many future discussions being much more healthy and productive.

Looking Back

Our American ways seem right to us, but sometimes when we look back over history we might wonder if we have helped or hurt ourselves. For instance, I lived through the "free love" era where morals became much looser. Before that time teen pregnancy, though still occurring, was not the norm. AIDS/HIV and other sexually transmitted diseases were not an epidemic. Promiscuity was frowned upon and teen pregnancies were dealt with harshly. With the hippie "love-ins" and the encouragement of sexual explorations, everyone relaxed their judgements. In many ways this seemed like a good thing. Girls weren't ostracized if they became pregnant. They weren't shamed, shunned, or shipped off to birth their babies in secret. This seemed much more humane and forgiving.

Unfortunately, there were other ramifications that came about. Having babies born out of wedlock became very acceptable. At least forty percent of first babies are from single moms here in America. In the black community that increases to seventy-two percent. That means there are generations being raised without the influence of a father and without the economic stability of a two-person household. Not that a single mother can't responsibly raise her children if a father is irresponsible, but child-rearing becomes more difficult when there aren't two adults to share the load.

Free love hasn't given us the freedom it proposed but has shackled us with a tangle of social problems. According to research, children of unmarried mothers are more likely to perform poorly in school, go to prison, use drugs, be poor as adults, and have their own children out of wedlock. So what is the balance between shame and punishment and widespread sexual encounters? We had to look at this when Victoria came to us pregnant.

Blog about Victoria:

Victoria was in the Help Primary School when she found out she was pregnant. She was a lovely young teen getting her education when an older man enticed her to have sex with him. This is against the Ugandan law so as soon as they were found out, he disappeared, leaving Victoria to face her new reality. Normally schools in Uganda do not allow pregnant girls to continue as they think it will be a bad influence on the other girls. Our Ugandan school leadership planned to send her home, thinking her pregnancy was the end of her schooling.

The H.E.L.P. board in the United States didn't agree with this plan. We recommended she return to school and finish Primary 7 and take her leaving exams. This would allow her to go on to secondary school if she passed. It took courage for her to go to school while pregnant, but she did it. H.E.L.P. got her support from another NGO in Uganda that is designed to help young women through pregnancy, birth, and early motherhood. She passed her exams just a very short time before the birth of her little one.

We used this experience to talk further with her classmates about the loss of opportunities and the difficulties of engaging in sex at such an early age. We stressed how following God's laws works best for our health and happiness. Hopefully, she was a great influence on her peers. She was challenged as she finished her schooling instead of being hidden away. But she also became an overcomer in the face of a difficult situation.

Attending secondary school is out of reach for many primary students, even if they pass their leaving exams. Those students fortunate enough to have a sponsor from H.E.L.P. during their primary years were given scholarships to attend secondary, usually paid for by their sponsors. Donations came in from people wanting to help students who didn't have sponsors so they could go on with their secondary schooling. These kids were offered a partial scholarship, and family members had to make up the rest.

There was one donor who wanted to provide a total scholarship to one student for their entire secondary education. This would be a huge blessing, but who would that student be? How do you decide who receives and who doesn't? We decided it would be best to leave this decision up to the Ugandan management team. Quite to our surprise and delight the same team that planned to send Victoria home from school awarded her this total scholarship. God works on hearts and minds in ways we would never expect. We are in awe of His plans and feel privileged to get to walk alongside Him!

I am hopeful that this incident doesn't lead to the relaxation of morals to the detriment of Uganda's future. We don't want to impose our culture, especially if it comes with pitfalls. How to include strictness and grace at the same time is a tricky endeavor. Once again, we sure don't want our helping to hurt, either now or on down the road.

Empowerment is our goal. The NGOs coming to the aid of this impoverished nation helped create a dependent people. Musana's website encapsulates both their mission and ours.

"Plagued by a history of colonization and foreign aid, Uganda's development has been paralyzed by a dependency mentality that has inhibited Ugandans from being their own catalysts for change. It is this realization and understanding of when helping hurts that has shaped Musana into what it is today. What Ugandans need is restored hope and dignity in their own economic and social capacity that will enable them not only to survive, but thrive."

Finishing Up

We proudly completed the fence. They painted it red and yellow. I think they saw it as elevating their community. Early on, the parents of the students voted to build a fence over having a school lunch program. We thought they were nuts; the kids were seriously malnourished. We chose to start the feeding program but kept their desire for a fence high on our list of requirements as we moved forward. It was good to have it now. The kids were less distracted and seemed to feel secure with their boundaries. The security guards breathed a sigh of relief and the staff could let down their guard a bit.

We had accomplished a feat we didn't know we could tackle. Much of the credit goes to Yeko and everyone knew it. He was confident from the beginning he could get this wall built and built well. Yeko worked tirelessly and kept his construction team focused. He showed Bruce his hands and arms—all chewed up after putting the razor wire around the top. We hated making this place look like a prison with that wire, but all the Ugandans said it was absolutely necessary.

Our security guard was protecting our property with his bow and arrows. He was afraid to carry a gun because it might get turned on him. He had been attacked by several guys and was happy to be alive. This guy still had challenges, but the fence with its razor wire made those challenges possible.

I thought a guard dog would help with these challenges, but I couldn't get anyone to run with that idea. By far, the majority of Ugandans are afraid of dogs. We could make that work in our favor, but our staff was equally afraid, so no one would take that on.

On this trip, we also made benches and tables for the school. It was a good chance to help some of the construction guys learn woodworking. A local man had been making them for us, but we were still short several. He became the teacher and even our American guys joined in the fun. Only simple tools were used, but the end product worked quite well. It was good to see all of our students finally off the ground!

We took clothes and gifts to the eight children at Zendia's House since Renee and her family couldn't come with us on this trip. We heard the Zendia kids recite Bible verses, sing, and dance. Winifred, the house mom, made a scrumptious meal for us with the girls' help. It was a heartwarming evening.

Pastor Frederick Ojiambo

Early in our time in Masese, the people of Masese advised us to find a spiritual overseer for our project. This fits well with our desire to transform the entire area for the cause of Christ. We wanted to bless each and every one we could reach. Not being able to reach everyone ourselves, we could help those ministering to groups, both large and small, thus expanding our reach.

These influencers were men of God, laboring, as they were equipped, in their own communities. We began with Pastor Frederick Ojiambo and fourteen churches. Currently, there are more than eighty congregations in this fellowship. With the help of Samuel, the Missions pastor of Rez Church in Loveland, Colorado, the Lord has blessed these churches both physically and spiritually. Jean Kaye mentors and blesses this group each trip. The unity of so many churches is impressive. They share with each other, train new ministers, and pray for each other and their congregations. It is a powerful alliance for this impoverished area. We want to empower them, standing with them as we can.

Pastor Frederick is the chairman of this coalition and the Spiritual Overseer of H.E.L.P. International in Uganda. Without his sage council, his trustworthy friendship, and his influence, we would never be where we are today.

Interestingly. I didn't think I trusted him at first. You will laugh when I tell you why ... He smiled and laughed too much! How could I trust someone who smiled so much? Was he hiding something? Jean knew immediately he was God's man. It took me a few meetings before I felt the same way. I had trusted and loved others who had disappointed me. I wouldn't be so easily fooled again.

Today I can truthfully say there is no one I would trust more. He is a true friend and a wonderful man.

His story is full of drama. It would, and maybe should, make a great movie. He was the oldest of seven children. His father worked in a factory making clothes and bedsheets when Idi Amin was being removed from power. Frederick's father aligned on the wrong side of the politics. The family lived in a village near the army barracks in Jinja. While Amin was being overthrown, many from this village were killed. There was a swamp that sat on the side of a hill, down a ways from the barracks. To keep from being beaten or killed, the family hid in the swamp. They built a small house from the grasses, but they practically slept in the water. They suffered from the cold since they didn't have any bedsheets.

Their father was being hunted. At one point the soldiers found him and were going to kill him. Frederick clung to his father crying. The soldiers took pity on the child and left. Terrified, Frederick's father ran away to his home village, Busia, where Frederick's paternal grandfather was born. The seven children were left with their mother until the mother left, too. She went looking for her husband in Busia. In Busia there were bullets flying because the war ending the Amin regime still raged. Frederick's father had run away again, this time to Kenya, abandoning his family completely.

The mother became blockaded in, unable to leave to get back to her children. The children didn't know what had happened to their mother or their father. Left with no one to care for them, Frederick had to provide for his four sisters, two brothers and himself. They had no food or anyone to cook for them. Times were so hard that one brother and two sisters died. The kids had to bury them. Sadness and tears dominate Frederick's memories as he tells this story to us.

After two years, Frederick took the remainder of his siblings to a church in the Walakuba area just outside Jinja, to hide. They lived in that church. Frederick and his younger brother left during the day to look for work and to find food. Life continued to be very hard.

When their mother finally returned, she could not find her children. They had been hiding in the church in a different area than where she left them. She thought they were all dead until someone directed her to the church. After the years of separation and all the suffering, this reunion was filled with joy. More tears flowed, but this time they were tears of joy and relief. The children huddled close to their mother as if to prevent ever being separated again. The loss of three of her children and the hardships her children had endured weighed heavily on this mother's heart.

Frederick became a Christian at this church and even sang in the choir. God showered favor on him and whatever he did in the church was blessed.

His mother took his siblings back to the village where she was living, leaving Frederick alone. He missed his family but stayed on God's path.

Frederick tells the next part of his story.

"God began using me in a supernatural way. I began seeing the favor of the Lord upon my life. There I started preaching. From the choirmaster, I became the youth pastor, and we planted a church called Miracle Center. After that I began going to Kampala, Northern Uganda, and Western Uganda. I started going into Kenya, preaching in Kenya, preaching the ministry, and that's when I was preaching in a place called Kakamega. I was telling them that even when you don't have the father, don't have the mother, the Lord is your father and I gave them my story.

"I didn't know that my father was in that meeting. He was in that place because the Lord just led me even to speak his name. And after that my father stepped outside because he was crying.

There the pastor asked him, 'What's happening?' The crying man said, 'The one who's preaching, Pastor, is my son.' They did not believe it. When the pastor came and said my father had been found, I thought, 'The Pastor is mad!' But when I talked to this man—he was my real father! When I came back to Uganda and told this story, no one believed my father to be alive. And let me tell you, I came back and my father came back. I brought him. All the people rejoiced. They thought he had died a long time ago."

Everyone thought Frederick was a hero, but he felt like God had done a miracle. God continued using Frederick around Uganda. He started about twenty churches in the mountains of Mbale, fifteen in the Busia area, and another ten in Walukuba. These were all "healing-driven" churches. Altogether there were ninety-two churches from his ministry. Because of his widespread ministry, he was chosen to be the chairman of all the pastors.

Frederick is married to Rosette. They have six children, three boys and three girls. His experience of being a driver at one point in his life helped him be hired to drive for us. Money earned from his driving helps with his family's expenses and gives us time with him on each trip. Rosette is wonderful. She is also free with her smiles and with her generosity. Sharing dinner with them is a true pleasure. Rosette is a good cook!

One day I noticed a pickup truck driving through the compound with several Ugandan men balancing something in the truck bed. I saw it was rather large and black. Not making sense of what I viewed, I moved nearer for a closer inspection. The guys had found a car engine for Pastor Frederick to use to teach automotive repair. I didn't know Frederick even knew car maintenance. This knowledge came from schooling earlier in his life. Other than the training for construction and brickmaking, the men of Masese had little opportunity for vocational training. Around thirty guys showed up for the first class, quickly increasing to eighty by the second. This was a huge hit with the men. I heard there were several who even stopped their alcohol consumption so they could learn. Often the use of alcohol stems from boredom and lack of hope. This opportunity remedied those problems for these men, eager to do something more productive with their lives.

Experiencing Pastor Frederick's preaching is a delight. He knows his Bible and loves his people. He never stands still but uses his whole body to emphasize his message. Always in a suit and tie, I have seen him jump in the air to make a point. The energy he expends must use mega calories every Sunday morning. I am never bored; he has something to say and says it with passion. It is twice the fun, if you can imagine, when his interpreter does his best to be his twin. They both move in unison putting on quite a show. I've been to a lot of churches in my life but never experienced his style of preaching. I love it. And I love him. He is a vibrant, bold, beautiful thread being woven throughout God's gorgeous tapestry.

October 2014

October 2014 a rather large medical team came to Uganda with Jean Kaye. They not only held clinics at the school for the Masese villagers, but they traveled to more remote locations spreading love and care. These medical teams are always a joy. Their enthusiasm to help the sick and hurting and to love on the people is inspiring. A dentist and her husband enlisted a dentist in Jinja, the father of our project manager, Richard, to work with them. He was honored to be included and always had a big smile on his face. Several of these medical people became sponsors of  students, too. At one point, one team member bought a goat, put it on the team's bus, and took it to Masese to give away. That was fun for everyone, and quite helpful to the recipient.

Sponsorship Program

Diana graciously volunteered to head the sponsorship committee. I signed up to be on that committee since I had experience with advocating for Compassion International's sponsorship program. Once Diana stepped up to this task, the sponsorship program soared.

It is quite a challenge from beginning to end. Diana and Ritah, our social worker at the school, work hand in hand. The first task is to choose the neediest children. Every family wants to have their children sponsored, so if we aren't careful, we are helping those who don't need help as much as others in less desirable circumstances. Resentment rages when that occurs. Even worse, parents abandon their responsibilities if they can get us to take on the care of their child. This is not our intent. We don't want to be the caretaker of all these children. We want to empower parents to take care of their own.

Diana and Ritah set up a group of villagers to vote and guide us in our choices. That was a good plan, but this group wouldn't meet without transport money or money for sodas or some reason to get payment, even though they were a "volunteer group." When we objected to that use of our money, it was difficult to get the input we hoped for. We finally relaxed a bit, and the committee stepped up to their task. It is important to have as many Ugandans taking part and being a part of this project as we can. It is their community and their problems we are attempting to solve.

Once a child is identified, their photo and a short bio are put on our website and added to a book Diana uses to show to people who are interested. She provided Delia and me with a book. I have not done as good a job signing up sponsors for these children as Diana. Once a child has a sponsor, Ritah purchases bedding (a mattress and sheets) and a treated mosquito net. The child is provided a uniform along with his or her school shoes. Yearly, they also get playclothes along with a new uniform. Ritah oversees the students' letter writing to the sponsors, makes sure their school lunch money is paid, sees to it they get to the clinic if they are sick, sets the child's family up for their weekend food (enough to feed the whole family a meal a day over the weekend), and generally looks out for the well-being of each sponsored child. We moved Ben from teaching to being Ritah's helper. He is especially good with nurturing the kids. In later years, we hired Patricia, another social worker, to work with the sponsorship program so Ritah could take care of the social work needs of the whole school. Now Diana is overseeing an entire department! Thank God for her heart for these children and for the sponsors who make this program work.

Albinos

Albinos are a hidden group in Uganda, but Jean found them. These shy people stay in the shadows. They are considered cursed and can be in danger from the superstitions surrounding them. In his 2017 article, "Ten Tragic Facts About Albinism Hunting in Africa" (www.listverse.com), Shannon Quinn wrote:

"There is an African superstition that albino people are not truly human. Many believe that they are demons or ghosts. They also believe that albinos are immortal, and their bodies contain magic healing properties. Witch Doctors still practice dark magic in many countries, although the persecution of Albinos primarily occurs in Tanzania and Malawi. Clients are willing to pay high prices for albino body parts because they are used in spells to bring good luck and success. Life as an albino is terrifying, to say the least."

Not only are the superstitions dangerous, just the seemingly freakish differences between their white skin and the rest of their family's darker skin set them dramatically apart. Then there are the challenges with the sun burning their skin and damaging their eyes. We take sunglasses, sunscreen, and hats along with clothes for the children. The medical team goes to a separate location to hold a clinic for these people so they aren't brought to the attention of other villagers.

There are about fifty Albinos in the Jinja area, hundreds over Uganda, and countless more all over Africa. An albino man named Peter has formed an association bringing this group together in Jinja and extending throughout Uganda. He and his friends are actively educating the general public along with the Albino community. They teach that albinism is genetic and not a curse. A black mother or father can give birth to an albino child as they pass on the albino gene. There are horrifying stories around the belief, from some old traditional African religions, that eating the flesh of an albino brings purification. Fear, superstition, and ignorance can engender craziness! Peter and his group are educating people that this belief is unfounded as they learn about the genetic origins of albinism.

As I entered the clinic, I felt a heaviness. Both the children and their mothers watched everything. They didn't chatter and play. With some encouragement, I could get a few children to smile for a photo. I loved seeing smiles light up their faces. I heard a story of a bus of Westerners who stopped in a village that rarely had Western visitors. When the white-skinned people disembarked, an albino boy nearby jumped up and down. He smiled and shouted, "They look like me!"

Tire Playground Legacy

A young Liberian boy, Osobie Borchert, one of four kids adopted by an American family, Katy and Jeff Borchert, noticed how many parks and playgrounds there were in America. He knew there were few playgrounds for Africans. Osobie raised money through his elementary school in Ft. Collins, CO, to build swings in Uganda. We had been a recipient of a swing. The kids in Masese dearly loved that swing. We had to teach them how to pump to swing themselves and how to take turns instead of piling six or so kids at a time on a swing. Sadly, the wood used to construct the three-person swing set either rotted with all the rain or termites got to it, so it had to be dismantled. To compound the problem, the small play area one of our teams had constructed earlier, consisting of a sandbox, three half-buried tires, and a rope swing was long gone.

One formation looked like an elephant (my favorite).

I found an African playground company in Jinja that made playgrounds out of car tires. Some of their structures were quite elaborate, but for the amount of money I had to invest in this project, we could get several smaller items.

As with the earlier effort, these structures were constructed by setting tires on edge and burying them halfway into the ground or laying them on their sides, in different formations. To finish, they are painted bright primary colors. They designed a tire obstacle course and stacked tires together forming a small climbing structure. A couple of "tables" and "chairs" were in another area. There were groupings resembling motorbikes (bodas), and another fashioned to look like a taxi with passenger seats. I not only loved the bright colors, but I loved the encouraging the imagination of the little ones.

Once the playground was all painted, the tires had to dry for a day or two. It was hard to keep the kids away from it! The playground looked so inviting we had to post a guard to keep everyone off the drying paint.

Once they were turned loose, the kids swarmed the playground! Big kids would leap from structure to structure. Older girls would sit at the tables talking. Tired children would lay themselves across the elephant or bodas to relax, once they were finished "riding" them. This was a big hit! I would still like to add a more permanent swing, so, maybe someday ...

It was pure delight to see the kids playing on this fanciful, colorful playground. It was equally special to show my mother what I had dedicated to her, halfway across the world. My mother is no

longer on this earth, but I still remember her in my heart and on this Ugandan school playground.

Graduations

One thing I have always missed on my trips to Uganda is a graduation ceremony. There are multiple graduations every year. Primary 7 students graduate from primary school. This is a really big deal! Remember, these kids would not have even been able to attend school without the help we brought in! Now they graduate, completing all seven grades and passing a comprehensive government issued test. It is a big accomplishment! Each graduate wears a rented graduation cap and gown. There is a party with cake, at the least, and a big dinner with meat, at the best. If we have the money, everyone celebrates—students, parents and teachers, and the whole school. It is an encouragement to the younger students to persevere in their studies so they, too, can one day be a graduate.

The preschool kids also graduate when they leave preschool to go into Primary 1. For a while, we rented smaller caps and gowns for them to wear. We received a donation which enabled us to have Rehema sew our own for yearly use. The preschoolers look adorable, as you might imagine. The graduating preschool class also gets a cake. Sometimes their parents come with a simple gift-wrapped present. The pride is visible in both parents and children, not to mention their teachers. All eyes dance with happiness.

Our preschool teachers do a good job loving the kids, helping them adjust to school, and learn some basics. These teachers are eager to learn new techniques and ideas to help their classes be the best they can be. Preschool  teachers don't go to teacher training schools for as long as primary school teachers. All of our teachers would like to go further in school.

Adults like to be recognized, too. Our vocational classes have graduations. Some of these adult students have never graduated from any level. This graduation feels very good. These students are even more grateful than regular students because they didn't know they would ever succeed at any schooling. All our senior staff and Pastor Frederick attend to congratulate these students, pass out their certificates of completion, and wish them success in their new vocation. I am as proud as I can be of these adults who overcome hardships to stay the course to better their future and the lives of their children.

Educating a Girl

Over fifty percent of our student population are girls and a greater percent are in our vocational school. Educating boys is essential but the education of girls has been seriously lacking. Education is such a strong force in the life of a person and the life of a nation.

Education unlocks the potential of African youth to solve their community's greatest problems of poverty, disease, and environmental degradation.

For every year after the fourth grade that girls receive education, child deaths drop by ten percent and a country's wages increase by twenty percent (WLP Women's Learning Partnership). The Urgent Action Fund for Women's Rights states that if you can raise a woman's income, child survival rates increase twenty times more than if you raise a man's income. UNESCO reports that a child born to a mother who can read is fifty percent more likely to survive past the age of five. In terms of improving health, girls' education is the highest returning social investment in the world. The video "The Girl Effect" published in 2008, states that when an educated girl earns income, she reinvests ninety percent in her family, compared to thirty-five percent for a boy. Yet over ninety percent of international aid money is not directed to her. It further states that after seven years of education, she marries four years later and has 2.2 fewer children. The population's HIV rate goes down and malnutrition decreases by forty-three percent. And if ten percent more girls go to secondary school, the country's economy goes up three percent.

Seema Jalan, Executive Director of the Universal Access Project, told the *Huffington Post* in October 2017:

> "The truth is, a ten-year-old girl is one of the most powerful people on the planet. She has the potential to shape our entire future. At the same time, she is often the most vulnerable. In many places around the world, the path to achieve her full potential is ridden with obstacles. Of an estimated sixty million ten-year-old girls on the planet today—more than the entire

population of Italy—forty percent are at risk of being left behind by our global development investments. This means they are systematically excluded from accessing services like health care, education, or jobs, which violates their basic rights and takes a toll on their families, communities and countries. Whenever a girl's potential goes unrealized, we all lose."

Ripples

These graduations make me think of ripples in a big pond. Each graduate will affect many others who will then affect many others and so on and so on. It is profound. Back in 2010 I wrote a blog I am reminded of as I celebrate the education the Help School is providing

Last summer I was sitting on a porch at a friend's house high above a lovely lake up in the mountains. As we watched, there were patterns on the water. Each pattern was unique, and each was lovely. Some were made from the wind blowing over the water. Sometimes it was a boat flowing through or maybe a fish jumping up from under the waves. Some lasted only a short while and others rippled clear across the lake. When the sun was at different angles, colors appeared to enhance these moving patterns. Never staying the same from moment to moment, you had to pay attention or you would have lost the opportunity.

From where we were there was no sound from these water drawings. If I had been closer, I could have thrown a rock to make my own patterns begin. It would have been fun if I could skip a rock across the water to make multiple ripples. I enjoy being involved. But more than being involved enough to throw the rock, I like knowing it will take on a life of its own. Add the color from the sun, the shadows from trees, interferences from other rocks or sticks, or bugs flying over—all make each ripple a wonder. My throwing of the initial break in the water is powerful, and yet, small in the significance of the evolving picture.

Can I apply this to my time on this earth? I am quite sure I will never know all the ripples I have initiated. It is mind-boggling to think about. I can't even follow one to any final conclusion. I love that I am involved and can observe from afar. I love that forces beyond me do the actual creating. I love thinking of my life as a thing of beauty. I certainly can't claim being the cause of that beauty. I just get to be a small involvement that God takes to a higher place. I also am aware that sometimes I "throw" something that makes a mess. I pray God can still take that mess and use it. Those things that created the ripples as I watched from high up were not even aware of causing a lovely show for our audience. They were just doing what they were doing; the sun rising and setting, riding in a boat, catching a bug, just their normal life. I like that. I can just do my normal life. I don't have to try to create patterns to create them. Things I do or say, and sometimes the things I don't do or say, have an effect somehow. I can make a mess or I can be a small part of a large beautiful set of responses. I most likely will never see the outcomes of my contributions, but just knowing I have made an impact is a good thing. At least I pray it is a good thing. God, please help it be a good thing. I can't always trust me, but I can always trust Him.

Church Camps

Summer church camps were a big part of my teen years, and I made sure each of my children got to experience them. I have great memories of both my camp experiences and hearing my kids talk about theirs. My Uncle Freddy started a church camp and ran it every summer, almost until he died. I firmly believe, as did he, that camp is a wonderful way to impact a teenager's life in a good direction. I even met my first husband at a church camp when I was just fifteen. That is another story, but knowing the positive power of a week at a good Christian camp, I was happy to learn of a camp in Jinja for the older sponsored kids. I rallied extra funds to send these kids to their first camp.

Blog for First Camp came during this trip in 2014:

Sometimes kids make you proud! If they are teens and young adults, even sweeter!

I was in the library, having returned to the Ugandan village in East Africa I have come to love. A bus drove up and unloaded some of my very favorite people. They were just returning from a church camp we had sent them to over their Christmas break. The camp is called SALT—Saved And Living True.

Teaching sessions and discussions focused on topics including Sexual Relationships, Pride, Missions & Evangelism, Goals & Ambitions, Attitudes, Obedience to Man, Love & Accepting Myself, Personal Relationships, Career Guidance, Growing Through Failure, Temptation, Addictions, Anger & Personal Rights. Each topic was power packed. With good role models leading the discussions, our kids learned volumes this week.

I remember camp well. I loved the fun times, inspirational times and the friends I made. I asked these campers to tell me their experiences. I expected to hear about the music and athletic competitions, the new friends and social times they had enjoyed. Instead, they were excited to tell me what they learned. Each gave a short report and all agreed that the lessons learned were the best part of their time. (I think the food came in second. ☺)

- I learned how to resist temptations.

- I learned I could defeat Satan by prayer and fasting and keeping God's Word in my heart.

- I learned to put God first in everything.

- I understood that sex is good inside of marriage but leads to death outside of marriage.

- I understood that even Jesus was tempted (Matthew 4: 1-5).

- I learned that if tempted, I can discern and if the temptation is bad, I can leave.

- I memorized the books of the Gospels and found out gospel means "good news." I also learned there are thirty-nine books in the Old Testament and twenty-seven in the New Testament, making sixty-six in all. In addition, I knew the first five books of the Old Testament were written by Moses.

- I learned that if something tempts me, I can put God's Word in my heart so I can overcome the temptation.

- I learned more about love and to love my neighbor as myself.

- I earned to worship God through singing.

- I learned to resist Satan, the tempter.

- I learned to overcome temptation by filling my heart with the Word of God and listening to the leading of the Holy Spirit. If I don't, then it will be like I am building my house on sand rather than on the Solid Rock (Matthew 7:24-27).

- I remembered John 15.

- I learned that when I believe in Jesus, I can escape from sin and can overcome temptation. I want to make God the center of life in all I do. I also learned the importance of keeping my body pure.

Now you can see why I am so proud! I pray they can follow through living their lives in God's everlasting love and knowing He is a forgiving God if they do fall into temptation.

Camp Pictures Taken

Lydia's Team

Blue Team

Yellow Team

A young woman named Kendri, from the San Francisco Bay Area, started a Nonprofit called Abundant Life Ministries to offer Christian camps in the Jinja area. She could use the compound of YWAM (Youth with A Mission) to hold her camps until she could purchase property. Our kids were invited to attend this camp in 2014. We couldn't afford to send as many as we wanted.

Kendri helped fund a class of students the first year.

Primary 6 and 7 was our focus as they were either already teenagers or soon to be. Her camp taught life skills, team building, leadership training, and spiritual development.

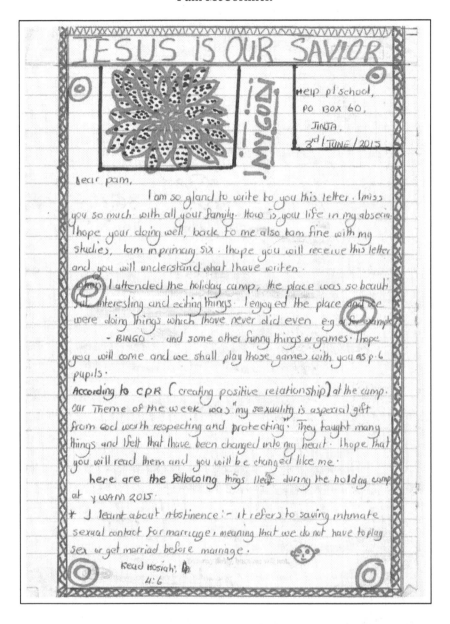

> JESUS IS OUR SAVIOR
>
> MY GOD!
>
> Help p/ school,
> PO BOX 60,
> JINJA.
> 3rd / JUNE / 2015
>
> Dear pam,
>
> I am so gland to write to you this letter. I miss you so much with all your family. How is your life in my absence. I hope your doing well, back to me also I am fine with my studies, I am in primary six. I hope you will receive this letter and you will understand what I have written.
>
> I attended the holiday camp, the place was so beautiful interesting and exiting things. I enjoyed the place and we were doing things which I have never did even e.g for example
>
> - BINGO. and some other funny things or games. I hope you will come and we shall play those games with you as p.6 pupils.
>
> According to CPR (creating positive relationship) at the camp. Our theme of the week was "my sexuality is a special gift from God worth respecting and protecting" They taught many things and I felt that I have been changed into my heart. I hope that you will read them and you will be changed like me.
>
> here are the following things I left during the holiday camp at ywam 2015.
>
> + I learnt about Abstinence :- it refers to saving intimate sexual contact for marriage, meaning that we do not have to play sex or get married before marriage.
>
> Read Hosiah;
> 4:6

These kids dearly loved this camp. I wish we could send them more years than just one. But with so many kids in the school, it is hard to have enough funding to do the extras like camps. We have committed to sending our P6 class each year. It is only about $10 per child for the week.

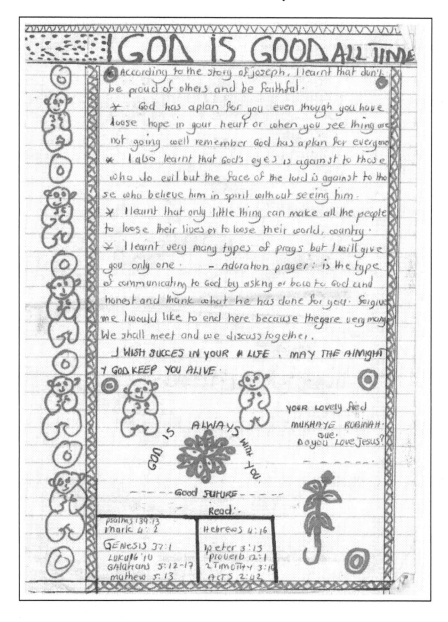

They receive a shirt, a Bible, personal toiletries and a feast of food each day. With about fifty students going each year, we need to raise $500.

I cherish letters from the kids who went to the Abundant Life Camp.

I think everyone talked about what good food they had and how much fun it was to learn new games and be a part of a team.

It amazed me at what all was taught in a week. Some letters went into detail about what they learned and enjoyed. Sexuality was a focus that impacted both the boys and the girls. They learned to create positive relationships and to know their sexuality was a gift from God to be protected, not abused.

Yeko Dies

The winter after this trip, Yeko had bowel problems. We didn't find out about it until several mistakes had been made both by him and by the medical community. Had we been there, or even been aware, there would have been a different outcome, but as I mentioned earlier in this story, Yeko died. Our Ugandan family and those of us in the States loved and valued him. We sorely missed him and mourned for him. A plaque was made and permanently attached to the fence near the entry to commemorate him. We reached out to his widow with help and also made sure his children in Masese were in school and had the care they needed.

2015

New School Building

Having a team here in the States who loves this project as I do has been a true blessing. Without them this project would have failed years ago. But with them, we have come a long way. Bob, and his wife Diana have been steadfast in their efforts and support. Every year they bring help to Masese in various, extremely beneficial, ways.

In 2015, Bob secured a grant to construct a new classroom building. Since we were using a new contractor for this endeavor, the project presented significant challenges for Bob and the Ugandan team. With the grant money, and some additional funding from H.E.L.P., we were able to complete the project by May.

By the time I got there in July we had three brand new classrooms and a workroom for the teachers. Our construction team used the interlocking bricks again to save the destruction of the already scarce trees that were important to us. There was a problem getting the foundation exactly right, but all in all, it was a very fine building. Everything else we were using had been an improvement of an existing structure and put together on a shoestring budget. This building, built from the ground up, was better than anything else we had by a long measure. We had actual floors, ceilings, and big blackboards painted on the walls. And there were desks. With windows and two doors to each classroom, there was enough light and air flow. The building was wired for electricity so lights could  be used. In the third room÷ there was even a ceiling fan. We put Primary 6 and Primary 7 in two of the classrooms and the third became a computer center. Yes, I said a computer center!

Bruce's Capstone

Before I met Jean Kaye, Bruce had decided to finish his undergraduate studies. He enrolled in a Regis University extension program in Ft. Collins, majoring in computer networking. He got stuck at writing the capstone paper he needed to get his degree. He simply didn't know what subject to write it on. Since Regis is a Jesuit institution with the slogan of "Men and Women in the Service of Others," his paper had to focus on using his education to give back to others.

He received a call with the news that if he didn't complete his degree requirements in a timely manner, some of his transfer credits would expire. His time had run out. I am quite sure he was led by God's Spirit when he searched the Internet for ideas for his paper and happened upon a site showing African village women seeing a computer screen for the first time. This article showed them ways of improving their gardening skills to better feed their families. The awestruck amazement on their faces touched his heart. If he could figure out how to bring the Internet to a developing country to widen their ideas and opportunities, give them the benefit of advanced findings from around the world, and teach them how to bring themselves up out of the gripping poverty they were mired in, he would have done a great service to others. He wrote his capstone and graduated. His children and grandchildren celebrated with us at his graduation ceremony, not having any idea where this would lead.

Computer Center

Thus, the computer center! For years we wanted to bring more computers to this project. We had tried in the beginning, but they had been gutted when the container was confiscated. Bruce decided that the desktop computers we had been sending just couldn't survive in the dusty, rainy environment available to us before the new building was built. So, he put his desire away until the conditions were more sustainable and the security was set up to keep them from being stolen or damaged. We did, however, bring a few laptops for the few staff members who had the desire and knowledge to use them.

With the new building, he felt more confident and went to work. The teams hand carried laptops over as we traveled. He brought in Internet access that had a better reach than some of our home providers offered, giving the whole compound access to the Internet. He networked the computers and found a young man from Masese, nearly graduated from Makerere University with a degree in Information Technology, to head up the IT department.

Arthur's Computer Program

Just a few years earlier I met with an American man, Skip Holloway, who was in Jinja touting the benefits of the Khan Academy, specifically the K-Lite program, to teach math and other subjects to our students with computers. Skip worked with Arthur to install this software and set up classes for the upper grades.

Arthur brought in Edmund, an intern, to help him, and set about training our teachers as well as teachers in the surrounding area. His greatest resistance has been the lack of enthusiasm from the teachers. They weren't taught with computers so they didn't know how to teach utilizing computers. Compounding that, they were afraid the computers might eliminate the need for them.

Even those who saw the place for computers in education found it hard to find time for their students to be gone from the classroom. They were under pressure to get their students ready for the government testing. The government needs to encourage the use of computer training in the primary grades before most schools will put much effort forth in this direction.

Since students could best use the center before and after school Arthur offered classes to the villagers during the daytime hours. They learned basic computer skills like word processing and spreadsheets and much more. We will never know the scope of the benefits of computer training for these eager to learn and forward-thinking, villagers, but I am glad we could extend our reach beyond the school. I would still like to see tablets in the lower grades as well as in the upper classes. I think the earlier we introduce computers and their superior educating capacity, the better. We have new volunteers, Lisa and Rob, planning on bringing Google Educate to the classrooms. That is exciting.

Education.com states: "Some experts suggest that allowing preschoolers to have computer time can be beneficial because computer use:

- Introduces educational skills

- Teaches spatial and logical skills

- Prepares children for future computer use

- Increases self-esteem and self-confidence

- Boosts problem-solving skills

- Stimulates language comprehension

- Improves long-term memory and manual dexterity

So, we are not the only ones who think this is important. In Uganda, the computer is primarily used in the universities and upper level secondary school, if at all. We are thankful for that but far from satisfied. Until Uganda catches up with their IT development as a nation, they can never compete on a global basis.

Ugandan Staff Gifts

Each trip we try to take gifts for our staff. This year we invited all our staff and their spouses to a dinner party in a garden area at our hotel. It was a beautiful night with Pastor Frederick in rare form entertaining us and emceeing. I can't remember what we gave the male spouses, but we gave the female spouses a bracelet. We brought red winter jackets for our employees. It may not seem cold to us who are accustomed to winters, but to the Africans, it is cold when the temperature drops to seventy degrees. They shiver and bundle up as best they can. These coats were not only red, but they had yellow lettering on them. It didn't matter that the lettering said Telluride; they were the same shouting colors worn by the schoolchildren. They loved them! There was laughter and celebrating. We were a big happy family that night.

Other years we brought watches, ball caps, several versions of red shirts, red ties for the male teachers and red scarves for the female teachers, to name a few. It is such a pleasure to delight our Ugandan friends. They work hard.

Two Babies

Life is precarious in Africa. On almost every trip we see death. When we arrived in 2015, there were two babies on the brink of death. One was Pastor Frederick's sister's child, and the other was a young girl baby Hillary's grandmother cared for. This child's mother died in childbirth. The father and grandfather tried to care for the baby, but she was near death when they brought her to Hillary's grandmother. Being the nurse she is, Jean Kaye did her best with both little ones. They were malnourished to the point of death. Pastor Frederick's niece didn't survive. Her loss was heartwrenching to all of us. If we had just been there sooner Jean might have been able to save her.

Our heavy hearts made the other little girl even more precious. Jean put Olivia on formula and prayed. I didn't know that it was unusual to have a baby on formula. We could hardly find formula in all of Jinja. The mothers all breastfeed their babies. We provided her nourishment, held her, and loved her with all our hearts. I couldn't help but feel a little sorry for Hillary's grandmother. She was old enough to be long finished with caring for a baby. In just a few days Olivia gained some strength. She was smaller than her age by a dramatic amount and very lethargic. She couldn't do the normal developmental tasks for her age, but by the time we left, she was laughing and gaining ground. I hated to leave her but was encouraged she had rallied so quickly. Later visits I would witness a delightful little girl, dancing and playing. I felt like a grandmother even though it was Jean who tended to her and made provisions for her to continue to receive food for a few years. I had connected on a heart level.

Dr. Harry and Leah

The 2015 trip brought Dr. Harry and his lovely daughter, Leah, with us to Masese. Harry was an emergency room doctor, but was now channeling his efforts toward creating new products to help the medical industry. He was fun to have on our team. Medically, Jean had him plugged in everywhere she could find as there wasn't a medical team focus for this trip. He didn't have any problem being valuable to the people in this land. He and Bruce made friends and brought out the playfulness in each other.

Dr. Harry watched our cooks as they labored over the massive school lunches and noticed how long it took to cook all those beans. With just a bit of inquiry he found out they didn't know to soak the beans overnight to shorten the cooking time. This enlightenment from him shortened their day, cost less for firewood, and helped all of us with digesting the beans. I didn't realize they didn't know this already.

Harry was a non-practicing Jew. His wife a Buddhist. Their daughter had never been to church. Leah was seventeen, and I was drawn to her from day one. This petite, pretty girl seemed like a granddaughter to me. I took her under my wing and helped her find projects to do and have a good experience.

Ugandan Church Service

One thing we like to share with our teams is the Ugandan church service. These services are a rich cultural experience. Everyone dresses their best. Guys usually wear a suit and tie. Women wear their best dresses and high heels. The children are washed and dressed in their best as well. Their clothes may be well-worn but they are clean and worn proudly.

In the Ugandan churches we attend drums and worship music play over loudspeakers to encourage everyone to sing with all their hearts. The volume on these speakers is often a bit more than our Western ears are used to. The night before, the music from the local bars dominated the air waves; but on Sunday mornings, the churches presided over the air space. With no solid walls or ceilings other than a tin roof, the sound travels all over the neighborhoods. Inside the church we sing and dance. If you thought you would just sit back and watch the Ugandans you would be surprised. I used to be caught off guard, but now I know to expect to be included in the fun. Dancing in church is all inclusive. I love the interaction.

Visitors always sit up front. I would rather just get lost in the crowd, but that is not protocol. We sit in special chairs off to the side of the stage facing the preacher and sideways to the audience. We are provided water to drink. I always feel guilty as the rest of the congregation doesn't have water to drink. However, if I don't drink it, I might seem ungrateful for their hospitality.

The music usually isn't in English as these services are for the poorer villagers and most of them don't know English. There is an interpreter for the sermon and other communications, but not the music. Sometimes a song will be in English. I thought they might include those songs on our account, but everyone knew the songs so I guess they sing them regularly. I am often in awe of the intensity of even the children's worship. This is not a show. It is from their hearts. The sweetness of their faces during the quieter worship songs makes me feel I am intruding on a special time between them and their Lord. There is always a time for the congregation to share their prayer needs or their praises for answered prayer. Often a visiting pastor gets time to speak. Sometimes several. No one is left out.

We are also asked to speak. Each of us gets up and at least tells our name and where we are from. If we have something else to say, we do. The more relational we are, the more they like it. Bruce and Jean preach a bit. Clapping, trilling, and amens from the crowd are frequent and demonstrate the exuberance of the Ugandan congregation.

Prayers are intense. There is much need in this community. Those needs are fervently brought before God. Their hope is in their faith as they have little other means to supply their needs. In America, we don't have to rely on God so much since we have our own resources. They only have God to rely on. Their opportunities are few, their government has other problems to attend to, and NGO's come and go, but God is ever present so they cry out to Him. They love having us come to "pray" with them (which just means attending church with them). It seems like an intrusion to me, but they are honored. The preaching is never a set amount of time. Between the guest speakers and the primary pastor and the singing, services can go on for hours.

I asked Leah if she wanted to try a Ugandan church service. She said yes so we went. I was curious about what she would think. Pastor Frederick had a great sermon, and the service went as expected. I gave her the option to leave without hearing all the guest speakers so she wouldn't be too overwhelmed. I was glad to have a reason to duck out as the longer services are tiring. She said she enjoyed it and was glad she attended. I wonder if she has been to a church in the United States since. The difference would be like the difference between night and day.

Clay from Kentucky

Clay was also seventeen. He came from Kentucky to spend some time with Jean Kaye at the warehouse and then travel to Uganda with us. He proved to be a good worker at the warehouse and seemed to enjoy learning the ins and outs of the nonprofit world. He lived on a Kentucky horse farm with private schools and privilege all about him. He was likable and capable. I thought for a moment he and Leah might connect, but they only crossed paths a few times.

Clay raised money to take to Uganda with him, so his time was directed at finding the exact thing he wanted to support. I don't know just what all he gave money to, but I do know that Kisima moved him. Kisima is an island just off the Masese 1 fishing village port. He found kids running everywhere on this island, as is common for Uganda. He also found relatively nice school buildings sitting unused. Apparently, the teachers weren't being paid. Clay determined to get that school back up and running. He gave money to start a feeding program and pay teacher salaries. He only had enough to cover a short time, so he pledged the remainder and raised it after he returned home. Within a short time, he had raised enough to cover a year. What a blessing kids can be when their hearts are touched and they have adults around to encourage and support them!

White Water Rafting Drama

Rafting is supposed to be fun!

White water rafting with my young boys in Colorado was such a good memory that I have wanted to check out the rafting on the Nile in Uganda. I was a little jealous when some young women from one of our earlier teams rafted while they were on a mission trip with us and loved it! I didn't think of myself as a thrill seeker but I do love to try new things.

Finally getting my chance to do the rafting on the Nile I had been wanting to do, I joined Dr. Harry, Leah, and Clay on their expedition for some adventure. I was nervous and asked if there was a way we could stay away from the extreme rapids. I was assured by the rafting team we could do a medium course. I emphasized I wanted to be in the boat not in the water. I felt a little guilty asking for the milder course since there were two teens with us who probably wanted all the thrill they could get. Dr. Harry didn't want to be in the water because many diseases lurked there. Nonetheless our rafting guide made us jump out of the raft to check our life jackets and teach us what to do if the raft flipped. He teased about crocodiles carrying us off, but all the animals on this part of the Nile had left for safer areas when local people began killing them for food.

We paddled across what seemed more like a big lake than a river. Never having been very strong and now being older, I was not sure I was pulling my weight, but we got into a rhythm and the four of us paddled while Abraham, our guide, handled the rudder. It had been lightly raining when we started, but the rain had stopped and the weather was lovely. We watched the Kingfishers and Cormorants catch their lunch and floated past some trees full of really large bats. Our guide slapped his oar against the water, startling the bats so they flew, entertaining us for a moment. Mostly, all was peaceful and relaxed. There were two kayakers on each side of us and another raft following that had muscular, fit Ugandans sitting on a platform, rowing with huge oars. Each had their role in our protection.

The state-of-the-art helmets and life vests we wore came in handy when the Ugandans surprised us by flipping the raft for a practice run before going over our first rapid. I took a knock to the head from the side of the raft. I was glad to learn how to find air while under the boat. When upside down, the seats where our feet were when we had been sitting were clearly designed to form a nice pocket of air. There were even illuminated lights around each area where the pocket of air was available under the raft, like airplanes have along their floor to show the way to exit. I was pretty impressed with the training, equipment, and knowledge of the guys with us. Abraham had white water rafted for thirteen years. I did the drill well and thought the upcoming rapids looked pretty.

Pretty scary in actuality! This was a level five rapid! I held on for dear life, and even though I was waterlogged, I made it through. However, there was a level three rapid, just a quick few meters past the level five. This one flipped the boat!

The flip happened so fast I didn't get a good inhale before being underwater so I was in a hurry to find air. I only had a fraction of time for panic as I found my way to the surface where, once again, I could find the air pocket under the boat, but the water was so turbulent it was harder to get a breath than in the practice maneuver. Gasping, I quickly pushed myself back under the water to emerge out from under the raft. As soon as I made it out, I was swept a little way from the raft. From inside the raft, Abraham stretched far with his paddle and pulled me to the boat. I clung to his paddle until he grasped my life jacket, and with one strong lift, he laid me in the boat while they finished retrieving my friends from the river.

I laid there, trembling, long enough to get my breath. It felt good to just rest, but I soon realized I needed to get back in place so we could move on down the river. As I started to get up, Abraham stopped me. He informed me I was bleeding and needed to lay still. Really? I had no idea! I never felt the paddle handle hit me, but I had a bloody nose and a cut on the bridge of my nose that says a paddle must have slammed into my face.

After Abraham opened a first aid kit, Dr. Harry asked for another pair of gloves and went to work doing his thing. He was such a comfort. I knew the Comforter Himself had provided this man in this boat just for me. After a quick exam, bandaging the cut on my nose and getting the nosebleed to abate, they moved me into the second raft where the Ugandans were doing the rowing. This raft was to take the easiest portion of the rapids. I was sincerely thankful for it. Even one of those easier rapids drenched me with an unwelcomed force. Each rapid was a Class 5, and there were five of those to make it through! By this time, I had swallowed more than my share of the Nile and am still amazed I didn't come down with typhoid or some other awful disease.

Lying in this raft as it made its way down the river was sheer pleasure. If I hadn't had all this infernal blood coming down my nose, I might have imagined I was some African Queen. I watched them fly through the air as every rapid catapulted them out when the boat was capsized. What an ordeal—I mean thrill.

I could hardly breathe until I saw each one surface and make it back into their boat. Seventeen-year-old Leah finally asked to be put in my boat. She had had enough!

When we finally made it to shore, we had to walk up a very slippery hill to the van. My knees were still shaky, but I had plenty of strong hands helping me each step. The concerned looks told me I must look a mess, but other than a headache, I still was not hurting. I wouldn't let them take me to a clinic. I would have Jean and Bruce get me the help I needed. Not all Ugandan clinics are the safest, but I felt good about the International Medical Clinic, otherwise known as the Jinja Clinic. Only one stitch was needed and the prognosis was that I did not break my nose. I would need to confirm that when I got to America.

You wouldn't believe all the beautiful colors breaking out over my face. It was incredible to watch the changes each day. I looked like I had been in a brawl and was NOT the winner! A week later my stitch was out and my face only looked a little bruised. My neck felt whiplashed for a few days, and I had headaches along with my tender nose, but I could do most of what I needed to do each day. Jean and Bruce fussed over me so I tried to take care of myself, but there is only so much time in Uganda. I didn't want to lose any more time than absolutely necessary. I looked worse than I felt, thank goodness. We even had a few laughs when I kept touting Abraham's strong muscles as he lifted me out of the water and mentioning how impressive the Ugandan rowers were as their strong bodies piloted the boats. Bruce was a bit chagrinned.

Once back in the States, I found out I actually broke my nose! But fortunately, it wasn't bad enough to require rebreaking it. Later I discovered I had a small tear in my rotator cuff as well. Altogether it could have been so much worse. I am thankful it wasn't. No more Class Five white water raft trips for this grandmother. But ... I have been wanting to try deep sea diving!

Mudvani Lodges Jewelry Order

Jean and I often talked about trying to find African markets for the bead women's jewelry. I thought I should take a Ugandan woman with me and go around Uganda looking for ways to sell in their own country. I wanted to train one of the bead women to be a salesperson and represent the Co-op. My sales career had been successful, but it was hard to train and motivate someone from an impoverished village, especially when I was only there a few weeks of the year. Jean didn't give up, though. She was able to connect with a man who just happened to be the buyer for the gift stores in five game park lodges.

These lodges are some of the nicest in Uganda. Their clients are wealthy people from all over the world. Jean set up a showing with this buyer. Even though my face was a mess from my rafting experience, we continued with business. We worked with the jewelry co-op leaders, and our social worker Ritah, to set up a display in one of the conference rooms at the Jinja Sailing Club. Mr. Ghei loved what our ladies made, especially the purses. He ordered six of everything we brought for each of his five lodges! Since we brought many samples to display, this was quite an amazing order. After he left, we danced and celebrated, hugging and praising God.

The next day we had to scramble! The workload had to be distributed evenly between groups and within groups. Each piece needed to be labeled and recorded. Prices had to be decided on. H.E.L.P. wouldn't make much money on this order but the ladies had a tremendous opportunity. We had to get an invoice generated. Quality control was a concern as was the need to accomplish everything quickly since the buyer wanted this order in time for Christmas tourists. Once again, I felt in over my head. Jean's prior business dealings gave her the skills she needed to head this up. Ritah took a leader's role as did the co-op leaders. Richard took on the financial responsibilities. Frederick did the transport. I took photos of each piece for our inventory. Bruce and I took the first of the order to Kampala to the Mudvani headquarters. We had to leave before everything was completed but the Ugandans did their jobs and made us proud.

It took a year for the ladies to get paid. Jean had to push to get this first order justly recompensed. We had a contract but there were still hurdles to overcome. Persistence won. She not only got every bit of payment, but they made another order just as large and with the payment up front this time!

Brianna, Christine, and Nancy

During the same trip, Brianna, Christine, and Nancy spent time in the classrooms. Brianna spent most of her time with the little ones. They adored her as she read books to each class. She acted like she was in seventh heaven. The little ones are so cute you want to stuff them in your bag and bring them home with you. Nancy and Christine taught in the upper grades. They assisted the classroom teachers and did some lessons on their own. It was a treat all the way around. The teachers got a break and could observe a different teaching style, the kids were enchanted with pretty teachers from America, and the gals teaching were happy to share their passion for education with these hungry-to-learn students. A music teacher friend of mine sent rhythm sticks for the preschool classes. The sticks were in bright primary colors and were quite a hit. We sat outside under a tree and made a happy racket. I love taking teachers to this school!

Sipi Falls

Jean left for a safari with our team while Bruce and I stayed to finish up some work. I was still working with the bead women, but we took the weekend off. Bruce was sick! He had the intestinal curse Westerners often get from the water in developing countries. I am not sure how he got it. This was the second time he suffered with this diarrhea. This time Jean wasn't around to doctor him. I found out later I had the medicine he needed. I just didn't know to give it to him. Poor guy! I felt bad for him. He felt just a little better on Sunday so we took off to see one of the sights in our part of Uganda, Sipi Falls.

Located near Mbale on Mt. Elgon, the falls were further than we had expected. Mbale is in a mountainous area so the drive was lovely. It was greener and lusher than around Jinja. Bright red flowers with deep green leaves stood out against the multiple shades of green throughout the mountainsides. Smaller purple flowers had been sprinkled throughout the valleys. The three waterfalls cascaded down the steep cliffs, their bright white a striking contrast to the green. Sunlight and shadows accentuated colors as they rolled over the landscape all around us.

Even so, Bruce was wishing we hadn't embarked on this venture. After he spent time in one of the squalid squatty-potties (how miserable!) at a Sipi Falls roadside restaurant, we hiked up the hillside to take a closer look at the falls. Two of the three falls are closer together. The top one is an easy hike with breathtaking views. I hated to be in the photos we were taking as my face was still pretty bruised. The blues, greens and purples on my face didn't match the gorgeous sights we were witnessing. Fortunately, a German woman staying at the Nile Hotel with us gave me some Arnica to use on my face so it wasn't as vivid as it started out to be. We were still quite a pair with Bruce sick and me all banged up.

Ugandan Police Encounter

Bruce rarely drives while we are in Uganda. When he does, he is quite good at it. I am not sure I can switch my brain to be able to drive on the opposite side of the road, but he does well, at least during the day. Driving at night is another story. The numerous Africans along the sides of the roads, the many potholes, and the glare of oncoming headlights, all make this a somewhat dicier proposition for him.

We cross a bridge over the Nile each day we travel from the Nile Hotel to either Jinja or Masese. There is a strict speed limit and usually quite a number of cars. No photos are allowed to be taken so you have to keep your phones out of site or the bridge police will stop you and take your camera or at least delete your photos. They stopped me once when they thought they saw me take a picture. When they couldn't find it on my camera feed, they let me go.

The police are decked out pretty smartly and look proud in their uniforms. The ones at the bridge wear a clean white uniform with the pants tucked into shiny black boots, a black beret, and matching black belt. There is always a gun attached to their belt and a rifle in their hands. I don't think I ever saw less than three bridge police at the beginning and end of the bridge.

One day Bruce was driving and I was in the passenger seat when we got signaled to pull over just after we crossed the bridge. I couldn't imagine what the problem might be. They generally don't hassle Westerners. They value the money we bring in and the help we are to their country. They do not see us as a threat.

But this day we were in trouble because Bruce was not wearing a seat belt. It didn't seem like big trouble, so Bruce and the policeman were having a friendly discussion. Bruce was shown a paper stating the fine for different infractions. The fine for not wearing a seat belt was $80,000 Uganda shillings, around $22. When Bruce offered 40,000 shillings to the officer to look the other way, the officer asked to see Bruce's driver's license. Bruce didn't have an international license, so he pulled out his Colorado one and handed it over. Looking at it for a minute, the officer smiled like the cat who was about to swallow the canary. Much to our surprise Bruce's license was expired! The policeman pulled out his list of infraction penalties again, adding the second infraction, all the while smiling his "gotcha" smile. Bruce smiled back and sheepishly palmed 40,000 shillings into the officer's hand raising his eyebrows in a questioning plea. The officer smiled back, pocketed his bounty, and waved us on. Ahh! Private enterprise in Uganda!

Pam McCormick

TEACHERS & STUDENTS

2016

Samson in Colorado—January

January 2016 brought some of Uganda to Colorado. Samson had stopped working for Compassion several years before. He did much the same work at an African nonprofit called Africa Renewal Ministries. After working there for a few years, he reapplied to Compassion to be a director. Samson came so close to getting that position (he was in the top two candidates) that he gave notice at his current job. Once the other candidate won the position, Samson had to return to his job and ask to stay. He could continue teaching in their Bible college, but not full-time. At this juncture, Samson felt he could do what he had always desired to do, start a church. I was pretty concerned since pastors rarely make enough money to live on and he had a family to support.

Hellen was working and Samson was working occasional gigs teaching seminars and preaching at tent meetings or other church events. He teamed up with some friends who had his same passion to start a church and start a church they did!

Samson named his church Set Free. Way back before he was married, when I was loading the container for Uganda and was able to put some things in for him, I had sent a leather jacket donated by a Christian motorcycle gang. On the back were the words "Set Free." Inspired, he had written and published a book on how to be set free by realizing your potential in Christ. Set Free Church started small and was growing slowly when some pastors from the United States came alongside him. Some of these supporters encouraged and enabled his first trip to the United States.

Samson had been given airline miles to get around once he got here. I was surprised to hear he had raised his own airfare to get to the United States. He just said, "God provided." I wasn't sure if he should have spent that much money to travel when his family and church could surely have used it. Getting a visa is difficult for

Ugandans coming here. Several we know have tried and been rejected. Some get their visas from a lottery. There are restrictions as to how many can travel. Samson was worried that he would be denied or postponed over and over until he paid "extra." As it was, he just walked in and was given a two-year visa within the hour. He took that as a miracle of God and confirmation he was supposed to make the trip.

We loved having him. I had been dreaming of sharing my part of the world with him ever since he was young. We had been to see him several times throughout the years. I had stayed in his home, played with all his kids, and come to love and respect his wife, Hellen.

I tried to prepare him for the airplane ride and the weather here. I told him we aren't as formal in our churches so he could pack mostly casual clothes. In Uganda, the pastors always wear suits and ties. I advised him to wear comfortable clothes on the plane since it is such a long trip. I tried to give him a heads-up about how to get around airports, what food on the plane he might like and anything else I could think of for someone who has never traveled. He was really grateful. I didn't think to help him understand the time change. He was aware we were in a different time zone, but he hadn't translated that to the extra time he would be on the plane. This African man thought he would never come out of the sky!

Samson landed in Atlanta where his friend had taken care of his itinerary for travel within the United States. Colorado was his next stop. We set him up with as much exposure as we could to help him raise funds for his new, fledgling church. But mostly, we just introduced him to our lives. He was very adventurous with new foods. Most Ugandans we know don't like variety in their food and aren't comfortable trying different things. Samson wanted to experience America fully, including American foods. He thought Mexican food was the most like Ugandan food. The beans and rice and flour tortillas were familiar to his rice and beans and chapati.

The only things he mentioned that he didn't like were shrimp cocktail and crusty bread.

We took him into Rocky Mountain National Park. Trail Ridge Road was closed through the winter, but the park was scenic and full of elk. Samson had never experienced mountains at all so everything he saw was intriguing. Being used to eighty-degree weather, the poor guy was frozen with January's temperatures in Colorado. The wind was blowing in the park, making it even colder for him. He had a good coat with a hood and a warm scarf we had gotten him at H.E.L.P.'s Warehouse, but he still shivered anytime he was out of the car. Regardless of the cold, he wanted to touch snow so we got a quick photo and he jumped back into the warmth of the car.

We also took a trip to the aquarium in Denver. He was fascinated. He didn't know any of this aquatic life was under the surface of the water. His praises of the God who had created all of this amazing world were continually on his lips.

Samson had heard a lot about my family but loved meeting them in person. He teased that they shared a mother. He calls me Mom now, and I have been OK with that since his relationship with his mother is in good standing. My family also enjoyed meeting him. He is good with people.

One of the "wows" for him on this trip was the letters I had saved over the years. He was able to read the letters he had written to me from the beginning of our relationship. He re-lived some of his own history. Samson had forgotten how young he was when he knew he wanted to be a pastor. I was glad I had saved these special letters and that I had remembered to share them with him.

Once Samson left us, he went on to other cities. I think the first and most important one was in California. His sponsorship program was started with those supporters. He was also determined to get to Missouri to meet my mother. He knew she was at the end of her days so he insisted on seeing her. I asked my cousin Janie to host him. She and her husband, Jim, quickly came to love Samson, as did my mother. The entire trip was full of making connections. Those seeds were nurtured via the Internet until he could return.

Which he did in July of the same year!

Samson's Second Trip

I was shocked that he came back so soon. I was also critical as it seemed too soon to be asking people for more support. It worried me that he was just indulging himself after his first taste of the "good life" in America. And he came without enough money to get around. He no longer had free travel from mileage and didn't bring enough money to even feed himself. He felt like God had given him the go ahead to follow up on his first trip's connections and God would provide.

Samson's story

It was in June 2016 when I was requested to go to Tanzania to supervise students I was teaching at Africa Renewal University. I was excited about the opportunity. I got barely enough facilitation to take me and care for me for two days. I went by road transport via Kenya. In one day, I crossed two borders. That is Uganda to Kenya and Kenya to Tanzania. It also meant changing money twice in one day. I successfully changed

Ugandan money to Kenyan money. When I reached the Tanzanian border, I also exchanged Kenyan money into Tanzanian money. It was at this point I got cheated of all the money I had. They were organized conmen with a makeshift office. By the time I discovered that my money was missing, they had already closed their offices. I felt bad. In that moment of wondering what next, I felt in my spirit that there could be a bigger divine appointment for me. I thanked God. I then alerted my host of my tragedy, and my host quickly arranged transportation to my final destination.

My host received a phone call from his pastor inquiring about my arrival. They had organized a big meeting/open air campaign of over 4000 people. He was requesting if I could give them one hour on my schedule. I said yes to the opportunity. I knew this could be the assignment I needed to accomplish. I checked into a hotel. The next day, we boarded a bus to go for the meeting. I felt so unprepared in all ways from dressing to spiritual preparation. I asked God to glorify himself which he did amazingly. Then they requested I extend my stay to the end of the meeting. I ended up being the main guest speaker. They booked me in a better hotel and gave a car for my transportation. They fed me like a king. At the end of the meeting, they gave me a very large gift. This was humbling. I felt encouraged to trust in the Lord more.

The next month, I felt encouraged to go to the USA even without funding. God had proved his faithfulness. I boarded a plane with $100. I had planned to visit Colorado, Missouri, and California. I had no funding, but God. My hosts Pam and Bruce could just not understand me. They made a statement that in time they would know whether it is God or my pride and ego. This made my prayers easier. We went to their church. I was praying for God to show up. When we reached the church, a stranger greeted me with a check of $200 saying God had commanded her to bless me. I knew God was with me. Many great things happened on that trip including getting $10,000 for our church roof and many children sponsored. God proved faithful. He amazed us all. He can be trusted across the borders and seas.

I must admit that my faith during this time was not as strong as Samson's. I told him I think God plans for us to use good judgement. But after the Sunday morning surprise donation I couldn't be sure I wasn't being shortsighted. When someone hears from God to do something and they only rely on their own resources to do that task, they might just be discounting their God. I told Samson I would watch and see whether he was being foolish or had actually heard from God. It was a test, and I failed.

From Colorado, Samson travelled to his next stop in California. He didn't need any money to feed himself here as we took care of that. This meant he had a few bucks in his pocket from the donation which made me feel a little better. In California, he was able to get many more kids sponsored and a $10,000 donation to put a roof on his church building! He flew on to Missouri where he got more kids sponsored.

All in all, I had to admit that God did have a plan for this trip. He blessed Samson's faithfulness and taught me I don't always have to take the safe road. Samson came needing and expecting God to provide. God's provision was over the top! He had been given confirmation while he was still in Uganda and possessed the faith to actually leave home for the United States, not knowing exactly how God would bring him back. God not only brought him back but with a sizable donation and promises for more. I stand in awe.

I was also really blessed when Samson told me I now have thousands of grandchildren from this open-air meeting in Tanzania. This puzzled me. He explained that without me he would never have been in the position of bringing God to these people. Since he is my son in the faith, these were my grandchildren. Remember the prophecy about having children, as many as the stars in the heavens? This is beginning to seem a reality. I thought those prophetic children would be ripples from the schoolchildren. Like Abraham was promised "descendants as numerous as the stars in the sky and as countless as the sand on the seashore" (Hebrews

11:12) but he didn't see them because they were future generations, I didn't expect to see them either. This sends shivers through me every time I ponder it.

Jennifer and Morella at Samson's—September

September 2016, Morella, Jennifer, Bruce, and I drove directly from the airport to Buloba, Uganda, to spend a few days with Samson. We planned on meeting up with the rest of the team later on in Masese. Whereas Jinja is a few hours east of Kampala, Buloba is on the outskirts of Kampala to the west. Jennifer is a nurse and had been on a medical trip with Jean Kaye in Malawi where she met Morella. Jennifer is from North Dakota. Bruce called her Fargo the whole trip. Morella is from Venezuela but lives in Florida. The four of us bonded and are still friends.

It was my first time to spend any time with Samson's ministry. The Buloba area is a mix of poverty and wealth. Most people live pretty humbly with poverty the norm. But right in the same neighborhood nice houses intermix with hovels. Samson's intent is to take care of the poor while attracting the ones with the means to support his efforts. He feels like if God builds it, they will come.

His building was larger than I expected. Far from complete, it will be quite a nice facility when it is finished. The small congregation made their own bricks and put up the walls themselves.

His school was being held in the church building. It was only a preschool with about thirty kids since it was his first year. I loved having a small number to work with and a roomy space to be with the kids. In Masese, the Help School is crowded and has many kids. We brought crafts and books to read. The teachers had good control of their students and seemed like lovely young women. One teacher was Samson's sister. The craft went well. We saw some of them displayed in homes later as we visited around the area.

Samson had several college students living in a room in his house just steps away from the church. His brother and sister were among those students.

Cycle Bracelets

Jennifer brought supplies for us to make "cycle bracelets" to help the women know when they are most fertile in their menstrual cycles. We made them together and talked about how to use them. Grateful for the help, the women worked industriously. They have better access to birth control than in the more remote villages, but they still saw value in using the bracelets.

The land around the church is hilly and green. There are several lodges nice enough for us to stay at. Samson showed us the simple well he put in for the community after his first visit to America. My cousin Janie and her husband, Jim, gave a donation for the well when Samson visited in Missouri.

Our team and ministers from the church (Samson and Stephen) visited and prayed for congregants of Samson's church. Bruce and I were especially touched by one family we visited. The husband/father currently lived in jail for having sex with an underage girl. Merriam, the wife, had five children and a teenage girl to care for. The oldest of the little ones was five. That five-year-old took care of all the younger ones while her mother worked. The mom took care of an elderly woman but would come home long enough to make food for her children so they could eat. When the school-aged children left for school, the younger ones stayed by themselves. I was aghast. They were way too young to be left on their own. Sometimes the teenage girl stepped up to help, but not often enough for my liking. The youngest child was just a baby learning to sit up. The father was Muslim, but the wife embraced Christianity and attended Set Free, Samson's church. At least they lived in a house. A very modest one, but it was better than a hut and even had a small yard out front, albeit dirt. Children had to carry water in jerry cans from some ways away. I didn't like seeing such little children carrying these heavy loads of water. Bruce and I decided to help this family. The five-year-old girl became our next sponsored child. Samson considers Nuliat his sister now.

Samson and Hellen and Their Growing Family

Hellen was pregnant. She took off work to help host us. She was glad for a reason to be at home instead of on her feet at work. Hellen still worked for Compassion in one of the projects where she had become the lead person.

All of us were charmed with Samson and Hellen's family. Angelo, the oldest, is a confident, engaging boy. He is responsible and a good leader.

Shalom Pam is taller than her brother and just as responsible. She is shyer but holds her own just fine. Noble is the youngest. He delighted us all. He loves visitors and all the attention he gets from them. Being the youngest, he is a little indulged, which might be a problem when the new baby arrives. He is not at all different from the baby of any family having to adjust to a replacement of their youngest status. I have sweet videos of each of the three kids singing "No more monkeys jumping on the bed!" My grandchildren sing that very song. I have a picture book of monkeys jumping on the bed and the doctor shaking his finger at them telling them to stop as each of them falls off the bed. I don't know where these Ugandan children learned this song, but we enjoyed hearing them sing it almost as much as they enjoyed performing for us.

When Samson and Hellen had their new little girl a few months later, they decided to name it Janie after my cousin in Missouri. Janie felt honored and thrilled.

Bruce's Birthday Celebration

Bruce celebrated a birthday while we worked in Buloba. Samson and Hellen bought him a lovely cake. Seldom does a Ugandan woman bake since ovens are rare. If you want baked goods, you purchase them from a bakery. It is possible to bake a cake in a clay oven. I have seen one outside a home where a cake was baked. It is

not common though. This cake had two large layers with decorative icing shaped as ribbon adorning it. "Happy Birthday Bruce" was written on the top. They wrapped the whole cake in cellophane like an Easter basket. The cake was quite an honor for Bruce and a delight to the children and adults alike. It was up to Bruce and me to cut and serve it. I couldn't figure out just what was happening when we had to press hard to cut through the icing. I think the icing must have been fondant and not too fresh as it was brittle and cracked when we tried to cut pieces to serve. The cake's texture was coarse but the flavor tasty. No one left a crumb uneaten in this crowd that rarely got a cake of any kind.

Baptisms

A highlight of this trip was the opportunity I had to take part in baptisms. Several of Samson's congregation wanted to be baptized. Samson asked Bruce if he would like to do the baptizing. Bruce

declined, so Samson asked me. I was thrilled!

Samson set up an afternoon at a small resort with a swimming pool not too far from the church. I didn't have a swimsuit with me so I got in the pool with knee pants and a shirt. I had never baptized anyone before, but I knew what to say because I had seen my dad and other preachers baptize over the years. With Samson on one side and me on the other I put my left hand on the brother or sister being cleansed from their sins and my right hand up to heaven and said, "Upon the confession of your faith that Jesus died, was buried, and was raised from the dead, and you understand Jesus is your personal Lord and Savior, I baptize you my brother/sister in the name of the Father, and the Son, and the Holy Spirit, for the remission of your sins."

Together Samson and I immersed each of them under the water. This symbolizes the washing away of their sins and is a picture of the death and burial and resurrection of Jesus. They were dying to their old selves and raising up out of the water to new lives in Jesus (2 Corinthians 5:17; Romans 6: 3-6). When Jesus was baptized, the Spirit of God descended from heaven, looking like a dove, and God spoke saying, "This is my beloved Son, in whom I am well pleased. Hear ye him" (Matthew 17:5). By being baptized these people followed in the footsteps of Jesus.

The Jews of ancient times would baptize proselytes to signify the converts' cleansed nature. Jesus tells us to go into all the world and "teach all nations, baptizing them in the name of the Father and of the Son and of the Holy Ghost" (Matthew 28-19 KJV). I got to do that this day! Full of gratitude to Samson and a deep emotional reverence, I could envision my dad looking on from heaven, bursting with pride. I couldn't help but look toward the sky and smile because this was a testimony of my dad's teaching and training. I felt really close to him that day and connected with a special kinship toward the souls being baptized. I bless Samson for giving me the opportunity and my dad for preparing me.

Samson Drives

Samson drove Bruce, Jennifer, Morella and me on to Masese. Samson had gotten a car a few years before. When he first learned to drive, he was timid and afraid. He prayed for "traveling mercies" before he even started the car. I can't even imagine learning to drive in Kampala! The traffic is aggressive and chaotic. Samson drove with such caution we thought the streaming traffic would run him over. By now, though, we felt safer with him as our driver. He still prays each time he gets into the car. I think that is a pretty good practice as traffic is dangerous everywhere.

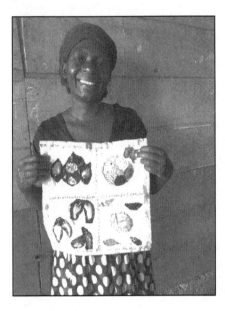

Making Quilts

Morella brought supplies with her to teach women to quilt. She had to learn to quilt herself before she came to teach the Ugandans. She learned a different style than pure quilting. Different fabric scraps were there to choose from. The women could pick out a picture or pattern from the fabric, cut around it and then stitch it onto another square of fabric. A piece of muslin fabric was attached to the back with a quilt, with batting sandwiched between the front and the back. The cutout piece was stitched through all the layers making the quilting pattern. Once a woman finished a square, she would do this process again three more times. After stitching these four-square pieces together using a cross stitch, a different piece of fabric was sewn around the outer edges to make a hem and a frame. Each woman would then have a small beginning of a larger quilt. These small four-square pieces could be used for an art piece. Adding a few more squares could make a baby blanket.

It was interesting to watch the women from the village. Most of them had never sewn anything before. Many had never even held a needle. Scissors were new to most of them. Getting the hang of cutting with scissors took practice. Stitches were not uniform, but perfect stitches were not necessary in this rudimentary beginning. At first, shyness kept the women from chatting. Our teacher, Lydia and social worker Ritah, attended the class. They had done some hand sewing previously and both could help us translate. They proved invaluable. The village women were eager to learn, so they watched and experimented and soon opened up with their excitement.

The classroom we used was in the preschool building. This is the roughest building on our property. When it rained the roof leaked like a sieve. When the sun shone the room heated up. There was never enough light. Since the preschool is only in session half days, we could use the room without interrupting classes. We had access to tables and chairs so, at least, we didn't need to sit on the dirt floor.

The creative part was not a struggle for most of them. Each of them had a good eye for what looked pleasing. Morella encouraged a theme for each mini quilt. Some followed her lead and others just made their own pattern, either around a color scheme or shapes. We were proud of each of them and, even more important, they were proud of themselves. Hopefully, they will take what they learned and use that knowledge to bring in some income for their families. We certainly had a good time helping them make their quilts. I absolutely love how much creativity comes from different team members. No one had thought of quilting before Morella came.

Lydia Receives Grace and Mercy

Lydia always attempts to get me to sit with her for a while each time I visit. Sometimes that is a challenge as I get pulled in many directions. She has been with us from the very early years. I love her and enjoy her friendship. She speaks pretty good English. That helps!

One year she told me she had gotten in trouble with the former headmaster. He withheld her pay until she agreed to write a confession. She was innocent and even had witnesses. But she couldn't use them or she would get them in trouble. She held out for three weeks but was too hungry to continue.

Now she needed to have her record cleared. It scared her to tell us. I hesitated to get involved between a headmaster and his staff. I agreed to get her an appointment but would not speak for her. I encouraged the headmaster to listen with an open mind.

He promised to review the issue and take appropriate measures. We left his office encouraged. She is still teaching today so I guess he removed it. Sometimes we just need to be heard. She trusted me to hear her.

Lydia loves teaching. You can tell it when she is with the kids. She also loves learning new methods. One year I showed her a simple leaf rubbing. I showed her how to take a leaf, put it under a sheet of paper, and then use a pencil or crayon (called a "shade" in Uganda) and color over the leaf. The form of the leaf "magically" appears on the paper. This thrilled her! For the rest of the day she scurried around showing other teachers how to do this magic. Their biggest problem was the lack of paper for the preschool. It's hard to do leaf rubbings without paper—hard to do so many things in an impoverished area.

From day one Lydia taught the kids songs and dances. I dearly loved hearing the kids sing their version of the Bible school songs I knew from my own childhood. I learned that their dances were tribal. I just thought there were different moves to different rhythms, but each tribe has their own type of movements. Now that I know, I can see the different styles when the kids dance. It is fascinating.

I asked what the Muslim students did while the class sang Jesus songs. I was told the kids can leave if they want, but instead, they all stay and sing together. I love that!

For a time, Lydia had an after school class teaching embroidery. I took her supplies when I could. Some of our team members taught her new stitches which she could teach her class. Lydia was one of the ones learning to quilt from Morella. Like I said, she loves learning.

It was a good thing she loved learning because we found out she hadn't gotten her certification to teach. She told us her husband had destroyed all her papers, but the truth was different. She didn't have those papers in the first place. Not only had she lied about that but we found out her name wasn't Lydia. It was Norah. I guess it is not uncommon for someone to change their name. Simon Peter, another teacher, also changed his name. I was upset. We had given her money to travel to her village to retrieve these papers. Lydia took the money and made the trip, knowing no papers existed.

It scared her into telling us the truth. She thought she would lose her job. I suppose she should have, but instead we sent her to a teacher's training college. (We sent several teachers to get their certifications so we could become a certified school.) It was difficult for her to go to school to complete her certification. The teachers getting this schooling would attend their college classes on their breaks from teaching. In Uganda, there are three terms a year with a month between most terms (more at Christmas). This enabled them to continue teaching and earning a living while they completed their schooling. It was a good system but hard on single mothers.

Lydia always had more children living with her than belonged to her. Elizabeth lived with her for years, along with several others. Those living with her needed love and attention and her home had to be cared for. While doing all this, she earned a small living and got her teacher training. Lydia has a big heart and could never be called a slacker.

Every day during the lunch break a group of kids, ranging in ages, meet in one of the preschool classrooms to participate in the

Scripture Union Lydia heads up. I confess I hadn't heard of a Scripture Union. I would probably call it a Bible Club. They get their lunches each day, bring them into an unused classroom and eat together while they sing, pray, and tell testimonies of God in their lives. Prayer requests are given, the Bible is read and a short lesson is shared. Sometimes Lydia gives the teaching and sometimes it is one of the older students. I am always touched at the deep spirituality these precious children have. At the end of their school year, in early December, they throw themselves a party. Those who can put in a few shillings to buy treats. H.E.L.P. contributes a few more shillings to encourage this group. We have taken Bibles to each child in the group who reads, and once in a while, I take a craft for them to do. Hobby Lobby has Christian supplies for reasonable prices.

I am eternally thankful for Lydia and her influence in the lives of the students at the Help School—not to mention the influence she has on my life!

Babies

I met babies during this October 2016 trip. Both Jackie and Marian birthed baby boys. Jackie could better care for her child since she had almost completed her social work certification. She also enjoyed the support of her family. I know she was disappointed that the father of her baby would not marry her. He is the biggest loser as far as I am concerned. I think Jackie would be a good "catch," and their baby was absolutely adorable. Even Bruce talked about stuffing this delightful little one into our suitcases and taking him home with us. Jackie enjoyed sharing him with us, and we gave her some baby clothes.

We also brought baby clothes for Marian's baby. I felt really bad for this mama and child. She could stay with her mom for this visit, but her dad would not let her live at home. Her guy was not being very good to her. He had her living away from people so she couldn't easily take care of herself. He was not much of a provider so life was hard. She didn't complete her secondary schooling and had no vocational training. Getting herself pregnant was not a good plan.

Marian's mother has a goiter on her neck. It is large and will kill her, choking off her breathing. I tried to get her help but once I left, nothing progressed. Her husband won't help. She is in a hopeless situation and I feel terrible for her and her younger children.

Bead Buy

The bead buy this year was not a large one. I didn't need many pieces. Never wanting to miss out on the new ideas, I set up a time to meet quietly with Alice and Sarah. I didn't want to spark jealousy with other bead women.

Alice wanted me to visit her new home. She and her husband, David, took the money she earned from the beads and invested in some land. They built a house and were building other rooms to rent. I saw the land when there was nothing on it but a small abandoned house.

Morella and Jennifer accompanied me since they both wanted to buy jewelry to take home. To get to Alice and David's house, we needed to park the car and walk through a field of maize. The maize was taller than we were, so their narrow footpath proved helpful. We were glad to see what these enterprising women had designed. They branched out from the paper beads. Some of their jewelry was an intricate design of small seed beads.

Meanwhile, our bead ladies received another order from the game lodges. We all pitched in to get that order together in time for the Christmas season.

Henry the Electrician

Henry came to the project and worked with an electrician from our team. It thrilled Henry to be of help, and he loved learning from this American professional. Henry used the time he worked with us as his practicum for his certification. We were so proud of him! His desire to please and his work ethic made him respected and liked. Henry had become a man blessed with a direction for his life. We rejoiced with him.

Microfinance

Unable to be integrally involved in everything happening at the school, I have been grateful and impressed with many of the programs and activities others have championed. One of those is the microfinance program started by Peter Garrity. Peter and students at Molloy College on Long Island, New York, formed the Molloy-Masese Partnership (MMP). This entrepreneurship initiative, founded in 2016 in collaboration with H.E.L.P. International Uganda, aimed to revitalize opportunities for entrepreneurs in Masese. They started with six enterprising women and $325 in donations. The program is designed to give a no-interest loan of $50-$100 to help start a business. This amount of money may not seem like much to us in America, as it sometimes takes thousands, if not millions, of dollars to get a business up and running. However, this amount overcomes a large barrier to the start-up of a small local business in this village.

Although the loans were defined as interest-free, the U.S. team established a payback model in which each payment had a small interest component. Once the loan was paid fully by the loan recipient, the accrued interest was returned to the loan recipient. The interest component was intended to act as a tool to help motivate entrepreneurs to save a portion of their proceeds to reinvest in their business. A trusted Ugandan team was established, mentors were set up, and business classes offered. Once repayment was completed, another small loan could be applied for. Not all the stories are successful, but everyone learned as they went, and many lives have been changed for the better. Peter and his student Chris set up a well thought out program, raised the initial money, established the Ugandan team, and did the oversight. Most of all, they cheered the fledgling businesses on. With God as the center and caring, socially conscious people putting forth effort, the ripples spread wider and wider and the tapestry became more and more beautiful. What a gift to the world!

Emotional Earthquake

A major shift happened during this trip. It felt like an emotional earthquake, like a knockout blow. My writing for that time sets the stage.

Bruce was worrying about retiring. He knew he wanted to do something different, something more rewarding and fulfilling, but he didn't know what that would be. His work was familiar and retirement was unknown. Without something to step into, it scared him to move. In the worldly realm this was understandable.

However, we serve a God who brings another whole dimension into play. He has the bigger picture and requires us to have faith. He will give us the faith we need, but without faith we settle for less than the best God has for us. I tried to help Bruce by telling him he has to let go of one before another could come into place—let go of the familiarity of his job and see what God brought along that would better meet his desire to make a difference in this world. This difference would bring meaning into his existence like never before. Stop sleepwalking and soar. Not just survive, but thrive! He needed to trust God had a plan, even if he didn't have a clue what that plan was.

Trusting is hard to do. Over the years I have fought God, trying to tell Him what I thought was best for my life rather than trusting Him with all my heart, soul, mind, and strength. I knew the Scriptures that said He has plans for my life that are "for good and not for evil, to give [me] a future and a hope" (Jeremiah 29:11 TLB). The Bible also says, "perfect love casts out fear" (1 John 4:18). So, if God is love, then why was I afraid to trust Him? I knew He loved me even more than I love my own kids. I would never do anything that wasn't the very best for them, so why did I think God, who really knows best, would not take care of me?

In Matthew 7:9–11 Jesus points out that if one of our children asked us for bread, we wouldn't give them a rock or if they asked for fish to eat, we wouldn't give them a snake. So, if we who are sinful wouldn't give bad gifts to our children, then why do we think our Father God wouldn't give us good gifts? Probably because we live in this world where we see deception, disrespect, and all sorts of malice and wrongdoing—a world where it's hard to trust anyone, where we learn to lean on our own understanding. It's difficult to make the leap of faith to trust in a God we can't even see. I remember Thomas, the disciple who couldn't believe Jesus had risen from the dead until he put his hand into Jesus side where the spear had pierced him on the cross. It is hard to believe without seeing. But if we can understand the heart of God and learn to know His nature, our faith builds. We begin to see Him working in our lives. We experience His faithfulness.

Bruce did retire but continued to wonder what he was to do with this newly found freedom. I planned a trip to Uganda with Jean Kaye, and we invited our husbands. Bruce reluctantly agreed to go, but again, he didn't know what his purpose would be. I wasn't worried. On previous trips, there were always more projects for him than he could get done. The construction and infrastructure projects had been his contribution. He would see the problem, find resources to fix that problem, get quotes, and get workers to get it done. He was ever busy and the school structures would never have been built if he hadn't taken on that role. Funds were limited, so he was at a huge disadvantage. On top of that, there were many opinions as to how each project should be done. Bruce persevered, and we have a school, teaching many children for many years now.

Closing One Door to Open Another

This trip turned out different. Jean's husband, Don, took over the construction role. Like two bulls locking horns, he and Bruce clashed. Jean and Don are the leaders of H.E.L.P. International and are powerful forces. Bruce stepped out of Don's way. Practically speaking, this was good. Bruce didn't have the frustrations he had experienced over the years, and Don did a good job.

Emotionally, it was harder. Bruce felt displaced and useless. He did not understand why he was even there. So he hid out in the computer center he established on the previous trip. While there, things began to unfold in a different direction. He and Arthur, the young man Bruce put in charge of the computer department, began to reach outward from the school to the greater community. Of the thirty primary schools in the Jinja area, only a handful have any computers. The ones that do, don't have support.

God woke me up one night and showed me what was happening. The construction door was clearly being closed, and none too gently. But if that door hadn't been closed, Bruce would have been busy with good projects—and missed the bigger role he was meant to play. God was opening another door. One perfectly suited for Bruce!

Bruce loves the information technology world. He can see ahead to how much difference computers could make. And not just computers themselves, but the bright minds that revolve around the IT community. Uganda has an outdated education system. Their neighboring countries have been embracing computers and the knowledge they bring. Uganda has been behind the curve.

But even the Ugandans who recognized the importance of computers didn't see the way forward. Bruce saw it and God is using him to develop a community who can bring Uganda into the 21st century in their schools. The words in my blog came back to me: "Letting go of one thing so God can throw open the next door. Not leaning on our own understanding, but understanding that Perfect Love has good plans for us."

Connecting the IT Community in Jinja

Shortly after our computer setup was operational, H.E.L.P. was requested by members of the Jinja municipal council to assist some of the other primary schools in this endeavor. They arranged a tour for us, and the lack of computer technology was disheartening, to say the least. The last two primary schools, each with over 1000 students, had one computer between them, and Bruce wasn't sure that it was even operational.

Bruce asked Arthur if they could visit some of the schools in the area that were also using computers. Arthur knew the IT instructors at Victoria Nile Elementary, one of the better government schools, so a meeting was set up. While there, they requested our assistance with their server. Arthur discovered a small problem with the IP configuration, which he was able to resolve in less than fifteen minutes. This issue had prevented the use of their computer lab for the last several months. A light came on for Bruce, as he realized these folks had local resources that they weren't aware of.

The last night we were in Jinja, H.E.L.P. International hosted a dinner that Bruce and Jean pulled together. This event was a faith producer for Bruce. The dinner didn't get planned until a few days in advance. Our Ugandan team had to give approval for something they didn't know much about. Letters of invitation had to be distributed, a program designed, a meeting place secured, and a goal set. Bruce could hardly sleep and was in the proverbial "cold sweat." But this fear, this feeling of impotence, this stepping into unknown territory with a total lack of preparation took him to his knees. He cried out to God for help. This was exactly what was needed both in this situation and in Bruce's life. His ego needed to be out of the way for God to step in and shine. The Bible says in our weakness, He is strong (2 Corinthians 12:10). Even though God had already equipped Bruce with all he needed, Bruce had to know he was incapable of greatness without God's leading. Being humbled can be painful, but it allows God to refine us and make us who He created us to be.

The dinner was a huge success. The deputy mayor, the director of schools, the RDC (Resident District Commissioner) who reports directly to the president of Uganda, several city council members, and other government entities came and even took notes. The director of schools and the deputy mayor stood up and spoke to the importance of this meeting. Arthur was there showing what we are doing in our school with K-Lite and the community classes. Hackers for Charity, a local NGO, gave a presentation and a leader of a Maker's club from a large secondary school doing robotics talked about what the kids were excited about in their school. Several teachers from local primary schools attempting to implement computers into their curriculum talked about the challenges they faced. Our Ugandan Help Staff shared.

The government, the IT community, the schools, and the NGOs all brought value to the group. They planned to form a user's group so they could all benefit from their different perspectives. Although Bruce would not be there to drive it, this was a large step in a good direction. The schools know about local IT resources, and the government recognizes the community's hunger for advanced technology.

We discovered and can interface with another NGO that has been bringing tablets to a few primary schools. Bruce may not be doing construction at the school, but he is constructing a movement that will impact this generation and only God knows how many more.

Arthur

To bring about this IT community, God brought us Arthur, a Ugandan member of the next generation. Arthur's bright mind, along with his desire to put his schooling to work for his country, made him the perfect counterpart to Bruce.

Arthur's story made his determination to better his world understandable.

> Hi, my name is Arthur Nsubuga. I live in Masese and work at H.E.L.P. as the IT manager. I'd like to share my story, but I'll break it down into where I was born, how I grew up, where I went to school, and how I ended up working at H.E.L.P.

> But first, before I tell you about myself, I'll tell you about my mother. She comes from a polygamous family. Her mother was murdered when she was still young, but she had elder sisters who were already married and who already lived in the urban centers of Uganda. One of her sisters happened to be employed and married here in Masese. She was a teacher in Jinja, so my mother started living with her and grew up with her. It's believed in Africa that for a mother to be blessed, they must bear boy children. My mother's sister did not bear any boy children for her husband, so that was kind of a problem for their marriage. Her husband wanted to force my mother to bear a boy child for him. My auntie was adamantly opposed, so they fell out with each other. Because of this my mother could not continue living with her sister.

> She moved to Kampala. She went to study to be a teacher, and that's where she met my dad. After she conceived, she got to know that my dad had another wife and several children out there, and that they wouldn't have a future as a couple. My mother didn't want to abort, so she kept me. When I was born, she took me to my father's home. My father threw us

out because he didn't want his marriage to be tampered with. From there my mother struggled to bring me up.

Unfortunately, when I was four years old, she passed on. I had nowhere to stay, but everyone knew me. They knew the family of my dad. His father was the first Ugandan archbishop of the Church of Uganda. They named me after him. That was the identity I carried with me that helped me wherever I went. Although they didn't know my father, that identity always kept me known to everyone.

When I was brought back to the place where my mother grew up, her sister's home, her husband would not allow me in there. He thought I would be his boy child, but that wasn't the case. He felt so angry he couldn't let me stay with him. I remember that argument. It was at night. They, my auntie and her husband, fought about me, and the guy said, "As long as I'm alive, this guy cannot live under the same roof with me." So they threw me out, and just like that, I started looking for where to stay.

I had another married auntie who was stable, but she was married to a Muslim. So when I was taken to his home the Muslim man said, "Okay, I can take this guy in, but only on one condition: that he also converts to Islam." My auntie didn't want that to happen because they knew I carried the identity of a bishop. She didn't want to bear the guilt of being the one who led me to Islam knowing I'm a grandchild of a bishop.

Because of not converting to Muslim, I couldn't stay in that home. I lived with various people. My uncles were not well off and were still in school so I spent all my time moving from home to home. I was just in Primary 3—that was when I was about six years old—when an uncle of mine was appointed the head teacher of a school in Kampala. That is Bukasa Primary School. And so I was lucky to go and live with him because he was the head teacher. I studied in his school for free throughout primary.

When I finished primary school, life again became tricky. My uncle also had two children who were studying. He felt he couldn't continue with my education. So he came and told me, "My son, you can see how our finances are. I don't think I can support you in school. You're gonna have to rest for two years as I look for a way forward." I had friends who also were not able to continue with school. We would go gathering mangoes on a farm near our school. The owner of the mango farm caught us taking her mangoes. She wanted to take legal action, starting with our parents. Fortunately enough, I carried the name of my bishop grandfather. When she asked me what my name was, I told her the names, and to her surprise that was her father. She was my auntie. So she asked me, 'Where did you get these names from?' I told her, "I just grew up knowing I was called Arthur Nsubuga," you know? So she got very concerned, wanted to know where I lived. She got in touch with my uncle, and she was the one who identified my father for us. She showed me to my father, and I moved to my father during that holiday, that long holiday.

When I met him, I thought everything was well, finally well. I stayed with my father for four years and was very happy. I thought when I found my father I was going to find a drunkard man or someone who was lame, someone who was so poor. But he wasn't everything I thought he was. When he returned from the army he did a course as a teacher and was appointed a head teacher somewhere in a different district. I was happy that one—he was not as bad as I thought, and two—he had a very beautiful home. Somehow, I thought life would be good again.

I think all this was just excitement for nothing because soon after that I started tasting the wrath of my stepmom. I think polygamy was still catching up with me. My stepmother didn't like me at all because she also didn't have any male children. She only had two girls, and my father also had children with other women elsewhere. Being my father's legal wife, she fought so much to see that no one encroached on her marriage. When they brought me in, I was a boy, very bright, and so loved by my father. My stepmom didn't like that. She waged war against me and we fought frequently.

In time, she forced my father to throw me out of the house. I had nowhere to go. I ran to school and explained to my teachers. They spoke to the priests because this school was Catholic-founded, and they allowed me to come and work in the seminary. I stayed in a small room there and would work for the seminary and then study in the school near the seminary where the seminarians went.

I started from there and finished my high school. After that, I didn't want to go back to my father's house because I knew my stepmom. She had tried to have me killed. She talked to the school nurse, the school where I was, and they planned to harm me. That next morning the sister to the nurse ran and told me, "Arthur, if you happen to fall sick right now, don't bother going to the sick bay because I heard my sister and your stepmom planning to do something weird to you. You'll either die or be paralyzed or something will happen, so don't risk going there the moment you fall sick." And that's how I knew how bad my stepmom's intentions were.

So when I finished my high school—here in Uganda we call it S4, senior four—I went to live with my uncle in Kampala who could not take care of my school needs. My father stopped giving me support because I didn't go back to live with him. So I struggled, doing odd jobs. I did everything I could find to raise money for my school fees. I started paying for my school fees as early as S5, or you could say—what you would call junior college in America.

After attending college for two years, I came out and continued doing my odd jobs to support myself. I would work as a casual laborer on construction sites. I worked in factories, Asian factories here, and I really couldn't find the purpose. My suffering was not going away. I tried so much to improve my life but I couldn't.

After I had gathered some little money, I trained in electrical engineering for two years in Leda. It didn't go well because by the end of the course, I had a very big balance of around five million shillings (about $1400) which I have not cleared even up to now. Without paying my five million shillings, they refused to give me my academy documents. I tried working as an electrician. I worked in factories and construction sites. They wouldn't pay me much because I didn't have any papers to present, although I could do the job. For two years I worked in the factories. I was very exploited. I came to realize that my wages should have been 25,000 UGX per day (about $7.00). They were paying me only 8,000 UGX per day (around $2.00), cheating me. At the end of the day, even my contribution to the products was very insignificant.

I needed something that would make me feel more relevant. I needed a job where I would be appreciated. I needed something that would make me feel closer to God, serve God's people in a better way. Yeah, I was prayerful. I'd go to church. I would sing on the worship team and I would attend fellowship with friends of mine, would read the Bible and go evangelizing around the place. But I didn't think this was enough for me.

When I left the factory, I left with around three million shillings ($800.). I started a simple business in town and I also enrolled at university again for information technology. After my first year I met Jean Kaye. I'd come to Masese to visit my auntie, my auntie where my mother grew up from. Pastor Frederick and Jean Kaye came to visit my auntie. My auntie was a retired teacher, and they needed a head teacher for their school. They came to visit her to see whether she would be able to take the job.

Jean Kaye started talking about IT. I explained to my auntie the IT aspect of their conversation. That's when Jean Kaye became inquisitive and asked me what I'd qualified in. I explained to her I did electrical engineering but right now I'm training in information technology at the university. She asked me, "Can you give me your resume?" Very quickly I put together something and presented the papers to her. And so that's how I started working with H.E.L.P.

At first my experience with H.E.L.P. wasn't that easy. First, the department was new. They didn't have any structures. Since I didn't have a job description, I didn't know what to do. I had to form everything from scratch, but with the help of Ronny, Richard, and Pastor Frederick. They explained the objectives of the organization and what they needed from me, and what the dream was.

I drew programs that would fit within the program—within the objectives of the organization. I drew up programs to help the youth, giving them skills, equipping them to be self-employed. I received many applications for the courses I put up. I saw lives being transformed because after the courses here they'd get simple jobs. Some of these students were encouraged to study at universities.

I discovered a friend, a friend of H.E.L.P., who had K-Lite. K-Lite is a database management system for a school. It has tutorials and tests for children. Our children would come and click on any test and the system would keep giving them tests. They try them out by feeding in the answers. The system analyzes how they perform. I installed it here at the H.E.L.P. computer center and put Kahn Academy on the network. Our children come to our computer classes, to do these tests. As they learn how to use the computers, we've seen them improve their performance in classes.

I feel so proud that, finally, I feel I'm a part of something that is causing transformation in this community. Every time I come across a child I have taught they tell me, "Arthur, we thank you—I thank you for what you made me. You taught me this, and this is what I'm doing." I feel so good.

I thank H.E.L.P. International for giving me an opportunity to be a part of something relevant, to be a part of the transformation happening in this community. My life has not remained the same. Just last year I married my wife. She loves me so much, and I love her. We are so proud to be a part of H.E.L.P.

Briefly that is my story. I wish I could tell you all, but that is my brief story. But as someone said, behind every story there is also a story. I hope next time I'll share more about my story, but that is briefly it. I pray that it blesses you and I wish you the best. Thank you so much.

Pam McCormick

Ugandan Visitors to Colorado
June 2017

2017

Political Visitors—June

The mayor of Jinja had changed and now we needed to forge a new relationship. Pastor Frederick had helped us become friends with the previous mayor, Kezaala, but this new mayor was another story. After multiple tries, Jean was finally given an audience, but for only five minutes! After hearing he had a trip to the United States planned in late May, she jumped at the opportunity to invite him to Colorado. Majid was the mayor of mayors. He carried a lot of responsibility. Not only was he the mayor of the second largest city in Uganda, he was over all the mayors in Uganda.

We were honored at his acceptance of our invitation. Jean and Bruce agreed to pay his way from the East Coast to Colorado. He had a few others in his party so they came as well. Jean housed them, and we helped feed and host them. This was a very different group than we normally interact with. These were movers and shakers. They were higher in the financial echelon and the political scene. Two of the guys were members of parliament. The others held Jinja government positions.

Then there was Leila. It took me most of their visit to figure out just who this young woman was. They introduced her as Majid's personal assistant. She seemed to know his schedule and be proficient at assisting him professionally. She was my guest to host. Jean and Bruce took the lead with the men while Leila and I hung out together.

Jean, Bruce, and I did the typical tour guiding of Northern Colorado but also kept them busy seeing possibilities for their country. We took them to an elementary school to show them the use of tablets by even the earliest of grades. Another stop introduced them to IT professionals integrating computers to teach and to interface in local schools. We showed them aquaponics and how it could help with fish and vegetable production for their country. They talked with other mayors in our area about tourism, trash management, and other strategies of city government. We even put them in touch with a member of the USGA because Benard, one of our Ugandan guests, wanted to establish a relationship with the golfing community in Jinja.

Jean and Don let them ride their four-wheelers around their property. The guys loved that, and Leila used it for a photo opportunity. Some friends of Jean's invited us all to their upscale condo high up over Denver for dinner one night. Another friend hosted us all earlier in the afternoon to meet their mayor and a few other interested friends. This one worried our Ugandan friends as there were only appetizers offered. They didn't understand we had dinner plans afterward. They were sure they would starve.

Taking them up into Rocky Mountain National Park and on up Trail Ridge Road was fun. Leila wasn't interested in sightseeing. She was tired of being dragged all over the place. However, when she got to play in the snow, her whole attitude changed. All the group tapped into their inner child and had fun! They were all amazed at the scenery on the drive up the mountain. It is impressive to even those of us who live here. We made sure everyone had a good warm coat, but they didn't have good shoes for snow. Regardless of cold feet and altitude fears, they grasped the beauty and vastness of the Rockies.

The guys started telling me about how talented Leila is. She is actually a musician giving concerts and making videos. Her singing and videos are the style of a pop star in America. She is respected in the fashion world as well. Her "day job" with the mayor is her steady source of income, but she is famous for her music. I got to view her YouTube page. She is definitely talented!

The men were quite interesting too. I wrote a synopsis of each of them while they were here and shared it with them on our last day.

Moses—Such an incredible leader, a Parliament member. Shows authority with wisdom. Has a wonderful human side while being confident of his own self-worth. Proud, but not needing to be in the limelight. Able to build others up. Impressive from the word go.

Majid—It was fun to see him break through his reserve to have childlike fun in the snow. I want to bless him in his role of mayor of mayors. What a tremendous responsibility that, as I can see it, can only be done with God's help. I pray for wisdom, boldness paired with empathy, and success in his endeavors to make his influence be for the good of his people. I see him willing to be led by those he respects and able to stand up and be counted.

Nelson—Impressed by his doing of the faith he believes in. He went from being a pastor, loving and leading his congregation, to putting himself in a position to make a difference in his country by serving it in a bigger way. As a Parliament member, his sphere of influence multiplied, and he is up to the task. He realized an opportunity to experience and grow by coming to Colorado and was even willing to fund his own way to catch hold of that opportunity. I love his humor and ability to make me smile.

Francis—What an impressive public servant, the town clerk! His skills are perfect for the role he has been appointed to. I have respect for the ones who saw this in him and set him in motion. He is grounded, meek, confident, and excited to learn. Jesus says the meek shall inherit the earth, and I believe that when I see Francis.

Benard—This is a likeable man, in charge of public works in the Jinja district! He will go far. His passion and servant heart show his ability to lead, even in the shadows. He has a confidence about him that speaks of depth and soul. Who wouldn't like a man who can look ahead to the future and do all he can to bring that future into being. He is generous and thoughtful.

Leila—As I become acquainted with this young woman, I felt like I just kept seeing the onion being peeled. From this quiet unassuming persona, at least compared to the high-powered politicians she was traveling with, into a powerful woman with a

sense of self many mothers would wish for their daughters. I observed her quietly clean all the dishes after dinner at my house with no praise expected or required. I saw her serve others in many small ways that were also not expecting any glory. Then I watched Leila's talent brought to the forefront, not from her, but from others giving her the due they believe she is earning. I wish her the best in that arena. She is not only lovely to look at but can bring out the beauty in music, and I expect also in the fashion ventures she is involved with. As she endured the schedules others set up for her, she showed patience and could find joy in the outcomes. You should have heard her delight at being in the mountains and experiencing the childlike joy of this new experience. Best of all for me was finding out she is a believer in Jesus. I didn't realize that I was feeling sad she didn't know Him, just to find out she does know this Son of God I so love.

It has blessed me to get a few days to begin to know these men and this woman. Uganda is blessed to have them call Uganda home. I will enjoy seeing what the future holds for each of them.

Buloba—July

In July 2017, my cousin, Janie and her husband wanted to go meet Samson's new baby. Bruce, after some discussion, went along.

Samson's love and respect for Janie had been brought to the forefront by naming his new little girl after her. Janie couldn't wait to get her hands on this child! She would have gone a few months earlier if I had been going because Baby Janie was born in December. My good friend Geri and Kendra, an elementary school teacher I met during a jewelry show, went with us. Jean travelled directly to Masese, but the rest of us were driven straight to Samson's. For the first time, I was able to introduce a member of my family to my African world.

When Janie and Jim decided to travel to Uganda with us I was both thrilled and worried. His health was good, but he was older. Her health was not as good. I worried about her digestive system since it was somewhat compromised. Her endurance also concerned me. Even though she was younger than me, she had to carefully consider the needs of her body.

Both the guest house/resort we stayed in and the church near where Samson lived were on a short, but steep hill. Janie and Jim took fewer trips up and down those inclines. They were happiest interfacing with Samson and his family. Baby Janie delighted us all. Nobel vied for attention but also respected his new little sister and her admirers. As Janie and Jim drove around Buloba, their hearts ached to see little children carrying heavy jerry cans full of water up the hills from the well to their homes. From one of Samson's earlier trips to the United States, Jim and Janie had helped pay for a well for the villagers because clean, available water is such an issue. Now they wanted to bring that water up the hill to help relieve the burden of carrying it. Jim and Bruce also looked at setting up rainwater collection at the houses of the children we sponsor. In the end though, they abandoned the idea because it would not help the majority of the people and cost more than they originally thought.

Attacked by a Gander

An amusing story from this trip happened on one of those steep inclines by our lodge rooms. As we walked to the building where we ate our meals, we encountered a few geese. They acted like they owned the road so we steered clear of them. One of them seemed pretty agitated when we came anywhere near. Geri knew geese better than the rest of us. She wisely told us to give them a wide berth.

Unfortunately, Bruce wasn't with us to hear this advice. One trip down the hill, when we encountered the geese coming at us from an adjacent path, Bruce decided to show his prowess by protecting us. He threw out his arms making himself big and ran toward the geese to frighten them away. The lead goose charged toward Bruce, aiming his beak at a very tender place on Bruce's anatomy. Quickly reversing his charge, Bruce tumbled backwards down the hill. It was an impressive backward roll with only a few scrapes and just a little blood. We didn't feel too guilty laughing at the whole incident. Retelling it over and over so all could enjoy Bruce's humorous misfortune has continued the fun to this very day.

Dancing in Church

One of my favorite memories of this time was the first church service. Samson's church had come a long way since we had last visited, with a new roof and several other construction advancements. Set Free had also grown as a leadership team. One showcase of this team was the kids' music performances. These performances reminded me of the Afritendo group I saw back in the beginning of this story. The kids were talented, enthusiastic, colorful, and upbeat. Samson's son, Angelo, and his daughter, Shalom (Pam), seemed like natural leaders.

Once the performances finished, we were all drawn into the singing and worship. I knew what was about to happen. I looked at Janie and Kendra and asked, "Are you ready to dance?" They both got a deer-in-the-headlights look on their faces and shook their heads with a panicked "No!" Regardless, each of us were drawn out onto the "dance floor." Everyone danced, so joining the crowd wasn't as intimidating as it seemed at first. In fact, we had fun. Jim was the hit of the dancers, interweaving his Missouri two-step with their tribal rhythms. We laughed and enjoyed being enveloped in the joy and inclusion of this loving African congregation. No sleeping during this church meeting!

When we sat after dancing, kids crawled up on our laps. God just wove them into our being in a way only God can do. I didn't recognize my sponsored little girl, but she knew me. As she sat on my lap our bodies melted together, physically bonding. I am not sure who got the best of that. No, actually I'm pretty sure. My mothering emotions and my need to be needed welled up in me with a satisfaction practically unexplainable. I can only guess that her need to be cared for and the security that came from our bonding filled a deep place in her being. God is like that! He has the whole picture from all sides of the equation. As I looked down the aisle, each member of our team had a bit of magic happening.

Kendra lost her heart to these children and to Samson's endeavors. She is a single young woman on a modest teacher's salary. A second job she had started would help pay for sponsoring two children, a boy and a girl. She visited their houses and met their families. Before she left, she bought a few things for them and left with a promise of returning.

Janie and Jim were the quintessential American grandparents to baby Janie and another family they assumed responsibility for. They brought fabric for Hellen and Bibles for Samson's team. Not just a small bit but whole suitcases of well thought out gifts and supplies had been hauled over the ocean to bless this ministry.

Geri already sponsored a family in Masese, but her brain went to work trying to figure out how to solve some construction problems she saw in Buloba. Geri and her husband have built houses in the States. She is a problem solver by nature. Being a teacher, she loved working with the children in their classes. There were three classrooms full of preschoolers, eager to learn. Geri brought Bible crafts for them which they did with excitement. It is hard to fathom how little these impoverished children get to experience. A simple craft is truly a gift.

Over the years I have known Geri, studying the Bible in classes has been important to her. One evening, we attended a women's Bible study class led by Hellen and some other women on the Set Free leadership team. Geri engaged with the women in that group on a level more meaningful than we are privileged to experience in many of our other activities. She blessed them and they blessed her.

Praise Akatukunda

An unexpected gift surprised me during this trip. My sponsored girl, Praise, had grown up and aged out of the Compassion sponsorship program. She had finished secondary, as well as a vocational school. She was born in November 1996 so she was almost twenty-one. Samson let her know I would be with him in Buloba. She took a seven-hour bus trip to meet up with me. I didn't even recognize her. She had grown into a beautiful young woman. Samson found a place for her to stay while we were there. Then we took her with us for the rest of the trip. She had a sister in the Jinja area where she could stay when we traveled there.

I loved her personality! Funny and warm, she won our hearts. Praise dressed fashionably, even in second-hand clothes. She had a cute sense of style. If I let her have my phone, she took selfies that made us laugh when we saw them. She never needed looking after while we worked at the projects. She simply made herself useful. I might find her singing and leading others to sing with her, animatedly teaching in a classroom, working with the cooks, or entertaining whoever was around. She would cuddle close to me and flash a million-dollar smile. Assisting with letter writing for the sponsored kids was very useful because she knew what that was like from writing me. We took her along everywhere we went until night time. She took a boda boda to her sister's house to sleep, meeting up with us again in the mornings. I loved my time with her and was proud of who she had become.

Generations

Before we left for Masese, Samson and Praise got my new little sponsored girl together with me to take generational pictures. Samson being the first generation, Praise the second, and now a new generation was beginning with Nuliat. Once  again, I felt humbled to see God at work in my life through these lives. Samson and Praise have grown up to be special people, giving God all the glory. It will be interesting to see how Nuliat progresses. Her mother is unstable and her father a non-player, at least for now. Samson considers her to be family so I trust he will be a big brother to her in my absence. He is a blessing to so many people. I am grateful to have played a part in his life.

Samson's Siblings—Graduates

Samson's siblings have been on his heart from the beginning. He told me he was responsible to educate his brothers and sisters since he had received help from Compassion. I didn't see how he could possibly live up to that responsibility early on. It seemed hard enough to support himself and then to support his own family. Nevertheless, he did all he could, and then some. This trip we got to celebrate some fruits of his faithfulness. Both his brother and his sister graduated from the Bible University where Samson taught as a professor. Not only did they look splendid in their caps and gowns but their faces lit up and they grinned from ear to ear. Both siblings work with him at his church/school. Jim and Janie decided to pay Samson's sister's salary as a teacher in his school. That sponsorship will bring children up out of poverty as they become educated and go on to be the future of their country. To sponsor a teacher is a gift that gives on and on and on.

On to Masese

Poverty is rampant in Buloba, but even more striking are the slums in Masese. Taking this team on to Masese further opened their eyes.

In Masese there are a few "nice" houses in the village, but the poverty levels go deeper than in Buloba. We watched as our team adjusted to the realities of this community.

Janie and Jim had been sponsoring Rehema and her tailoring class for a few years. After they met her and her current class, they bought another sewing machine, gave money for graduations, and blessed Rehema for her efforts with supplies. They recognized what a good work Rehema is doing for the women she trains. These women have no way to support themselves and their families. This class bridges the gap from hopelessness to sustainability. Janie and Jim are leaving a legacy in this world through their generous hearts.

Kendra and Geri at Work in Masese

Kendra and Geri went to work teaching. They visited classrooms and worked with teachers. I don't think they had planned on going

to every classroom, but once the word got out, no classroom would let them skip their room. It was a joy for both our team members and the students. One classroom asked to go to the Jinja Agriculture Fair.

Kendra made that happen!

Crutches

One afternoon Jean brought a young man to the office who she found along the road to the office. He'd hurt his foot and was trying to walk with the help of a big stick. Jean had brought crutches from home. This young man didn't know us but trusted Jean enough to ride with her to our school. He didn't know what she had in mind until he saw the crutches. His face filled with gratitude and his eyes with tears as she threw away his stick and handed him the crutches.

Geri had had surgery on her knee that past winter and knew how to use these crutches. She taught him how to go up and down stairs, turn around, sit, and stand. God was using the design He was weaving of her life experiences to bless this young man.

Extracurricular Activities

One day I saw a line of kids in front of the porch where Kendra and Geri were sitting and taking a break. Kendra had asked for some tape to mend a shoe. We had given our Ugandan leaders some duct tape, but they never used it. I guess they had not been shown the versatility and strength of this

291

tape. The sole of this student's shoe was almost totally separated from the top of the shoe. Kendra taped the sole onto the shoe in need of taping, and the student ran away happy. Before she even looked up, there was another shoe, and then another, until the line that had formed finally dissipated.

Another day, Geri and Kendra hand-mended rips in clothes the students were wearing. Rehema provided two needles and a bit of thread. The kids often just make do with tattered clothes. Buttons get ripped off while playing. I have seen sweaters with big holes in

them from rats. Seams come apart and fabric rips. Only a few parents have the means to repair these uniforms.

Tailors are available in the village. I have seen extra-large shirts tailored to fit a small built man as if that shirt had been designed especially for him. I don't know whether the kids' parents are just neglectful or truly unable, but many of our students have ragged uniforms. At least until a generous, dedicated, couple of "can do" women with big hearts came along!

Giving the Shoes Off Her Feet

One place we scheduled Geri to do her craft was on the island of Kisima. There is a preschool there where Help funds the lunches. The conditions are rougher than at either the Help preschool or at Samson's, but she could still give them a good experience about how God loves them. After leaving that island we went to a different Kisima island. This was my first time to this Kisima. As we were getting off the boat, I noticed a young teenage boy with a bleeding foot. I was distracted getting to the shore but noticed him again while he was carrying some donations we brought with us up the hill to the school. After we gave the clothes and toys we were donating to the pastor, I pointed out this boy to Jean.

Jean usually has a medical bag with her as she often finds someone along the way she can help. Sometimes they have wounds she can address. Sometimes she might have them get in the car, instructing the driver to go to the nearest clinic where she pays for their treatment. Sometimes she will take them to a pharmacy to get them "scripts." There are untold lives or limbs or bodies that have been touched by her love that would have otherwise been unrepairable. She is a wonder to watch.

This time she had nothing with her! Jean sat the boy on a table in an unused room. With no protective gloves, she used extreme care to keep from coming in contact with the blood oozing from this wound. One of us had water in a bottle she used to rinse his wounded foot. Geri had some antibiotic ointment in her purse. She also had some toilet paper Jean used to wrap around the foot in lieu of a bandage. At first we couldn't figure how to keep the toilet paper wrapped until Geri remembered she had some masking tape for the craft they had done. Once the wound was cared for as best we could, Jean wanted to send someone to get shoes from his house for him. But he had no shoes! How was he ever going to be able to keep his wound clean? Kendra took off her own shoe and measured it against his foot. It was a soft style and large enough he could fit it on over the wrapping. We wouldn't let Kendra walk without a shoe so she wore her shoe to the boat and sent both shoes back up the hill by way of one of his friends.

As we were leaving, I saw many children either without shoes or with one shoe. I think they would take one shoe for themselves and give the other to another child. Once back across the water I had a pair of sandals for Kendra to wear from the boat back to the hotel. Jean bought some antibiotic meds and  sent them back to her patient via one of the pastors from that island. We were all amazed at the provision God had given us to help this young man. He has his whole life ahead of him now whereas he may have died from infection without God's interference. It is a true blessing for God to use us in this way. We were all rejoicing as we headed back to our village.

Returning Our Hospitality

Since our political friends had just visited us that very spring, they were anxious to return some of our kindness.

We met Bernard in Jinja where he bought our sodas. Never before had a Ugandan bought Jean her drink. She always paid for their drinks. It was a small thing but noticed and appreciated. Bernard took Bruce for a game of golf (and beat him).

Magid, the mayor, took us on a boat excursion on Lake Victoria. He provided drinks for all our team and then bought our dinner at the lovely Jinja Sailing Club.

Nelson picked us up in his car and drove us to visit his school and former church.

Frances invited us to a BBQ dinner at his house. We all ate outside like they had at our house. It was a fun evening both for us and for the team.

Leila gave a concert at our school. The kids were so excited! She is a celebrity there. The older kids could sing all the words to her songs with her. She admonished them to do well in school, not for their parents but for themselves. She told them they had worth and to believe in a good God. They listened.

An Audience with the First Lady of Uganda

Moses had a bigger agenda. He was able to get us an audience with the First Lady of Uganda. Janet Museveni is the Minister of Education and Sports for Uganda, as well as being the wife of the President of Uganda. Moses wanted her to know us—H.E.L.P.

International, our work in Masese, and the IT Initiative Bruce was proposing using computers to aid learning, that could affect the whole of Ugandan primary education. They met at the State House. I didn't go because ssomeone had to stay with the team. Jean and her husband, Don, went along with Ronny, our

Country Director, Pastor Frederick, Morella, and Bruce. The meeting went very well. There was a nice article in the Ugandan National News the next day. The reporter told all about what H.E.L.P. was doing in their country. He quoted the First Lady saying, "God is forever looking for people to send and when he gets them, you truly see amazing and inspiring stories. If everyone was willing to extend a hand of help to a person in need, then the face of the earth would change." This was a monumental meeting. Now we just had to take the next steps in partnering with the Ugandan government to achieve our shared dreams.

Samson Versus the Cage Buffalo

I didn't go on most of the safari trips with our teams. As long as Jean could take the team, I usually opted to stay and work in the village. However, since my cousin and friends from home were going on this trip, Bruce and I went, too. I never tire of being in the park and seeing the animals in their natural habitat. Some of our group stayed at Red Chili's campground, and some of us stayed at the Sambiya Lodge. Both are comfortable, but the campground is more rustic and the bathrooms are outside. I have heard tales of hippos coming around as you find the bathroom during the night. Sambiya is nicer, but not nearly as expensive and luxurious as the game lodges like Paraa or Chobie. You might also run into a cage buffalo at night as you leave the main building where we have dinner at Sambiya, so there are Ugandans who walk you to your little cabins.

As Samson drove us to meet Jean and the rest of the team, he stopped abruptly in the middle of the road. This was Samson's first safari. We were excited for him to experience some of his own  country's natural wonders. However, we weren't getting very far because there was a big cage buffalo, much like the one in the picture, standing in the road looking right at us. Samson was backing up! He didn't think our car was any match for the big horned animal in our path. We had a call from Jean while Samson was moving backwards. "Where are you? You are going to miss the ferry." Bruce answered in his sarcastic way, "At the moment, we are going backwards."

Both Geri and Bruce had been around bulls in the States. It took some persuasive coaching to get Samson to venture forward. As he did, the animal slowly sauntered away, leaving us a clear path to our rendezvous point.

Murchison Falls Safari by Land and by Water

We took a motorized boat up the Victoria Nile (which bisects Murchison Falls National Park) to the base of the falls. Murchison Falls is the centerpiece of the largest wildlife preserve in Uganda, over two thousand square miles. The entirety of the mighty Nile River flows through an opening of less than seventy feet. It's just one of the many reasons Churchill referred to Uganda as the "Pearl of Africa."

On the way we saw many hippos, some crocodiles, and a wide range of aquatic bird life. We often saw land animals coming for a drink. It was lovely out on the water and exotic. The hippos group together as they walk by the shore along the bottom of the river, submerging and reappearing. A fun photo to capture is the hippo's huge open mouthed yawn that reveals formidable teeth. I would not want to be caught in those jaws!

Next we drove to the top of the waterfall. Some adventurous people walk to the top of the falls from the river. I am sure that is fun. I have only driven. The falls are nearer to us at the top. Their power is tumultuous and loud, both before and during their cascade. The waters violently compress through a narrow gorge, spraying mists along their wake over an eight-mile radius and dropping four hundred feet. Whether at the foot of the falls, in the boat, or at the top watching the roaring decent, I am always impressed at the beauty with which God blessed this place. The raging water has an energy and a beauty that surges through me to my core. Glistening rocks sparkle from the sun, smaller pools of water wait their turn, small critters scamper while the butterflies flit about. Lush greenery borders the bright white of the water. I love it all.

The next day we took a safari vehicle onto the savannah. Grasses, shrubs, and widely spaced acacia trees comprise the landscape framing the wildlife. This park is home to seventy-six mammals, including the Big Five. I have only  seen a cheetah in Kenya, but they are in this park. Giraffes are a favorite as are the elephants. I would just as soon the elephants keep their distance. They are interesting to watch, but if they get close, I feel too vulnerable. They don't look especially friendly to me. It is pretty cute to see a mama elephant and her little one though.

As giraffes get older, their spots darken. I didn't know that before our safaris. They are continually munching on leaves from the taller trees. When they move, they are like poetry. We find lions most trips but not on this one. In Kenya, I saw them close up. A lioness was lying on the berm beside the road. We stopped but stayed in the vehicle. I didn't even have to zoom my camera. She was right there!

In Kenya, we viewed the migration of the wildebeest who look a lot like buffalo. That was impressive, but in Uganda we saw herds of the hartebeest (a type of gnu like the wildebeest). I read that there are between 4000 and 5000 in Uganda whereas there are just under 3000 elephants.

The giraffes, Bruce's favorite, number only about 250. Over the savannah there are herds of Uganda kobs, waterbucks, cape buffaloes, bushbucks, and the ugly warthogs. We saw an occasional hyena typically causing some consternation among the other wildlife. The rhinos are rare because of poaching. We have never seen one. Since they are slow breeders, giving birth to one calf every two to four years, we may never see one.

I must say that as amazing as the animals and the birds are, sometimes our team is the most interesting of all. Janie and Jim dressed the part. Especially Janie. She had on a flowing, tye-dyed red, orange, yellow, green, and blue summer top and a wide-brimmed hat in a camouflage print. The brim was flipped up on one side for style or down with a veil covering her face to protect from bugs and sun. With her big beautiful smile, she looked like something out of a movie. Well, I guess that fits since the movie *The African Queen* was filmed near the falls.

Power of One.

One evening, back in the States, Jean was leaving my house when she ran back in and handed me a small box saying she had thought of me. I opened the box to find a dainty silver starfish necklace. Have you ever heard of the starfish story? It is a simple, but profound tale.

A little boy and his mother were walking along the shore one day. The night before the tide had washed millions of starfish up on the shore. As they lay dying, this little boy was picking them up as fast as he could and throwing them back. His mother surveyed the vast number of dying starfish and told the boy not to bother as he could never make much of a difference. He bent down, picked up another starfish, and threw it as far as he could, saying, "It made a difference to that one!"

I tell this story to groups that visit the H.E.L.P. International warehouse so they can see the importance of just one person. This 9,000 square-foot warehouse full of humanitarian aid for the nations was started from just one woman whose heart was broken for the poor. The power of one is really hard to grasp, but it is the way God usually works. While shelling with a friend in Florida a few years ago, I found a starfish on the beach. I wanted to take one home with me but didn't want to kill any. This one was stiff and dry so I stuck it in my bucket with the other shells. That night we covered our shells with water to help them soak off the sand and ocean. The next day I almost dropped my bucket in surprise when my hand touched this live thing in with my shells. My starfish hadn't been dead after all! I reverently picked him up, walked over to the ocean bay, and threw him back in the water! I had saved a life, and it felt fantastic.

There are so many needy people in the world, it often seems overwhelming. It would be easier to walk away thinking I can't do much. Sometimes I get tired and discouraged, but Jesus said to not grow weary in well-doing, so I keep helping each starfish/needy person I can. It feels good to do my part even if it doesn't seem like nearly enough. My necklace is around my neck to help remind me that one person can save a life, even if it is one life at a time.

Sometimes we don't feel up to the task. Actually, most of the time, I wonder what God is thinking. "Why did You put me in this position?" "How can I possibly do what You are asking?"

Those times bring the story of Esther, the Queen of Persia, wife of King Ahasuerus (or the fifth century Persian king, Xerxes 1) to mind. Unbeknownst to her husband, Esther was a Jewess. The king was being influenced to kill the Jews in his kingdom. These were her people. Since she was in the position to be heard by the king, she was called on her to save her people. She had been an unknown young girl found, because of her beauty, when the king was looking for a bride. She was prepared and taught to be a queen. However, being queen put her in danger. If she didn't honor the king properly, she could be executed. When she was called on to help her Jewish people, she was scared. She was told that she had become queen so she could save her people. "Yet who knows whether you have come to the kingdom for such a time as this" (Esther 4:14 NKJV).

So, who knows, maybe we were brought to Masese "for such a time as this." People there needed to be "saved." Saved from hunger, disease, illiteracy, hopelessness, and generational poverty. We were unknown and unprepared. With God choosing us and consequently preparing us over the years, we were in a position to do His work.

We were blessed to help H.E.L.P. International do their amazing work as they have sent aid to 121 countries around the world, as well as our work in Uganda. Maybe Samson's ministry has been blessed by God through us. Would he have a church of hundreds and a thriving school if we hadn't heard God's call to sponsor him? It seemed like such a simple thing at the time. God multiplied our small contribution to unfold it into a widespread, life-changing, and ongoing work of art. As Samson put it: "un-erasable marks of transformation."

"Religion that God our Father accepts as pure and faultless is this: to look after orphans and widows in their distress and to keep oneself from being polluted by the world."

James 1:27

2019

Tenth Year Trip

In June 2019 Kendra returned with Bruce and me, along with my longtime friend, Ginger. We met up with Jean after first spending a

few days with Samson and his loving clan. Bruce spent Father's Day with Samson, a treat for both of them. It is true that we have parented this person, but it is also true that, like all kids, he has taught us lessons we needed to learn. He was the gateway to our work in Uganda, opening up our legacy in a

way we never dreamed. We are grateful for him and his part in our lives. It is encouraging to see all God is accomplishing in and through him. He and his wife's outreach encompasses other pastors, women, and youth in all walks of Ugandan life. Between Samson's church, his mission efforts, and his primary school, his influence spreads wider and wider. Who knew (but God) that the little boy Compassion sent for us to sponsor would become such a force for good?

Ever aware of the ten-year mark, my heart was full as we spent time in Masese and Jinja. There was a large, two-story, eight-classroom school building nearing completion. We celebrated as we remembered the beginnings. First a tree, then an open pole barn with a leaky roof, and then our ISSB brick six-classroom modification of the other pole barn. Along the way we have renovated other existing rooms to accommodate our bulging

301

enrollment and built a new three-classroom block building to house our computer center and upper grades. Trying to find classroom space for five hundred and fifty students and find room for our staff and adult education efforts required some considerable scrambling, especially with our limited funds. I pray we were good stewards of what funding we have received throughout the years. I continually pray for sustainability for this place we have given our hearts to. I am ever grateful for each one who took their time and talents to bring this about. They are my heroes.

The Busoga Kingdom

Speaking of heroes, in many of the fairy tales there is a king, central to the story. Our story has a true king—the King of Glory, but we also had a night with the king of the Busoga tribe. I have heard the

Busoga tribe is the third largest of the fifty-six tribes in Uganda with eight percent of the Ugandan population belonging to them.

Jean had been connecting with several Busoga elite through our political friends in Kampala. She was excited for them to meet Bruce and Dr. Larry on this trip. She arranged a meeting with the prime minister of the Busoga tribe. From that, H.E.L.P. was given a room in the Busoga complex for computer training and ICT advancements.

We were invited to the Kyabazinga Royal Banquet, celebrating the third anniversary of the coronation of the current king, William Wilberforce Kadhumbula Gabula Nadiope the 4th. The invitation was quite an honor!

Not being prepared for such an event, we needed appropriate attire. The Ugandans dress in evening clothes for such events. Kendra, Ginger, and I took Rehema, our tailoring instructor, to Jinja town to purchase what she needed to make us presentable. We each found fabric we liked and a style for her to replicate. She measured each of us and went to work with only two days to sew all three dresses. Even sick with malaria, Rehema finished our fashions in time for our big night. Ginger bought some shoes to go with her dress, but before dinner was over, the sole had come unglued, rendering it practically impossible for her to walk without tripping. We wished for some of Kendra's duct tape. Bruce had to rent a suit and buy a shirt, bow-tie, and shoes. Never having seen Bruce in anything other than his safari style work clothes, our Ugandan friends were impressed and remarked, "How smart you look!" I'll admit I, too, thought he looked quite distinguished.

The king, a nice looking man born in 1988, is still young and unmarried. He is getting some pressure to marry, and the current

favorite seems to be Quiin Abenakyo, a Ugandan model who won Miss Uganda in the 2018 beauty pageant, was crowned Miss World Africa also in 2018,

and finished 4th at the Miss World contest. If they married, she would become the queen consort, sharing her husband's social rank and status. But she would not share the king's political and military powers.

Miss Abenakyo accompanied the king on this celebration night. She is drop-dead gorgeous. If they do marry, they should make beautiful babies.

We only saw one other mazungu in the sophisticated gathering. Everywhere we looked there were important Ugandans dressed to the max. We were not in the "castle" but outside in an elaborately decorated tent. The eighteen of us were a curiosity to the otherwise ethnic crowd. I was running around boldly photographing the festivities along with media guys. We were not inconspicuous!

After the royalty made their appearance, there were speeches and entertainment (not in English), and then the celebrities retreated to a smaller room to eat their dinner.

By and by, sixteen of us were escorted into this room. One of our group had fallen, breaking her arm, so she and another of our team

members left to go to the hospital. We had been granted an audience before this esteemed group.

H.E.L.P. was introduced by the Busoga official who invited us. On her knees, our Busoga social worker, Ritah, gave an overview of who we are and what we have done throughout the years. At least that is what I think she was saying—she addressed them in the traditional Busoga language. Bruce was surprised when he was called to speak about his ICT initiative. He wasn't prepared but did a good off-the-cuff talk. It was well received, and we may get some partnership funding from the Busoga. Favor with God is an amazing thing. What will this section of the tapestry be like when it is taken to its fruition?

Glasses Clinic Recollections

While helping at a medical clinic in a remote village in rural Uganda, my world collided with another's reality. I haven't been able to get this woman out of my mind.

We were fitting people with reading glasses. Compared to the more dramatic work of the nurses and doctors in the medical care area, our help with reading their Bibles and doing close-work seemed less significant. At least that was what I was thinking. However, we had a waiting line all day for those hoping to see better.

I had been trained in another clinic to pray for anyone who wanted prayer after we finished fitting their glasses. So I held each of their hands and looked in their eyes as they told me their prayer requests. My interpreter was a pastor who relayed their words with unflinching honesty.

Everyone desired prayer. No one passed by without a prayer. Some even stopped who weren't getting glasses.

I was humbled. Who was I to pray for them? I don't have the gift of intercessory prayer. I am not in the flow of dramatic miracles more than any other person who loves and believes in the goodness and power of our heavenly Father. This was my way of loving these lovely people. Letting them know they are important. Touching them both physically and heart-to-heart. I wanted God's overwhelming love to flow through me to infuse their lives in a way only God can do.

Most were older adults and the elderly. The young rarely need magnification for close work. If they do experience a problem with their eyes, it probably is a more serious vision impairment than my readers can accommodate.

It is interesting that many of the men asked for wisdom. I wonder how many of the men in our country ask for wisdom above anything else. These men might have had other requests, but wisdom came first. I think that is pretty wise of them!

Other prayer needs were for provision, school fees, health, and "family matters." One man's wife had run off, leaving him with a young baby to care for. Another's husband had abandoned the family. Everyone thanked me profusely. I am always impressed with the gratitude of the Ugandans I meet.

But this one lady was different. She dressed the same, albeit her dress was a little more faded. Her eyes were dull. Her shoulders drooped. The voice speaking to me was very quiet, almost as if she didn't have the energy to speak or the will to be there. With few words, her message to me for prayer was, "I have a miserable life." Oh, my goodness! I could feel the misery. I could see the hopelessness and despair in her demeanor. No explanation came from her. No description of her misery, no specific requests. Just, "I have a miserable life."

With empathy, I reached for her hands. As she slowly reached out so I could enfold her hands in mine, she looked downcast and worn. How do I pray for her? With all my heart, I petitioned the Father to bring joy into her life. Joy unspeakable. Joy overflowing. For her to feel His love and see His provision for her. For her to take in the beauty around her and bring that radiance into her being. For life to be easier and for friends to surround her. I don't remember all my words. My spirit groaned for her as she disappeared from my sight, but not from my memory.

Prayers for this woman still well up in my heart. I ask God to give her purpose and renewed energy to meet her challenges. As I feel my own slight aches and pains, I pray for her, knowing her road to travel is so much more difficult than I can even imagine. The inequality makes me cringe. I am sorry for the life she has lived that led her to such a state of mind. I wish I could roll back time and help her find her way.

But I can't.

I can continue to pray for her and direct my efforts to others who I have more opportunity to bless. If I can help stop the tide that brings such misery, please, God, help me do that. I can remember her and focus on gratitude for my good life. Those who contemplate suicide must feel some of that despair. I wonder if they were to walk a mile on her path, would they see things differently? I am sure they would see with clearer eyes. Reading glasses help one see the words, but I was seeing the soul.

Catching up

Elizabeth just happened to be having her eighteenth birthday the day we saw her. She was in our very first class ten years ago. Now she is a young woman. We took her to eat at the Sailing Club and even ordered a cake for her. It was fun to treat her with a nice dinner and spend some time together. She is in a culinary vocational school and says she will only marry a white man because they treat their wives better than black men do. I argued with her about that. There are plenty of black men who are good men and there are plenty of white men who aren't. We will see what she does.

Hillary was around. He was busy trying to get his tourism business off the ground. I wished him well!

Jackie brought her new baby to see us. Now she has a boy and a girl. She looked good and her kids are adorable. Her guy has stuck around. No wedding, but they are what we would call common law. She seems well. Our years of support paid off with her.

Olivia, the baby who was left almost dead with Hillary's grandmother, is thriving. We still were paying for her nutrition. It feels good to think Jean was able to save that life. Olivia is an embodiment of many lives Jean has saved throughout the years.

Henry was in the hospital so I didn't see him. Bruce got to visit with him one day when I was gone with the medical team. I brought him some good sandals to help make up for the ones that were stolen years ago. He was thrilled. As an electronic installer, he will be helping with the electrical on our new school building when that is ready for installation. I was sorry to miss him.

I tried to see Juma. He was around but wouldn't come to the project. He has been making some poor choices and didn't want to face us. I would have liked to see him.

I missed Marian too. Painfully so. She hurt my heart.

Kids are growing up and new ones are coming along. I don't know so many of the newer ones. I am sad about that. With so many kids, I don't get personally involved like I did in the early days. There are others loving on these children for me. I am blessed.

Safari

The safari this year was excellent. The team stayed at the lovely Paraa Lodge. We took a videographer from Kampala. He had been filming the school and medical clinics for us. David was talented and eager to please. He used a drone, so we were excited to have him producing our videos. His footage of the lions, the sunrise over the savannah, a hyena with the carcass she pulled into her den to keep us from helping ourselves, the herd of giraffes running from the drone, hippos doing their thing, and an alligator up close and personal were all keepers. He even has a romantic photo of Bruce and me with the sunset over the Nile framing our smiles to each other.

Saying Goodbye

This whole trip had an air of goodbye to it. Ten years have been a good run. Much more will happen, but it is a wrap for this decade.

Praise personified these truths. The only possibility she could travel to connect with me was on Saturday, the day we were leaving. We planned to meet near the airport for a few hours visit. She traveled by public transportation from her home in Western Uganda with her three-month-old baby daughter and her cousin. The trip took hours longer than she planned. Over ten hours! With a new baby, ugh! She almost missed us. We needed to check in when she arrived at the airport. I eked out about fifteen minutes to be with her and her sweetest of babies. I was frantic. She had come far and spent much energy just to have a short visit with Bruce and me. When I expressed my regret at the shortness of our visit she said, "Thanks for everything, Mom. I really appreciated. I also would love to have stayed longer, but I failed." She came all that way because she "appreciated." She and her baby will be fine. They have a whole life ahead of them. We just played a small part, but it was significant. She has a permanent place in my heart. However, we needed to go home. Maybe I will see her again and get to see her baby grow and maybe not. Only God knows. But for now, it is goodbye.

Too Many Bags!

Diana and Ben's Ezra

3 Amigos
Ronny, Frederick,
& Moses

Celebration after a Clinic

Life Changes in the Past Ten Years

My life has been speeding past. I buried my parents and my mother-in-law. Bruce and I had surgeries. My fourteen grandchildren have grown up way too fast. Some have babies of their own.

Just for the fun of it, Bruce and I have taken some wonderful trips. Jean and I, too. Bruce has moved from the everyday grind of his career to the luxury of retirement.

Masese has grown as well. Hundreds of kids were given the chance to get their education through primary and beyond. Hunger has been abated at the Help School and on two islands. Hundreds of women improved their economic situations by selling their beads or starting profitable businesses. Others became tailors. Our staff has profited from their employment. Men learned viable skills to support their families. The community at large has benefitted from the flow of funds. Pastors are being blessed and growing their congregations. Both adults and students have made life decisions to follow our Lord. Our leadership for Help Uganda has matured and our standing in the community is strong. The health and well-being of this community is better than ever before.

Balancing and intertwining my life at home and my love for Uganda has been an ongoing affair. I have tried to be true to both, trusting God to guide me at every turn. Not only has God guided Bruce and me, but there is an entire board successfully leading and blessing as they turn to the Weaver to further the tapestry's beauty beyond our greatest expectations. Thanks go to each member of every team who went with us, every financial supporter, the sponsors of the children and of the teachers, everyone who bought jewelry, and the families of us all.

My tapestry is only one of a collection of designs. All of them are, intricately and meticulously, incredible works of art. And none of them are finished!

Legacy

Jump out of a plane or see the pyramids along the Nile. Any number of experiences can be on a list of things to do or accomplish before we die. Is this the definition of a bucket list?

Maybe I need to take it further. It is more of our heart desires accomplished before we die. Well, what are my heart's desires before I leave life as I now know it? I suppose I could simplify it and just say my heart's desire is to love. But what does this look like? I could love life, love people, love my God. But what does that all mean? What will my legacy be? Do I even care what people remember after I am no longer here? After all, I won't be here so why should I care?

My dad was determined to leave money behind for his children. It was important to him. I didn't understand that since we would so much rather have seen him spend it on our mother. Money is here today and gone tomorrow. The love behind his wanting to leave us an inheritance means much more than the actual money. I hope he knows that.

So I am back to love again. I do dearly want my family to know that I love them. That is definitely on my list. Accomplishing that to the degree I would like is the challenge. Sometimes it is a tough call. I may want to lavish love on them so much I spoil them. Then they never become the people they would be if I had left them to develop their own strengths. Rescuing is a part of my nature but not always a healthy part. My goal is to love them with a godly love so they will see and know Him through my love for them. I feel inadequate for that. But I keep trying. My best bet is to get as close to

Him as I can so He can teach me to love the way He loves. Maybe that should be first on my list.

Next, I'd like to make some kind of positive difference in this world. Duh! Don't we all? Maybe I am giving the rest of mankind credit where credit isn't due. Maybe many are too caught up in themselves to care about others. But I suspect that the vast majority would like to leave a good footprint where they can. There seems to be a lack of something that keeps this from happening. I don't want that "something" to rule in my life. Even if I am forgotten soon after I am gone, I want to be a part of something good that continues.

And if you want to know my heart, I would most like to be part of something that counts for eternity. Not only now, but forever. I don't want much, do I? I am not a preacher or an evangelist, but I want my life to preach for me. I want who I am to help others beyond time. This life is like a vapor that vanishes, a flower that soon withers, but then there is the life beyond. That life is the one that counts.

So, what can I give on my giving bucket list? Love, honor, attention, respect, wisdom, good times, family gatherings, a life lived well, a chance for a better life, health and healthy choices, and eternal understandings.

About the Author

Pam McCormick has been traveling to Uganda once or twice a year since 2007 with H.E.L.P. International, a small Colorado NGO. Her previous volunteer work advocating for children with Compassion International and her personal dedication to sponsoring children in developing countries led her to Uganda, where she was instrumental in birthing a primary school for the children of the impoverished village of Masese. Over the next ten years, the ministry has grown from forty-five to 550 students and from one teacher to a staff of over thirty, ultimately empowering not only the *children* of Masese, but the entire village.

Pam holds a bachelor's degree in Education, and a Lifetime Achievement Award signed by President Obama from the Corporation for National and Community Service for her lifelong commitment to building stronger nations through volunteer service. She also received a Certificate of Heroism from Rotary International.

Contact Pam at www.accidentalmissionarybook@gmail.com and follow her on Help Uganda-Masese Facebook page. Go to Instagram at Accidental_Missionary to see more pictures.

Find more information on sponsoring a child of your own at Sponsor a Child www.help-uganda.com.

Gallery

Kids Reading

Friends in Donated Shirts

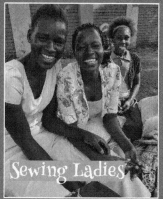

Sewing Ladies

Sewing Class

Street Kid

Nursery Sports Sack Race

Girls Soccer Team

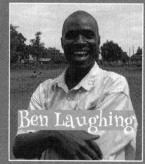

Ben Laughing

Ways You Can Help!

Pray for the ministry, the Ugandans, and the teams.

Recommend this book to all your friends.

Write a 5-star review on Amazon.

Sponsor a child. $30/month

Send a classroom to camp. $500

Sponsor a teacher. $60/half or $120/full month

Help with school lunches. $0.20 cents/meal per day or $10/month for 50 lunches

Buy supplies for the tailoring program.

Pay for a scholarship to send a student to secondary school. $25/scholarship

Buy jewelry from the biggerthanbeads.com web store.

Purchase school shoes. $15/pair

Contribute to the microfinance program.

Adopt a pastor and his church. $60/month

Contribute towards our building fund.

Invite Pam to be a keynote speaker.

Recommend this book to all your family.

Purchase mosquito nets. $10/treated net

Buy new uniforms for the students. $8/uniform

Purchase sweaters for school uniforms. $10/each

Invest in the future of Uganda through the Information Technology Initiative.

Help get tablets into school classrooms.

Buy projectors to be used with Google Classroom.

Send a monthly amount to be used where most needed.

Pay the entrance fee for a craft fair to sell the jewelry. $250-$550

Send a classroom on a field trip—like to the zoo or to parliament. $500

Send a classroom to the agricultural fair. $185

Treat a graduating class (Primary 7 or Nursery) to a celebration party. $400

Advance our gardening program.

Host a jewelry party.

Organize a fundraiser.

Recommend this book to all your social media friends.

Adopt a farmer. $50/month

Adopt a well. $5000

Find and write grants.

Come and see what is happening in Uganda.

Questions for Further Discussion

When have you seen the power of one used for good?

How should couples resolve significant disagreements like Pam and Bruce had about going to Africa?

What should be considered for your legacy?

Have you seen instances of helping that hurt?

Have you experienced miracles and/or prophecy in your own life?

Does God's faithfulness ring true for you?

Is there value in sponsoring?

How do you reconcile the disparity of those that have and those that don't? Can you relate to Pam's musings on money?

Do you know ordinary people that do extraordinary things?

Can you see God's design in your own life like the tapestry Pam writes about?

How much does the time and place of your own story affect your beliefs about other races or poverty?

How have your parents' views shaped your own?

Do you have others that you share your life with that can stand with you through good and bad times like Pam and Bruce's Kinship Group?

Is God "knitting" your heart toward something that will be your destiny?

Have you seen the face of Jesus in someone? How did that affect you?

Have you ever tried to do a good thing but had a force doing its best to stop you like H.E.L.P. and the MWA? Have you been betrayed by a friend? Did God redeem those times?

Are there songs that especially touch your heart like Bruce's "I'll Be Somewhere Working?"

Have you been a "fool" by taking on an impossible undertaking just to find God provided all you needed and more?

How do you feel significant or do you?

Is time and pressure making you a diamond or a pearl? Are you still a caterpillar? Or are you in the cocoon stage or are you flying?

Have you ever experienced a God complex? Have you seen others fall into this temptation?

Have you ever lavished love on someone and had it backfire from jealousies like with Sam and Juma?

Are you part of a ripple or are you making a splash causing a ripple? What are some of the things you do or say that affects others?

If you needed to write a capstone what would be the subject?

What do you think about Samson coming to the US in 2019 without enough money? Just his faith.

How does perfect love cast out fear?

Are you feeling displaced or useless like Bruce was? Could God be opening another door to greater things for you?

Love does. Do you believe that?

Made in the USA
San Bernardino, CA
08 January 2020